MECHANICS·
MERCANTILE
LIBRARY.

Arthur F. Mathews '06

Unjust Enrichment

Unjust Enrichment

How Japan's Companies Built Postwar
Fortunes Using American POWs

Linda Goetz Holmes

STACKPOLE
BOOKS

Published by
STACKPOLE BOOKS
5067 Ritter Road
Mechanicsburg, PA 17055
www.stackpolebooks.com

Printed in the United States of America

10 9 8 7 6 5 4 3 2 1

FIRST EDITION

Library of Congress Cataloging-in-Publication Data

Holmes, Linda Goetz.
    Unjust enrichment: how Japan's companies built postwar fortunes using American POWs/Linda Goetz Holmes.
        p.cm.
    Includes bibliographical references.
    ISBN 0-8117-1844-1
    1. World War, 1939-1945—Prisoners and prisons, Japanese.
2. Industries—Japan—History—20th century. 3. Prisoners of war—Japan. 4. Prisoners of war—United States. 5. Forced labor—Japan—History—20th century. 6. Industrial mobilization—Japan—History—20th century. I. Title: How Japan's companies built postwar fortunes using American POWs II. Title.

D805.J3 H58 2001
940.54'7252—dc21
                                                                                          00-058375

To all the men

who endured being a prisoner of the Japanese

during World War II

and

To the families

who waited, hoped, and prayed

for three and a half long years

this book is respectfully dedicated

Table of Contents

List of Illustrations

Acknowledgments

MANY PEOPLE SHARED THEIR EXPERTISE, INFORMATION, AND TIME TO MAKE this book a reality. John E. Taylor, senior archivist and our national treasure at The National Archives, has offered constant, invaluable guidance on so many occasions. I also appreciate the help of Milton Gustafson and researcher Mia Waller at the Archives.

I am especially indebted to Robert J. Hanyok, senior historian at the National Security Agency Center for Cryptologic History for his assistance in locating and interpreting literally hundreds of signals intelligence messages.

I am grateful for the extraordinary amount of information, photographs, and material supplied to me by ex-prisoners of war John Aldrich, Frank Bigelow, Jack Edwards, Harold Feiner, Terence Kirk, Edward Jackfert, Andrew Miller, Charles Pruitt, Robert Renfro, Melvin Routt, Otto Schwarz, and J. O. Young; and my thanks to an additional several hundred ex-POWs for sharing their recollections.

For their assistance in supplying information about the secret relief funds, I am thankful to Vincent Crettol at the Swiss National Bank, Bern; Swiss historian Michele Coduri; Asataro Miyake at the Bank of Tokyo-Mitsubishi, Tokyo; Archivist Rosemary Lazenby at the Federal Reserve Bank of New York; archivists Martin Morger and Jozef Palkovic at the Geneva headquarters, International Committee of the Red Cross (ICRC); Bruno Zimmermann and Patrick Zahnd in the New York office, ICRC; and Jay N. Woodworth.

I appreciate the time, recollections, and referrals extended to me by Maj. Gen. John K. Singlaub, USA (Ret.); Geoffrey Jones; and members of Attachment 404, Pacific Office of Strategic Services.

For her assistance in facilitating my access to transcripts of the Tokyo War Crimes Trials, I thank librarian Whitney Bagnall at the Columbia University Law Library.

Richard A. Long, Chief of the Oral History Unit, U.S. Marine Corps History and Museums Division provided invaluable help, as did Judith Petsch at the museum.

I am deeply grateful to Frederick H. Taylor for reproducing and supplying originals of the extraordinary rescue photographs taken by his father, L. Henry Taylor.

The expertise and time given to me by Jeanne Randall at the Executive Option, Shelter Island, New York, was key in keeping the production of this work on schedule.

For being willing to write a preface, I thank Pacific War historian Bruce Lee.

Finally, my thanks to copyeditor Tony Hall for his insight and precise verbiage; and I have especially appreciated the cheerful guidance, patience, and wisdom of my editor, Leigh Ann Berry.

Preface

IT USED TO BE AN AXIOM IN THE CITY ROOM: GOOD JOURNALISM COMFORTS the afflicted and afflicts the comfortable.

Unjust Enrichment fulfills these requirements—and goes further. It is excellent investigative reporting. It also is a book of historical significance, because it fills a major void in what is known about World War II. Carefully researched, written with understatement, this book documents one of the most depressing stories of the war in the Pacific—the dreadful fate of American civilians and military prisoners of war (POWs) who became slave laborers for the Japanese throughout the Far East and especially in Japan itself.

Worse, these slave laborers never had their day in court. The U.S. government prevented it. Instead of seeking justice for those wounded by war's experience, our State Department decided not to punish or seek financial retribution from some seventy-nine major Japanese corporations, which are still operating today, and which, according to official Japanese records, turned American civilian and military POWs into slave laborers.

Unjust Enrichment reveals how the State Department's decision caused Japan's leading industrialists, or *zaibatsu*, to be omitted from the list of war criminals to be prosecuted after the war. Not one executive has ever been held accountable.

It is ironic that in Europe, a corporation such as Nestlé will, in the year 2000, contribute $14.6 million to the $1.25 *billion* already raised to settle claims on behalf of Holocaust-era victims. The Swiss-based food giant declared it was making the payment because it is "either certain or it may be assumed" that some of its companies under Nazi control employed slave labor during the war. Meanwhile, to date not one penny in compensation has been paid by any Japanese corporation to the Allied slave laborers who were beaten, starved, and worked to death in the factories, mines, and shipyards owned by Japan's industrial giants. Today, these companies—among the richest in the world—are household names to American consumers.

The author also compares the fate of American POWs in Europe with those interned in the territories occupied by the Imperial Japanese forces. Her findings are equally horrifying. Only 1 percent of our POWs died in Nazi hands. But nine out of ten of our POWs who died during the war died in Japanese custody.

During the course of writing *Unjust Enrichment,* author Linda Goetz Holmes also uncovered another scandal: how, during the course of the war, a Japanese bank, working under instructions of the Japanese government, duped the Swiss into turning over to them millions upon millions of dollars contributed by Allied nations. The Japanese had promised the Swiss that these monies would be used to provide relief for Allied internees and POWs. Instead of using the funds as promised for humanitarian purposes, however, the Japanese used them to finance their war efforts. The author's reporting of these events for the working press in recent years has already made headlines around the world. But the full story, as revealed in this book for the first time, will garner even more attention.

Perhaps the most controversial section of the book deals with what would have happened to the 200,000 civilian and military POWs who were in Japanese hands as the war ended. According to Ms. Holmes's carefully documented account, radio messages sent from command headquarters in Tokyo to POW camp commandants, dated from April 1942 through August 20, 1945—or five days after the emperor of Japan had announced the nation's surrender—were explicit in this regard. The author points out that no prisoners or civilian internees were to be allowed to be freed by Allied forces. The orders from Tokyo read, in part: "In any case, it is the aim not to allow the escape of a single one, to *annihilate them all, and not to leave any traces.*"

These orders—to kill all the civilian internees and military POWs in Japanese hands—were turned over to General MacArthur's staff on September 19, 1946, in plenty of time for the forthcoming war crimes trials. But instead of being brought out in open court at the trials, they were submitted to the court merely as Exhibit 2015 without explanation. The reporters covering the war crimes trials were deviously blocked from understanding that some 200,000 Allied internees and POWs had been saved from certain death by America's use of atomic weapons.

Also, at that time, the American public did not know that the Allies had been breaking the Japanese diplomatic and military ciphers throughout the course of the war. The press did not comprehend that Washington had learned about Tokyo's threat of death to all the internees and POWs prior to President Truman's order to use atomic weapons to end the war in "a quick and decisive manner."

Yet another fact the general public did not know at that time was that immediately after the war ended the next Japanese government set out on a new course of propaganda aimed at keeping Emperor Hirohito from being tried as a war criminal. This was linked with Tokyo's desire to hide the many atrocities committed throughout the Far East and especially Japan's mistreatment of internees and POWs.

As I revealed in my book, *Marching Orders*, the Americans kept intercepting Japanese diplomatic radio traffic *after* the war ended. Thus, the American government—but not the public—was fully informed about Japanese intentions to influence world opinion and propagandize the use of atomic weapons against America and Great Britain. On September 13, 1945, for example, Prime Minister Shigemitsu began Tokyo's exploitation of the issue by sending a message to the Japanese legations in Sweden, Switzerland, and Portugal. His message said in part: "The Japanese leaders intend to play up the atomic bombings not only to explain Japan's surrender [to an army that does not believe it was defeated in combat], *but to offset publicity on Japan's treatment of Allied prisoners [of war] and internees [and countless other atrocities]. . . . Since the Americans have recently been raising an uproar about our mistreatment of prisoners, I think we should make every effort to exploit the atomic bomb question in our propaganda.*" (SRS Files 1791, September 15, 1945, National Archives, emphasis mine).

This intercept began Japan's clever postwar propaganda campaign. It is still in use today. No country has ever spent so much as did Japan for lobbying in Washington in this fashion during the 1980s. As one expert on Japan wrote: "A large proportion of academic research by Western scholars who concentrate on Japan is funded by Japanese institutions. The idea the scholars and commentators can remain objective because no formal conditions are attached to what they receive is mostly an illusion when the money comes from Japan." (Karel von Wolferen, *The Enigma of Japanese Power* [New York: Knopf, 1989], 12–13.) The Japanese government suppressed this writing. One wonders if *Unjust Enrichment* will suffer the same fate.

The ultimate question posed by *Unjust Enrichment* is this: Our POWs were improperly forced into slave labor to keep Japan's war machine operating. Our military and civilian POWs have never received a dime from these Japanese corporations for their labor, for their starving, for the beatings and the subhuman living conditions they endured. Their plight is worsened by the fact that our government has failed in its duty to protect the rights of these people and seek compensation from the corporate giants of Japan who prospered on slave labor. If the American government can marshall its judicial strength to force German companies to pay for the Nazi use of slave labor in World War II, why won't our government do the same against Japanese corporations on behalf of our ex-POWs who are still alive today?

Unjust Enrichment is an excellent book that demands answers and action.

Bruce Lee, author of *Marching Orders: The Untold Story of WWII* and coauthor of *Pearl Harbor: Final Judgement*

Introduction

MOST AMERICANS DO NOT THINK OF WORLD WAR II AS HANDING THE
United States one of the biggest military defeats in its history. We remember
how it ended in victory over Germany and Japan; but we find it harder to
recall how that war began in total disarray, with one Allied defeat after
another.

Japanese forces not only caught the U.S. Navy by surprise early on a Sunday morning in December 1941, decimating the Asiatic Fleet, but within
months, the Imperial Japanese Army had also cut off, killed, or captured all
U.S. ground forces stationed in Asia. By May of 1942, Gen. Douglas Mac-
Arthur's entire Army of the Pacific was either dead or in enemy hands; and
the general himself (against his own wishes) was ordered by President
Franklin D. Roosevelt to flee to Australia, so that America's most senior army
commander in the Pacific would not also become a prisoner of war.

As 1942 drew to a close, 26,943 Americans had become prisoners of the
Japanese. During the course of any war, fighting forces usually capture some of
each other's troops. But never before had so many Americans become captives of
an enemy in such a short time. Never before in our history had so many Americans remained prisoners for an entire war: three and a half very long years.

A total of 36,260 American soldiers, sailors, marines, airmen, and construction workers became Japan's prisoners, along with nearly 14,000 American civilians: men, women, and children who had been living or working in
territory occupied by Imperial Japanese forces. To compare the fates of
American prisoners held in the two major theaters of war from 1941 to 1945,
nearly 40 percent of U.S. military prisoners died in Japanese captivity, while
just over 1 percent of American POWs died in Nazi hands.[1] *Nine out of ten
prisoners who died in World War II perished while in Japanese custody.*

Approximately 25,000 American prisoners were sent to do slave labor in
the factories, shipyards, and mines owned by Japan's industrial giants, now
among the richest in the world: Mitsui, Mitsubishi, Showa Denko, Nippon
Steel, Kawasaki Heavy Industries, and at least forty other Japanese companies.
Our POWs were crammed into merchant ships bound for the home islands

of Japan or territories under Japanese occupation: Taiwan (called Formosa by the Japanese), northeast China, Manchuria (Manchukuo), Korea. Some Americans initially sent to work on the infamous Burma-Siam Railway were later shipped to Japan. But not all arrived alive: of 55,279 Allied POWs transported by merchant ships, 10,853 prisoners, including 3,632 Americans, drowned when their unmarked transport ships were torpedoed and at least 500 died at sea from disease and thirst in the hellish conditions aboard those merchant vessels. International law requires that vehicles or ships transporting prisoners be clearly identified. But there were no markings on these ships— except, according to POWs who worked at the docks, when merchant ships carried Japanese troops or weapons and supplies.

Even when they arrived "safely" in the port city of Moji, Japan, all of the prisoners were dazed, diseased, disoriented, and sometimes naked. They had been at sea for a month at least, sometimes two; one ship held POWs at sea for sixty-three days. Japanese civilians often threw stones, spat, and jeered as prisoners stumbled, shivering, through the streets to waiting trucks, trains, or ferries, which would carry them to a company worksite: 800 men here, 400 there.

According to official Japanese government records, in 1945, the final year of the war, 12,180 Americans were laboring at company worksites in the Japanese home islands. But many of these were replacements for fellow Americans who had already died at their work. Throughout the war, the population of prisoners laboring in Japanese companies was a grim revolving door: sick men arriving to replace those who had been cremated. General MacArthur reported recovering 19,202 Allied POWs, including 11,295 Americans, from Japan in September 1945.

An American who survived slave labor in Japan sees daily reminders of Japanese postwar prosperity: driving behind a pickup truck with the name "Mitsubishi" emblazoned in big letters across the tailgate; or along I-95, passing a fleet of huge container trucks bearing Mitsui's distinctive logo of three wavy lines—the same logo he may have seen each grueling day on that company's buildings and ships. Or if he rides in a brand new subway car in New York City manufactured by Kawasaki, and realizes that his tax dollars helped to purchase it. Kawasaki Heavy Industries used at least 250 American POWs for slave labor at its shipyard in Kobe, but the company was awarded a $190 million contract in December 1998 by the Metropolitan Transit Authority of New York to build 100 new subway cars. Kawasaki was awarded even larger contracts by transportation departments in Maryland and Boston, but our ex-POWs never got a dime from their former "employer."

Mitsui, Japan's largest exploiter of wartime prisoner labor, now operates the world's largest container fleet, and is the world's largest integrated trading company. Not only is the Mitsui family the most powerful in Japan outside the Imperial Palace, but this family-owned conglomerate has over recent years been ranked the third richest corporation on Earth—just behind General Motors and Ford. Several thousand Americans believe they were disabled helping to make that prosperity possible.

So eager were the industries of Japan to get white prisoners, especially Americans, into their wartime production workforce that they paid the Imperial Japanese Army a daily fee for each POW released to the company. They also provided living quarters for the prisoners—if you could call flimsy, unheated, vermin-infested barracks by that name. And some of the companies that owned merchant fleets were contracted to transport the prisoners in their own vessels, designated by the Japanese government as "auxiliary navy" ships.

Despite elaborate promises to the POWs, despite the pay sheets prisoners were forced to sign (written in Japanese), and contrary to statements in official Japanese government records, few prisoners ever saw any money from Japanese companies for their years of brutally hard labor. The words "forced labor" are commonly used to describe the work Allied POWs did in captivity. The term "slave labor," until now, has been applied only to civilians who are forced to work without pay. But the Japanese did everything possible to make prisoners of war feel like slaves, without any rights at all.

Japanese captors denied prisoners soap, hot water, and even toilet paper—then called the POWs "dirty Caucasians." Prisoners were issued a number, which they had to display pinned to their clothing at all times and were required to shout—in Japanese—at the daily *tenko* (roll call). No prisoner was addressed by name. During three and a half years of captivity, most prisoners had no change of clothes. They worked in the mountains of northern Japan, with snow up to the rooftops, in the same cotton clothes they were wearing when captured in the tropical climates of the Philippines or Java (Indonesia). They often had no shoes and were issued no safety equipment for their hazardous work in mines, at blast furnaces, shipyards, or factories.

When prisoners got sick (or became sicker than they already were), medicine was not made available, even if they were lucky enough to have a doctor in their midst. And no matter how sick he might be, a prisoner was forced to work, or he didn't eat—unless a fellow POW sneaked some food to his bedside.

The Japanese government agreed to distribute relief supply funds for prisoners, contributed by the U.S., British, and Dutch governments and placed in secret bank accounts set up through the Swiss National Bank. But the Yokohama Specie Bank was ordered not to release the funds, while a heartbreaking number of prisoners perished each day from starvation and disease.

Exceptions to these general conditions were very rare. After talking to more than 400 ex-POWs, what strikes this author is how very alike the experience was for prisoners of the Japanese, from Tamarkan in Thailand, to Taihoku in

Taiwan, to Tsuruga in the home islands. This was centrally organized, deliberately instigated slave labor.

The industries of wartime Japan profited enormously from prisoner labor: most POWs were highly skilled workers who could operate complex equipment; the seemingly endless supply of these unpaid workers made it possible for a Japanese company to keep production going at full tilt throughout the war—at least until American bombers found their targets. Prisoners were usually made to work long hours, even through air raids. Twelve- and fourteen-hour days were common. Sometimes a shift worked around the clock. Days off were virtually unheard of. And these prisoners could be pushed to the limit: if one died from overwork or starvation, there were plenty more available to take his place.

How were Japan's companies able to use so many prisoners in war-related jobs, in violation of international law? Why did their employees beat prisoners so brutally, steal their food, and lock up mail and Red Cross packages? And why weren't the heads of these companies prosecuted after the war for making such treatment standard policy? How did the companies of Japan literally get away with murder?

It was not until very recently, when this writer gained first access to newly declassified Japanese messages and other documents from the National Security Agency and the National Archives, that it has been possible to begin connecting the dots and showing that prisoners were sent to company property, at the companies' request, to live and work. Only since 1996 has it been possible to help ex-POWs learn where, precisely, they went, and why, and for which companies they toiled. This writer has been the first to do so, and to help build a record showing the pattern of deliberate abuse to which these men were subjected.

Some clues can be found in the pattern of America's own postwar policies, reflected in how some liberated POWs were told not to discuss their captivity experiences; how the Americans orchestrated the Tokyo War Crimes Trials; and how the U.S. government manipulated the 1951 Treaty of Peace with Japan. But much of the record has been constructed from razor-sharp recollections by the ex-prisoners themselves: the diaries they secretly kept; the photos they dared to take; and the many pictures of prisoners actually taken by Japanese company photographers—showing Japanese executives sitting, smugly, and the gaunt prisoners standing in rows behind their "employers."

The Pacific War record exists, but not all of it has been made public. Even after over half a century, some U.S. government agencies insist upon keeping certain material relating to Pacific POWs classified. After several boxes of documents relating to the Pacific War were declassified in 1996, the direct link could finally be more strongly established between wartime slave labor by Allied POWs and the Japanese companies responsible for it. The first clues, as mentioned earlier, were in newly declassified secret Japanese wartime messages, indicating how eager the industries of Japan were to get large numbers of white prisoners to their sites, as quickly as possible. An examination of official Japanese records showed a company name at nearly every POW camp. But it was only after detailed interviews with hundreds of ex-POWs that a consistent pattern emerged, showing that the control, supervision, and assignment to duties for POWs were made by company employees, not members of the armed forces.

"Who provided your living quarters?" I would ask during interviews. "Who escorted you to work? Who supervised you during work hours? Who administered discipline?" (a reference to often brutal beatings). And the answer was always company employees—except in cases of an occasional road or rail project or dam, though after completing those tasks, prisoners were usually sent on to industrial sites. Most American POWs were moved around several times during their captivity.

So the full story of what really happened to American and Allied prisoners, and why, is still being pieced together. Even some Japanese are surprised now and then by the blur of their country's own wartime history. A Japanese couple I know, professionals in their sixties, grew up in Tokyo and remember vividly the fire bombings they survived as children. For many years they have lived and worked in New York; periodically they take a vacation in Hawaii. Recently, they were strolling down a street in Honolulu when a pair of young Japanese honeymooners rushed toward them.

"Please help us, we are so confused," the newlyweds begged. "We have just been to some place called Pearl Harbor, and there seems to be a memorial involving an American navy ship. Tell us please, were we ever at war with the United States?"

Incredulous, the older couple exchanged glances, then answered softly, "Yes, we were at war with the United States over fifty years ago."

"Then tell us please," the groom asked, "Who won?"

If you're talking in terms of economics, the answer would have to be Japan, hands down. And the companies that used Allied prisoners for slave labor during the war had a big head start for their spectacular peacetime prosperity. Every major Japanese company's balance sheet has a hidden column that should be marked: "Unjust enrichment from the labor of another."

Five Japanese corporations have been selected for special focus in this book: the three that exploited the largest number of American prisoners, Mitsui, Mitsubishi, and Nippon Steel; and two others, which also used American POWs at their worksites and which do a large volume of business in the United States, Showa Denko and Kawasaki Heavy Industries.

In the following pages, a shocking story will unfold of how Japanese companies laid the foundations of their postwar fortunes on the backs of prisoners of war, and how hundreds of American ex-POWs have finally found the voice, strength, and evidence to sue those companies in the United States, where they do multibillion-dollar business each year. It will be a story told fully for the first time.

Chapter 1

"A Personal War, A Dirty War"

In mid-1941, a group of Japanese diplomats bowed politely, one by one, as they departed from a meeting at the White House with President Franklin D. Roosevelt. As soon as the door clicked shut, the president is said to have remarked to an aide: "They hate us. Sooner or later they'll come after us."[1] And come after us they did, with a vengeance, on December 7, 1941.

But "us" was not just the Asiatic Fleet at Pearl Harbor; or the ground and air army units scattered from the Philippine Islands to the Dutch East Indies; or the Marines guarding diplomatic communities on mainland China. "Us" was also civilian construction workers on Wake, Guam, and Cavite Islands; "us" was American businessmen, church missionaries, doctors, nurses, travellers, embassy officials—along with their wives, children, and office staff.

Within hours of attacking the U.S. naval base at Pearl Harbor, Hawaii, on Sunday morning (Pacific time), December 8, 1941, Japanese military forces throughout Asia began rounding up American military and civilian personnel. By nightfall, even a garrison of Marines guarding a remote outpost in northern China had been ordered to surrender. By the time the U.S. Congress declared war on Japan the following day, territories under the American flag in the Pacific were under attack. Before Christmas, 1,146 American civilian construction workers on Wake Island, along with 379 Marines, were captured when Wake and Guam islands were overwhelmed by Japanese naval, air, and assault forces. During the first week in March 1942, a field artillery unit from Texas, along with some members of a California field artillery battalion, sent to help the Dutch hold Java—was forced to surrender when the Dutch gave up and capitulated to the Japanese, hoping to avoid total slaughter. They were soon joined by a handful of survivors from the cruiser USS *Houston,* sunk offshore in the Java Sea after a fierce naval battle that lasted two days. By March 6, over 700 Americans had been captured on Java; most being sent to work on the infamous Burma-Siam Railway.

American captives, mostly civilian construction workers, on Wake Island are made to sit out in the open on the airstrip for two days and nights, December 23–24, 1941.
SKETCH BY JOSEPH ASTARITA

By April 9, 1942, after the last of their food and ammunition ran out, 11,796 exhausted, malnourished, and sick American defenders of Bataan, along with some 66,000 Filipino troops, surrendered to the Japanese, who lost 10,000 men taking the peninsula in a five-month campaign. Less than a month later, on May 6, Corregidor, the last Philippine holdout under the American flag, fell to the Japanese, and another 6,000 Americans became prisoners of war.

Americans back home were stunned to learn that Gen. Douglas MacArthur's entire Army of the Pacific had been killed or captured in just six months. It was the greatest defeat of land forces in U.S. military history, and it meant that over 20,000 Americans were now prisoners of the Japanese.

What the home front was less quick to learn was that 5,000 Americans perished in Japanese hands during their first six months of captivity. In fact, news of Japanese mistreatment of American prisoners was so suppressed during the war, and so swept under the rug afterward, that public awareness on this subject remains relatively low, to this day.

By early 1942, nearly 14,000 American civilians were also caught in the dragnet as Imperial Japanese forces swept through Southeast Asia and the Pacific—rounding up every Caucasian man, woman, and child in their path. Expecting deportation, then desperately hoping for rescue, non-Asian families realized to their horror that house arrest was being replaced by jails and prison camps. Civilians were treated as harshly as military prisoners, and classified as enemy aliens, or spies.

Worse still, the trapped civilians were not protected by the 1929 Geneva Conventions, not only because Japan's Diet declined to ratify the agreements its government representative had signed in Switzerland, but also because the documents specified standards of treatment only for military prisoners of war.

No provision had been made for civilians; after all, interning civilians is not supposed to be part of a nation's war strategy. And besides, governments are supposed to keep their overseas civilians out of harm's way, and evacuate them at the first sign of trouble.

How could the U.S. government leave so many of its people in harm's way? Couldn't they see what was coming? Couldn't the military forces have been more alert? Americans have been asking themselves—and their successive leaders—these questions for more than half a century.

What happened to U.S. citizens, civilian and military, in the Pacific in the first dark months of 1942 was the result of wishful thinking, a woeful misreading of the situation, outright deception, and fear.

Wishful thinking was what some of the State Department officials indulged in, as they tried to assure each other that the United States' previous actions would merit special consideration from Japan. After all, the U.S. had acted as Japan's international advocate and sponsor as far back as 1871 in Hawaii; and again during the Russo-Japanese War in 1904-5, when it had arranged for the release of 2,000 Japanese POWs; and at the outbreak of World War I in 1914, when the U.S. government saw to it that every Japanese civilian trapped in harm's way in Europe was returned safely to Japan.[2] Surely, they thought, the Japanese government would remember these acts, and protect U.S. citizens, should hostilities erupt in the Pacific.

Francis B. Sayre, U.S. high commissioner to the Philippines, told Congress after the war that it had been impossible to predict in 1941 whether Japan would make a direct attack on the Philippines, and that he was advised by Washington that it would not be in the national interest to issue a warning notice to U.S. civilians living and working there. When Americans asked his advice, he said, he told them they should decide for themselves whether or not to stay.[3] Similarly, our ambassador to Japan, Joseph Grew, issued a series of "suggestions"—not warnings—throughout 1941 to Americans living in the region.

High Commissioner Sayre and Ambassador Grew apparently didn't see an article written by Japanese general Kiyokatsu Sato in the August 1940 *New Current Digest,* published in Tokyo. The general had it all figured out: how to conquer the United States in several stages. Key to his plan was to take possession of Hawaii, relying on a navy that would be swifter than ours. Next would come the Panama Canal; then landings on the West Coast. Japanese troops would then mass along the Rocky Mountains, and on to New York! The whole campaign would take seven years, by the general's estimate. Melvin Simons, one of the few Marines to survive the bloody battle on the tiny island of Peleliu, found a map of the United States in a dead Japanese soldier's pocket, which showed little Japanese flags up to the Rockies, and little American flags from there to the East Coast. So General Sato's plan must have been widely used to inspire the emperor's fighting men.[4]

Much has been written over the last five decades about whether President Franklin D. Roosevelt "allowed" the United States to be attacked, so that the country would turn away from its isolationism and be willing to enter another world war, after rebuffing calls for help from Europe for over two years.

Throughout the summer and fall of 1941, both the United States and Japan rattled sabers at each other, diplomatically. Frustrated by Japan's refusal to halt her advances in Asia, President Roosevelt froze all Japanese credits in the United States on July 26, 1941, and a few weeks later, on August 17, he warned Japan that further expansion in the region would force the United States to take immediately "Any and all steps necessary to protect American interests in Asia."[5]

Tighter restrictions were placed on registration requirements for Japanese doing business in the United States, and Japan imposed similar restrictions on Americans traveling in and out of Japan. Despite the increase in tension, American officials still continued to issue only "suggestions" to U.S. citizens about leaving the region.

But by far the most illuminating information about Japan's intentions in 1941 was rediscovered in 1998 by Takeo Iguchi, a professor of law and international relations at International Christian University in Tokyo, who gained access to recently declassified documents in his country's Foreign Ministry archives. The papers show that factions within the Japanese government prevented a proposed warning to the United States from being delivered as written. In a Final Memorandum dated December 3, 1941, four days before the attack on Pearl Harbor, the original wording stated that Japan was forced to terminate negotiations [concerning its continuing expansion in Asia] and that the United States "[w]ould be responsible for any and all of the consequences that may arise in the future."[6]

Professor Iguchi also noted that the war diary of Japan's General Staff (comparable to the U.S. Joint Chiefs of Staff) displayed an ongoing debate in Tokyo over whether to notify Washington of Japan's intent to cease negotiations and start a war, in compliance with the provisions of the Hague Convention of 1907. Since military members were given equal status with civilians in Japan's cabinet, and enjoyed direct access to the emperor, their views usually prevailed. The apparent compromise was to draft a revised Final Memorandum, with much weaker wording, on December 5 and send it to Washington. This draft was intercepted by our intelligence, and read by President Roosevelt, who interpreted it as a declaration of war. But his aides disagreed, saying the memo contained nothing new, and their collective "wisdom" dissuaded the president from ordering an increase in preparations and a standby alert for war to our military forces stationed in Asia and the Pacific.

On the day before Pearl Harbor was attacked, an entry in the war diary of the Japanese General Staff reads: "Our deceptive diplomacy is steadily proceeding toward success." Japanese diplomats in Washington were deliberately not notified of their government's plans.

Professor Iguchi further found that the staff in Tokyo specified that the watered-down message be delivered to our State Department at 1 P.M. Washington time on December 7, but records show it was received by Secretary of State Cordell Hull at 2:20 P.M., about one hour after most of the American Asiatic fleet lay sunk or burning in Pearl Harbor, and 2,403 Americans were dead. Professor Iguchi maintains that the hour-and-twenty-minute delay in delivery of the memorandum was also deliberate, because it contained purposely garbled wording difficult to translate.

So at long last, Professor Iguchi's research, which received scant attention in the Japanese press, would appear to lay to rest the theory of a calculated plan on the part of President Roosevelt to sit back and allow the attack on Pearl Harbor to take place. To the contrary, it would seem that President Roosevelt was more alert than his aides to the bellicose plans of Japan toward the United States. For example, the president, a former naval officer and past secretary of the navy, became alarmed by intelligence reports showing an unusual increase in Japanese naval activity during October and November 1941—but again, his concern was deflected by "cooler heads," notably General MacArthur himself. According to Joseph Della Malva, a Corregidor survivor who was an army intelligence agent in the Philippines in 1941, General MacArthur was convinced that the Japanese attack (of which most were certain) would come no earlier than April 1942, and he "tamped down" a standby alert issued to forces there in October 1941. MacArthur's view prevailed at the White House, and the president was dissuaded from following his Navy-trained instincts.[7]

Probably the communication that has most fueled the speculation that the United States deliberately waited for Japan to attack first is the cable transmitted by army chief of staff general George C. Marshall to General MacArthur and Lt. Gen. Walter Short, commander of the Army of the Philippines, on November 27, 1941. It read in part: "Negotiations with Japan appear to be terminated . . . Japanese future action unpredictable. Hostile action possible at any moment . . . If hostilities cannot repeat cannot be avoided, the United States desires that Japan commit the first attack."[8] Wishful thinking in Washington, combined with misreading obvious signs of trouble, helped the Japanese deception to succeed.

Also, contrary to the impressions of many historians, U.S. intelligence really couldn't accurately decode everything the Japanese were saying to each other in the weeks before the attack on Pearl Harbor. U.S. intelligence cryptologists had broken the initial code of the Japanese Navy, known as JN25-A, but they had mastered only about 800 of the 35,000 values of the newer code, designated JN25-B, which was in use by December 1941. So when the coded attack message: "Climb Niitakayama 1208, repeat 1208!" was repeatedly flashed to the Japanese fleet on December 2, 1941, our cryptologists could not decode its full meaning, which was to attack Pearl Harbor on December 8 (Pacific time; December 7 on the U.S. mainland). Several crucial weeks would go by before JN25-B was finally broken, in early 1942.[9]

And then there was the fear. So often history is an exercise in hindsight, viewed from a safe distance, and the context of the times is overlooked. For those of us who did not live through the uncertain months of 1942, it is hard to imagine the genuine fear that gripped the United States and its leaders in the aftermath of Pearl Harbor. The fact is that throughout most of that year, until cryptologists broke the Japanese Navy code, and until the military and manufacturing industries could fully mobilize, the West Coast of the United States was very, very vulnerable to Japanese attack; and despite reassurances, most people knew it.

Nine days after the fall of Bataan, on April 18, 1942, Brig. Gen. James H. Doolittle led a daring daylight air raid on Tokyo. On May 28, Secretary of War Henry Stimson held a press conference in Washington, in which he said the War Department considered a retaliatory attack by Japan on the United States to be inevitable. The Associated Press, in a wire story reprinted in newspapers throughout the world, quoted Secretary Stimson as saying the U.S. Army was doing everything possible to meet the attack, which he indicated was being expected on the West Coast. "Whatever happens, we shan't relax our most effective defense—our preparations for a major offensive," he said. Secretary Stimson also told a questioner that despite the great distance the East Coast lies from Japan, an attack on the national capital was "not inconceivable. . . . The 'loss of face' Japan suffered from the army air attack led by . . . [General] . . . Doolittle made a vengeance blow inevitable," he contended.[10]

All the American people needed to fan fears were the reports of espionage by Japanese in their midst: a cache of weapons and uniforms found in the barn of a Japanese farmer in California; dozens of suspected Japanese saboteurs arrested in the Naval yard at Pearl Harbor; newly captured American prisoners in the Philippines recognizing the face of a Japanese guard who the previous week was a shopkeeper in Manila; a soldier on patrol defending Bataan hearing a Japanese soldier nearby calling out mockingly: "I'm a graduate of UCLA!" A number of ex-POWs have told this writer that the worst beatings they received during their captivity were administered by interpreters with degrees from American universities.

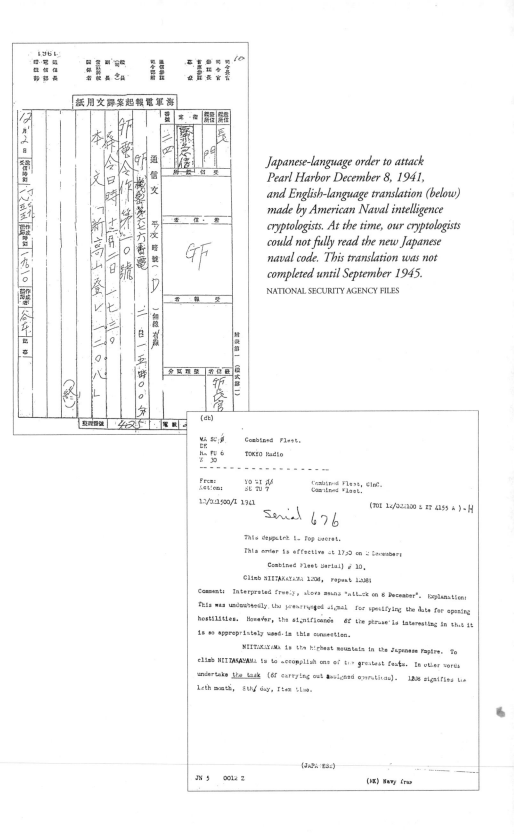

Japanese-language order to attack Pearl Harbor December 8, 1941, and English-language translation (below) made by American Naval intelligence cryptologists. At the time, our cryptologists could not fully read the new Japanese naval code. This translation was not completed until September 1945.

NATIONAL SECURITY AGENCY FILES

Before Pearl Harbor was attacked, the Federal Bureau of Investigation already had a list of 770 Japanese living in the United States who were considered a threat to national security. By nightfall on December 7, 1941, both the president and the attorney general had authorized FBI director J. Edgar Hoover to detain those individuals, and he promptly did so. California attorney general Earl Warren stated that in his view all people of Japanese descent living in the United States were a potential threat, whether they were citizens or not.[11]

A week after Pearl Harbor was attacked, Congressman John Rankin declared on the floor of the U.S. House of Representatives: "I'm for catching every Japanese in America, Alaska and Hawaii now, and putting them in concentration camps. . . . Damn them! Let's get rid of them now!"[12] Little did the congressman know that the Japanese felt exactly the same way about Americans and other Caucasians living in Asia.

But despite the nationwide clamor, President Roosevelt did not issue Executive Order 9066, declaring the West Coast a military zone and establishing the War Relocation Authority, until March 2, 1942, nearly three months after Pearl Harbor, and after seeing with dismay that the Japanese were not making any effort to send American civilians home, out of harm's way. Instead, the Japanese had already interned over 14,000 American men, women, and children by the time President Roosevelt issued his executive order—a fact that is often overlooked in discussions about the wartime internment of people of Japanese descent in the United States.

The ethnic cleansing carried out by Japan in the Pacific War was part of its Greater Eastern Coprosperity program, under the slogan "Asia for the Asians." It became apparent very early on to the Caucasians held by the Japanese that they were not only unwelcome in Asia, but were very deeply resented, and had been for a long time. White women were a special target of Japanese anger and contempt, partly because women of European descent living in Asia had households full of Asian servants. The Japanese perception was that Caucasians looked down upon all Asians as servants, and turning the tables was one of the main aims of their conquest.

Japanese civilians, as well as military personnel, often seemed to take special pleasure in finding daily ways to humiliate and mistreat the thousands of military prisoners suddenly under their control. Within six months of the attack on Pearl Harbor, the remnants of America's Asia/Pacific fighting force, along with over a thousand civilians, were being *leased* to Japanese companies for forced labor. At least seventy-nine Japanese companies used POW slave labor, according to the official records of the Japanese Prisoner of War Information Bureau. Prisoners were loaned, like chattel, from one company to another.

Each day, each man knew he was expendable; the company could just send for more prisoners to replace the ones who died that day from disease, starvation, and from being worked to death. Over 4,100 Americans died while on forced labor; many were so weak from starvation and disease that they died within a few months of again becoming free men. At least 11,532 American prisoners perished in Japanese captivity.[13]

Military prisoners who understood Japanese sometimes overheard guards reassure one another that it was all right to mistreat prisoners, or skim from their food supply, because "They're only dirty Caucasians."

Ken Towery, a Texan captured on Corregidor with his army unit, still remembers the speech with which the Japanese commandant greeted prisoners at the vast Mitsubishi factory complex in Mukden, Manchuria. The yellow and the white man are eternal enemies, the Japanese officer announced, and as long as the white man was in Asia "There will be no peace in Asia." At Towery's camp, the Japanese did their best to assure a peaceful future in Asia: of 1,500 POWs who began the journey to Manchuria with Towery aboard the merchant ship *Nitta Maru* in January, 1942, 500 were left in Japan, deemed too weak to be any good for work. An additional 80 were dropped off at Pusan, Korea—too sick to bother transporting farther. Several died at sea due to the dreadful conditions in the sealed hold of the ship. Only 1,100 arrived alive at Mukden, including 920 from the *Nitta Maru*. Of these, 300 died the first winter in the extreme cold, and from being forced to live in unheated semiunderground mud barracks, built some years earlier by Chinese soldiers. "We buried 176 in one day that first winter," Towery recalled in a March 2000 interview.[14]

Before the day of liberation came, it was the Japanese plan that no white prisoners at all should survive to resettle in Asia—or anywhere else. How early in this very personal Pacific War that policy was formulated, and how precisely it was carried out, is revealed by some of the men, women, and children who weren't supposed to live to tell about this holocaust in the East—but somehow they did, and their stories are backed up by the messages Japanese military leaders never expected to be intercepted, recorded, or retrieved.

In a 1995 panel discussion at the Overseas Press Club in New York, Marine Corps veteran John Rich, who spent twenty postwar years in Tokyo as NBC news bureau chief, commented that in the Pacific, World War II was "A personal war, a dirty war." And a very racist war, on both sides of the ocean—right from the very beginning. Nowhere was that racism more evident than on Japanese company property. Yet unlike German companies and the German government, which together have paid billions to their wartime slave laborers, not one Japanese corporation has paid ex-POWs a postwar dime for such unjust enrichment.

Why? Because no one has ever asked them to—until now.

Chapter 2

"We Don't Recognize the Red Cross"

"ARE YOU GOING TO LET THE RED CROSS KNOW I'M ALIVE?" LEROY SIEGEL asked after his B-29 was shot down over Nagoya, Japan, on April 7, 1945. Siegel, a gunner, was twenty years old, badly bruised, and thoroughly shaken, facing his interrogators in an old castle used for the purpose—and wondering if any of his fellow crew members had survived.

"We don't recognize the Red Cross," was the Japanese interpreter's chilling reply, according to Siegel.

That wasn't quite the response the world's leading nations had in mind when they met in Geneva after World War I to tighten the rules, or conventions, governing the treatment and deployment of prisoners of war. In 1929, the Geneva Conventions were adopted and signed by Japan's delegate, Hasahi Kobayashi, who later became a vice admiral in the Imperial Japanese Navy—the man later held responsible for the massacre of 139 U.S. Marines at Palawan Island in 1944. But back in 1929, Kobayashi was still playing the diplomat and was signing, on his country's behalf, conventions, which stated in black and white that prisoners of war should be protected by international law.

Unfortunately, some members of his government didn't entirely agree. When it came time to ratify the Geneva Conventions, the Japanese Diet [parliament] ratified the Red Cross Convention, which was part of the 1929 document; but militarists, who prevailed in the Diet, argued that detailed regulations involving treatment and deployment of prisoners would never apply to their nationals, because no Japanese soldier (or sailor or airman) would dishonor himself by surrendering to the enemy. Death would be preferable. So that section of the Geneva Conventions made no sense to this powerful section of Japan's lawmakers, and they refused to ratify it.

This omission made the U.S. government very nervous in the weeks following Japan's stunningly successful attack on Pearl Harbor, and its lightning advances into Southeast Asia, including the Philippines. With thousands of American military personnel already in Japanese custody by mid-December 1941, the U.S. legation in Bern, Switzerland, sent the following urgent request to the Swiss government as our designated representative, or Protecting Power:

> Please request the Swiss Government through its representative at Tokyo to make a communication in the following sense to the Japanese Government:
>
> It is the intention of the Government of the United States as a party to the Geneva Prisoner of War Convention and the Geneva Red Cross Convention, both of July 27, 1929, to apply the provisions of these conventions.
>
> It is, furthermore, the intention of the Government of the United States to apply the provisions of the Geneva Prisoner of War Convention to any civilian enemy aliens that may be interned, in so far as the provisions of that convention may be adaptable thereto.
>
> Although the Japanese Government is a signatory of the above conventions, it is understood not to have ratified the Geneva Prisoner of War Convention. The Government of the United States nevertheless hopes that the Japanese Government will apply the provisions of both conventions reciprocally in the above sense.
>
> The Government of the United States would appreciate receiving an expression of the intentions of the Japanese Government in this respect.

The message is signed by Secretary of State Cordell Hull. After seven weeks of anxious waiting, our State Department finally received a reply to its query, on February 4, 1942, from the Swiss Foreign Ministry in Bern:

> Reference Department's [message no.] 331, December 18. Swiss Minister, Tokyo, telegraphs January 30 as follows:
>
> Japanese Government has informed me: First. Japan is strictly observing Geneva Red Cross Convention as a signatory state. Second. Although not bound by the Convention relative [to] treatment of prisoners of war Japan will apply *mutatis mutandis* provisions of that convention to American prisoners of war in its power.

Japan's foreign minister, Togo Shigenori, had the previous week offered the same assurance to the United States via the embassy of Spain (Japan's Protecting Power) in Washington, D.C. But several months later, on December 11, 1942, the Japanese government gave an ominous clarification to *"mutatis mutandis,"* usually translated "as the situation arises." Responding to American protests about treatment of our prisoners of war in China, the following telegram was sent by Japan on December 11, 1942:

> Japanese government has informed American government [it] had decided to apply *mutatis mutandis* Geneva Convention [of] July 27, 1929, regarding treatment [of] prisoners of war but without any way changing Japanese laws in force.[1]

And Japan's policies regarding POWs were being formed as fast as prisoners were being taken. On December 27, 1941, four days after the American flag was lowered on Wake Island, an official Prisoner of War Information Bureau was established in Japan's government, by Imperial Decree. But the bureau was supervised by the Ministry of War, which quickly created its own Prisoner of War Management Bureau, headed by the most powerful man in Japan and architect of its war machine: Gen. Hideki Tojo, minister of war, minister without portfolio, and—throughout much of the conflict—prime minister as well. On January 8, 1942, Tojo issued a Field Service Code order that set forth how every Japanese, military and civilian, was expected to view prisoners of war. "To live as a prisoner of war is to live without honor," Tojo proclaimed. And to a Japanese, life without honor is a worthless existence. Prisoners, therefore, were worthless—expendable—not deserving of any consideration.[2] As historian Gavan Daws put it, a white prisoner of the Japanese became "A thing with a Japanese number."[3]

Despite the reassuring words of Foreign Minister Shigenori, Japan's Ministry of War had already wrested away responsibility for prisoners of war from the diplomats; and within the first month of America's involvement in World War II, the fate of U.S. prisoners in Japanese hands had been sealed.

It took until April 1942 for the International Committee of the Red Cross to obtain information from Japan's Prisoner of War Information Bureau about the nearly 1,200 civilians and 379 Marines captured on Guam on December 10, 1941, and on Wake Island on December 23. As for the terrified Wake prisoners, they sat on the tarmac, stripped to the waist, for two days and nights, two days before Christmas, with a few sips of water and bits of bread. Meanwhile, Japanese officers argued whether to kill them or to accede to international law and frantic U.S. State Department demands that the civilians be released—or to capitalize on their luck and put these skilled construction workers to good use in Japan. It is no coincidence that many of the Wake Island civilians found themselves work-ing for Fujinagata Shipbuilding, Tsuruga Stevedore, Kawasaki Heavy Indus-tries shipyards, and Nippon Ko-Kan.

Families of Americans captured in the Philippines only received word that their loved ones had survived the hideous sixty-five-mile Bataan Death March of April 1942 eight agonizing months later, in December. Some fami-lies did not receive positive confirmation that their sons, brothers, or hus-bands were prisoners of the Japanese until a year after their capture. The official 1948 postwar report of the International Committee of the Red Cross (ICRC) states: "Communications from the Japanese Official [POW Informa-tion] Bureau about military personnel taken prisoner . . . came in slowly all through the war. No news reached the [ICRC] concerning wounded and sick prisoners. The Japanese Official Bureau also failed to send any death certifi-cates." In a classic understatement, this section of the report concludes: "The situation was far from satisfactory."⁴

Despite the fact that the Japanese government had notified the Swiss ambassador Camille Gorgé, in Tokyo on January 30, 1942, that "Japan is strictly observing the Geneva Red Cross Convention as a signatory state," the Japanese Red Cross refused to cooperate with the ICRC headquarters in Manila, using as its reason the fact that the Philippine office had initially been set up under the aegis of the American Red Cross. A hastily issued new char-ter from Geneva, making the Manila office autonomous, still didn't speed up cooperation from Tokyo. On February 1, 1942, the beleaguered commander of the Army of the Pacific, Gen. Douglas MacArthur, informed Secretary of War Henry Stimson that Americans in the Philippines were receiving "Extremely harsh and rigid measures [characterized by] abuse and special humiliation [designed] to discredit the white races."⁵

And it wasn't any better for Americans taken prisoner on Java [Indonesia] in early March 1942. The Texas 131st Field Artillery unit, captured there when the Dutch command capitulated, became known in the local press as the Lost Battalion, because no one had any official confirmed information about them for so long. Most Americans are astounded, even today, to learn that 668 Americans, including a National Guard unit from California and survivors of the cruiser USS *Houston,* toiled with members of the Texas bat-talion building the Burma-Siam Railway. Because a Japanese radio broadcast in May 1942 mentioned the abuse of USS *Houston* survivors, the Office of War Information's Facts and Figures (OFF) Unit in Washington released the text of remarks made by Rear Adm. Mitsuo Matsunaga, partly because it gave American families reason to hope that their loved ones might be alive as pris-oners. The Associated Press put out the story on its news wire, and it was picked up by papers all across America.

PLEA TO ROOSEVELT

Maharaja of Indore Asks Aid in Indian Problem.

Bombay, May 28 (A. P.).—The Maharaja of Indore appealed to President Roosevelt in an open letter today for joint American, Chinese and Russian arbitration in the autonomy dispute between India and Britain. Pledging himself "without question to abide by any decision," the Maharaja proposed that the United States, China and Russia send two representatives each to India to study the problem and advance a solution.

The ruler of one of India's most important States, he described himself as "by the accident of birth, a ruling prince" but "an internationalist and democrat by conviction." His wife is the former Miss Marguerite Lawler, of Fargo, N. D. She is in New York.

broadcast was designed for home listening and might have had a domestic propaganda purpose.

"Nevertheless, the information is disclosed in accordance with the policy of announcing all substantial evidence relating to prisoners of war and interned civilians."

OFF said the Japanese admiral described an inspection trip by plane from March 3 to March 30 in the "southern countries" under control of the Japanese. Special visits were made, it was said, to the Philippines and the Netherlands East Indies.

"Many Suffer From Hunger"

The text of the statement by Matsunaga, identified as a former aircraft carrier commander, was quoted by OFF as follows:

"What kind of work are American prisoners from the Houston engaged in in this sector? They are engaged in the work of filling the holes of the airfields. They are engaged on comparatively easy jobs. There are many who are suffering from hunger because they are not used to Japanese type food and there are some who get very lazy because of the extreme heat.

Some "Severely Beaten"

"Those who do not do their part are beaten by the Japanese guards who are placed on watch on a ratio of about one guard to one hundred prisoners. Those who are hard to handle are severely beaten with rope which is similar to rope used by sailors. Because of the pain lazy Americans continue the work with expressions of suffering on their faces."

The OFF statement noted that the Navy Department had announced that it had not been in communication with the USS Houston since the battle of the Java Sea February 27 and February 28.

A Later Report

The most recent report by the State Department, on May 23, said

that, on the basis of statements from neutral observers in places where investigation was permitted by the enemy, the Axis nations appeared to be abiding by the Geneva convention on treatment of prisoners of war.

"However," OFF said, "the State Department report specifically explained that it had been impossible, because of the refusal of Japan to admit neutral observers, to obtain first-hand information concerning the treatment of prisoners of war held in Philippines, in parts of occupied China, in Hongkong, Malaya and the Netherlands East Indies."

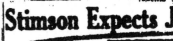

Stimson Expects J

Thinks Retaliatory Blow Inevitable—Says Defen

Washington, May 28 (A. P.).— today the War Department conside on the United States to be inevital Brig.-Gen. James H. Doolittle's att Japanese cities.

The Secretary told a press conference that the army was doing everything possible to meet the expected attack, which he indicated was looked for on the West Coast.

"Whatever happens, we shan't relax our most effective defense —our preparations for a major offensive," he said.

Mr. Stimson also told a questioner that despite the great distance the East Coast lies from Japan, an attack on the national capital was "not inconceivable." He did not discuss the possibility of attacks by Japan's Axis partners.

May Strike to Regain 'Face.'

"The 'loss of face' Japan suffered from the army air attack led by Gen. Doolittle made a vengeance blow inevitable, he contended.

"The United States, through Gen. Doolittle, inflicted a stinging, humiliating, surprise blow on

Jap Radio Tells Of Beating Of U. S. Prisoners

MAY 29 1942

[By the Associated Press]

Washington, May 28—The Office of Facts and Figures today quoted a Japanese broadcast which, it said, was intended for home consumption, as saying that American prisoners from the cruiser Houston were being forced to do manual labor and, if laggard, were beaten with ropes.

The OFF cited this broadcast, by Rear Admiral Mitsuo Matsunaga, as describing such treatment as "contrary to all international agreement and all humanity."

"This evidence," the OFF cautioned, "differs from reports of neutral observers who have been permitted to inspect prisoner conditions in a limited portion of Japanese territory."

Domestic Propaganda

It added:

"The Office of Facts and Figures also cautions that the Japanese

Associated Press wire story telling of Japanese admiral Mitsuo Matsunaga's boasting about mistreatment of USS Houston *survivors, May 29, 1942. The* Houston *was sunk off Java on March 1, 1942, and no official word about surviving crew members had been received until this message was heard over Tokyo radio. Secretary of War Stimson's remarks about expected Japanese attack on U.S. mainland appear in the adjacent column.* ASSOCIATED PRESS FILES

Apparently Admiral Matsunaga couldn't resist gloating over the airwaves about the abuse and humiliation the surviving crew members of the *Houston* were being subjected to. The cruiser had been the flagship of the U.S. Asiatic Fleet and its sinking was a point of particular pride to the Japanese Navy. Between December 8, 1941, and March 1, 1942 (the night the *Houston* actually went down), the Japanese Navy claimed to have sunk her about eight times, prompting the crew to nickname their ship "the Galloping Ghost of the Java Coast." One can almost hear the mockery in the admiral's voice as he gives this account:

> What kind of work are American prisoners from the *Houston* engaged in[,] in this sector? They are engaged in the work of filling the holes of the air fields. They are engaged on comparatively easy jobs. There are many who are suffering from hunger because they are not used to Japanese-type food and there are some who get very lazy because of the extreme heat.
>
> Those who do not do their part are beaten by the Japanese guards, who are placed on a ratio of about one guard for 100 prisoners. Those who are hard to handle are severely beaten with rope which is similar to rope used by sailors. Because of the pain the lazy Americans continue the work with expressions of suffering on their faces.

The Associated Press story goes on to say:

> The OFF statement noted that the Navy Department had announced that it had not been in communication with the USS *Houston* since the battle of the Java Sea on February 27 and 28. The most recent report by the State Department on May 23 said that, on the basis of statements from neutral observers in places where investigations were permitted by the enemy, the Axis nations [Germany, Italy, and Japan] appeared to be abiding by the Geneva Convention on treatment of prisoners of war. However, the State Department report specifically explained that it had been impossible, because of the refusal of Japan to admit neutral observers, to obtain first-hand information concerning the treatment of prisoners of war held in the Philippines, in parts of occupied China, in Hongkong, Malaya and the Netherlands East Indies.[6]

The Office of Facts and Figures may have speculated that Admiral Matsunaga's boasting may have just been propaganda for home consumption, but Melvin "Ollie" Danner, a civilian construction worker captured on Wake Island, remembers receiving it. Apparently there was enough ship's rope handy at the Tsuruga Stevedore shipyard in Osaka for the rope punishment to be used on him—for having a rice ball in his possession. Here is his account of that awful day in 1944, when he received a rope beating, which left him permanently injured:

> I received a ration of three cigarettes, but believed that food was more important to me than tobacco. I found a [Japanese] convict working in the same area who had a large rice ball for lunch, but was not allowed to have cigarettes, so we made a swap. I started to the latrine to eat the rice ball where I would not be seen. A little Japanese soldier stopped and searched me and found the rice ball. He took it away from me and made me stand at attention while he got a rope and tied knots in the end. Then he stood back and struck me repeatedly so the rope would wrap around my head and snap in my face, and he would then give it a jerk. He did this until he was tired. As the result of this beating I am now legally blind in both eyes.[7]

Article 40 of the Geneva Conventions stipulates that prisoners should be permitted to send and receive mail, but this provision must have interfered with existing Japanese policy, because rarely in Japanese-occupied territory was there such a thing as "mail call." Occasionally, a family member might receive a preprinted postcard, signed by a POW as much as a year earlier. The printed, cryptic lines would read: "My health is (good, usual, poor). . . . I am (have been) in hospital. . . . I am working (not working) for pay at ———" (this line was always crossed out by the POWs, since they were hardly ever being paid.) The prisoner was allowed to write up to twelve carefully chosen words. But family members said that by the time his message reached home, so many months had passed that a mother or wife could only wonder if her loved one were still alive. In an act of particularly malevolent cruelty, Japanese camp commanders would accept sacks of mail for the prisoners, but refuse to distribute them. At one company worksite in Japan, the staff amused themselves by pinning photographs of wives, sweethearts, and babies all over the inside walls of the guardhouse, then throwing away the letters—a discovery the infuriated prisoners made the day they were liberated.

And the folks back home let it be known that they weren't hearing anything from their loved ones in Japanese custody—in sharp contrast to those later held in German military stalags, or fixed POW camps. Apparently a Swiss inspector had actually been allowed to visit a POW camp in Hokkaido where most of the prisoners were British, and had been assured by the Japanese camp commander that prisoners were permitted to send two postcards per month. When this information was passed on to the British Legation in Switzerland, it prompted the following response: "Despite the information contained in your [communication] that prisoners at Hakodate [Hokkaido] may send two postcards monthly, no correspondence has been received from this camp in 1944 . . . the last correspondence from Hakodate appears to have been dispatched in August 1943, and a considerable amount of mail should have been received this year if prisoners write at the rate of two postcards or even one a month."[8] But inquiries and protests from Swiss representatives in Japan had absolutely no effect.

American POWs felt that they were always singled out for harsh treatment. Bataan survivors knew that they were the object of special wrath, because their fierce defense cost the Japanese five months of combat and 10,000 casualties to win the battle for that peninsula. Two weeks after Bataan fell, on April 14, 1942, the *Japan Times and Advertiser* ran the following editorial:

> They surrender after sacrificing all the lives they can, except their own, for a cause which they know well is futile; they surrender merely to save their own skins. . . . They have shown themselves to be utterly selfish throughout all the campaigns, and they cannot be treated as ordinary prisoners of war. They have broken the commandments of God, and their defeat is punishment. To show them mercy is to prolong the war . . . an eye for an eye, a tooth for a tooth. The Japanese Forces are crusaders in a holy war. Hesitation is uncalled for, and the wrongdoers must be wiped out.[9]

From a description by Bataan survivor Kenneth Calvit of a road-building detail at Tayabas in southern Luzon in the Philippines, it would appear that some Japanese commanders were trying their best to eliminate as many prisoners as possible, if they had managed to somehow survive the Death March:

> The detail was made up of 295 men from Camp O'Donnell (these men had just come from the Death March and were in terrible shape). Five of my group . . . were added to the group when five of them died. After riding flat ass, we started marching in the afternoon and marched until 7 A.M. when we arrived at Tayabas. They marched us onto a dry river bed covered with large smooth rocks and said this was our camp. No cover, no protection from the elements at all. The camp soon became a hell hole. Everyone had dysentery, pellagra, beri beri, scurvy and malaria. The flies were everywhere (most of the men were covered with excrement) and the stench was overwhelming. At night you were kept awake by the moaning of the dying men. What a way to die! After six weeks there weren't enough men left to work so they abandoned the detail. The

last truck could only take 20 men to Bilibid. There were 5 or 6 men who were comatose and the Japs wouldn't take them, so a Captain Ashton gave them an overdose of morphine to put them out of their misery. I figure that less than 100 men survived Tayabas.[10]

It appears as if General MacArthur's concerned report of February 1942 to Secretary of War Stimson was a correct observation of a deliberate Japanese policy to "discredit the white races." Barely two months later, the chief of the POW Information Bureau in Tokyo issued these instructions to the army chief of staff on Formosa [Taiwan], who was responsible for all POW administration in the region: "We will use the POWs principally as laboring power . . . and on another hand as material of education and guidance of local [people]."[11]

Even more revealing are the instructions issued by the chief of staff on Formosa [Taiwan] to all POW camp commanders in July 1942:

Although the white prisoners of war on this island will of course be used as labor for the expansion of production, the effect they will have on the governing of Formosa will be even greater than has been instructed previously. Namely, in spite of forty-seven years of administration the accomplishment of forming Japanese citizens of these people [the Formosan Chinese] has been as yet incomplete. However, with a certain delinquent group, it is a regrettable fact that the victory of the Chiang Kai-Shek regime [on mainland China] is secretly desired and under these circumstances in order to make them realize the true power of Japan we must let them see with their own eyes the fact that we are able to use white people. In the use of the guards also, this must be observed. However, care must be taken to plan methods for the fulfillment of this objective at every opportunity, for the general public and at times for Japanese.[12]

Probably the most explicit example of how white prisoners were to be treated was found in a booklet issued in 1943 and captured by British forces in Burma in 1944. It is entitled, "Notes on the Interrogation of Prisoners of War," intended as a guide for officers interrogating British, American, and Indian POWs. A specially marked passage citing threats to be used contains this sentence: "That he will not receive same treatment as other prisoners of war; in event of exchange of prisoners, he will be kept till last; he will be forbidden to send letters, will be forbidden to inform his home that he is a POW, etc."

In a mastery of diplomacy at which the British seem to excel, the British Foreign Office asked Switzerland's ambassador to Japan, Camille Gorgé, to

"Bring these extracts to the notice of the Japanese authorities; Mr. Gorgé, should point out that the Japanese government recently indignantly denied that they used torture. It is presumed, therefore, that these instructions which envisage the use of torture when interrogating POWs were issued without the knowledge of the Japanese government. The British government, therefore, expect that Japan not only will cancel these instructions, but will punish the person or persons who issued them without authority."[13]

As for Leroy Siegel, the airman shot down over Nagoya in April 1945, he is lucky he wasn't shot or beheaded. On July 16, 1944, Tokyo Radio broadcast a warning that Japan was executing American fliers who had become prisoners of war as a result of a recent air raid on northern Kyushu, and any Allied aviators who landed in Japan would be condemned to death.[14] The Japanese treated aviators as captives, not prisoners of war, saying they had no rights, and were war criminals. They were segregated from other POWs, isolated even from each other, and kept in solitary confinement. Most ended up in Omori prison, on a small island in Tokyo Bay, set aside for aviators. B-29 crews who were not executed were treated with special harshness. Siegel was made to "Sit at Japanese attention": kneeling all day, keeping his back straight, until bedtime. He was not allowed to wash, to have a toothbrush, or to change his clothes. This is how Siegel spent the five months of his captivity, every day, until he was liberated.[15]

Even at the time of Japan's surrender in August 1945, Japanese authorities still had not provided a nominal list of captives, or those who had died in their hands, to the International Committee of the Red Cross. Conversely, the ICRC postwar report in 1948 notes that throughout the entire conflict, the agency did not receive one inquiry from the Japanese government concerning any of their prisoners in Allied hands.[16] A secret message sent December 2, 1944, from Japanese foreign minister Mamoru Shigemitsu to his Naval attaché in Bern, and intercepted by Allied intelligence, may explain why. It reads, in part: "At home, we take the position that the enemy has no Japanese prisoners of war." The message goes on to note that "It would be difficult to carry out any exchange of sick and wounded prisoners, . . . the Japanese have therefore no intention at present of establishing the committee [an international committee being proposed for the exchange of sick prisoners] in question."[17]

After the war, Japanese individuals put on trial for mistreating prisoners often complained that no one had told them any details of internationally accepted standards about treatment of prisoners. Some claimed to know that a document called the Geneva Conventions existed, but said they had no idea what those conventions actually were.

~~TOP SECRET~~

From: Tokyo (SHIGEMITSU)
To: Bern
2 December 1944

#329

Reference: your #520.[a]

As you know, we must also consider the fact that at home we take the position that the enemy has no Japanese prisoners of war. And even if the New Zealanders should set up this committee, it could serve no purpose. We, therefore, reserved our reply.

Will you please reply that for the present it is believed that it would be difficult to carry out any exchange of sick and wounded prisoners, and that the Japanese have therefore no intention at present of establishing the committee in question.

a - Available if requested.

Inter 2 Dec 44 (5)   Japanese   H-154640
Rec'd 2 Dec 44
Trans 4 Dec 44 ~~TOP SECRET~~ (2)

Japanese foreign minister Shigemitsu's message to the Foreign Ministry in Bern, December 2, 1944, intercepted by American intelligence, saying that the government does not intend to cooperate with the International Red Cross on the exchange of sick prisoners. NATIONAL SECURITY AGENCY FILES

No one seemed to mention the treaty Japan's delegate to Geneva signed in 1930, which the Japanese Diet ratified on November 21, 1932: the International Labor Organization Convention concerning forced or compulsory labor. This convention does not condone slave labor, and it spells out in detail that those working as forced labor must be given adequate housing, food, training, safety equipment, and medical treatment. If a government finds that a company is not following those guidelines, the government is supposed to levy a fine against that company. And if a government decides to exercise its periodic option to withdraw from this treaty, that government is supposed to enact similar regulations in its place.[18]

Japan apparently found it convenient to be a signatory nation to this treaty until April 1, 1938, when it enacted the National General Mobilization Law, and began conscripting Korean laborers a month later. Once again, a treaty was in force until it conflicted with Japanese interests—a precedent already in place, which set the framework for the horrors awaiting white prisoners of war just three years later.

Chapter 3

"The Use of White POW is Earnestly Desired"

ON SEPTEMBER 8, 1942, ALLIED INTELLIGENCE INTERCEPTED A TOP SECRET message from Japan's transportation and communication chief to the Shipping Transport Command. It said: "Due to a serious shortage of labor power in Japan, the use of white POW is earnestly desired. Therefore it is required to render consideration to send some white POW to Japan by every returning ship (including both transport and munition ships). The Shipping Transport Command is requested to report . . . the possible amount of personnel expected to be sent every month (*special technicians should be classified*). . . . It is also desired to send as many personnel as possible by every means such as loading them on decks."[1]

So eager were Japan's industries to get increased numbers of prisoners into their factories, mines, and shipyards that merchant ships had been mobilized to expedite the process, and classified as "auxiliary navy" by the Japanese government. In fact, some of the companies that built a number of these vessels, notably Mitsui, Mitsubishi, and Kawasaki Heavy Industries—became the biggest importers of white POW slave labor; effectively transporting their new captive workforce on their own ships.

Shortly after the urgent message of September 1942 was transmitted, American and other Allied POWs began arriving in larger numbers in the Japanese home islands. But POWs were being deployed to company-operated worksites in the home islands and occupied territories as early as January 10, 1942, when the Mitsubishi-built *Argentina Maru* sailed from Guam to Japan with 400 American POWs aboard, many of them civilians. Two days later, the *Nitta Maru,* also built by Mitsubishi, sailed from Wake Island via Manila to Japan, Korea, and China with 1,500 POWs aboard, mostly Americans.

White prisoners continued to be sent to Japan throughout 1942, but the message on September 8 signalled a frantic cry from the manufacturing industries: they needed many, many more POW laborers if they were going to meet the increased output demanded by wartime production quotas.

Mindful of the industrialists' needs, War Minister Tojo had already convened a conference of POW camp commanders in Tokyo on June 25, 1942, during which he announced that "The labor and skills of POW should be utilized to the development of industries."[2]

A most telling record showing the sequence of instructions issued to POW camp commanders throughout the war regarding the treatment and deployment of prisoners is a file that was never intended to survive. It is the personal file, fourteen documents in all, kept by the camp commandant at Taihoku, Formosa (Taiwan), near the Kinkaseki copper mine where nearly 1,200 POWs, mostly British, toiled from 1942 to 1945. The commandant burned all his papers and set fire to his headquarters, per instructions, after the surrender was announced. The file, charred but still readable, was discovered in the rubble at the site by an ex-Kinkaseki POW, Jack Edwards, while searching for War Crimes Trials evidence in January 1946. Most of the documents are addressed to the commanding general for POWs in the region, who was headquartered on Formosa, and he frequently queried Tokyo for instructions. The replies, addressed to him, were radioed to every POW camp commander in the occupied territories, as updated clarifications of policy. So the Taihoku camp commander's file offers a unique glimpse into the evolving use of POWs as company laborers.

On April 2, 1942, while the battle for Bataan was still raging, the chief of the POW Information Bureau in Tokyo radioed the army chief of staff on Taiwan: "Plans are now being pushed on projects for the use of POW in production, etc., in Taiwan. We think you want to apportion as many as possible to your island. We want you to report immediately a list of the requisite strength."[3]

Five days later, on April 7, the Chief of the POW Information Bureau in Tokyo radioed Formosa: "We wanted for the time being two to three thousand [POWs] . . . however, the Governor-Generalship wanted to use them in Public Works construction and mines, too, so . . . [the request] comes to about 7,000."[4]

On April 29, the chief of the POW Management Bureau radioed further instructions: "The Army will take responsibility for control and supply but the POW camp facilities with the exception of repairs . . . will be the responsibility . . . *of the companies which use the POW* [emphasis added]. This will be the framework."[5]

By August 1943, the Prisoner of War Management Bureau was getting picky. The bureau circulated a request in another secret message: "Not to send those POW officers who do not submit to labor work [a provision of the

EXHIBIT 2009

Document No. 2694
(Certified as Exhibit "G" in Doc. No. 2687)

TO: Taiwan Army Chief of Staff

FROM: Chief of POW Control Bureau, Tokyo
        Coded Radio #17
        29 April 1942

We acknowledge your radio #929 dated 7 April, further please consider the following points, and also report the approximate number of POW's that can be confined on Taiwan.

1. We went to confine as many POW's as possible on Taiwan.

2. For the purposes of control, the number in each camp should not exceed 500.

3. The army will take responsibility for control and supply but the POW camp facilities with the exception of repairs and additional construction will be the responsibility of the Governor-Generalship or the companies which use the POW's. This will be the frame work.

Chopped by: HIGUCHI, TANAKA and YOKOTA.

　　　　—　　—　　—　　—　　—　　—

I hereby certify that this is a true translation of a radio the fifth entry in Taiwan Army H.Q. Staff Files concerning POW's. Vol. 1, 2 April 1942 to 24 August 1942.

                    Signed: Stephen H. Green
                               STEPHEN H. GREEN

　　　—　　—　　··　　—　　—　　—　　—　　—

This is Exhibit marked "G", referred to in the Affidavit of

JAMES THOMAS NEHEMIAH CROSS,

Sworn before me this 19th day of September, 1946.

                        /s/ A. L. Vine

                             Major, R.A.O

Message sent April 29, 1942, from the chief of the POW Management Bureau, Tokyo, to the Taiwan army chief of staff, who was in charge of all POWs in the region. Copies were sent to all POW camp commanders. It states POW facilities will be the responsibility of companies that use POWs. FILES OF INTERNATIONAL PROSECUTION SECTION, TOKYO WAR CRIMES TRIALS

Geneva Conventions that was occasionally observed in POW camps]." The department also asked that camp commanders should not send "POW of mixed blood whose appearances be mistaken for Orientals."[6] In other words, only white prisoners should be sent to Japan, to minimize the risk of escape.

In the final months of the war, prisoners were sometimes worked around the clock in a frenzied effort by companies to keep up with the demand for vital war materials: "In view of the fact that the demands of the situation more and more make necessary a display of the highest degree of efficiency in the prisoners' service, from now on the duty hours of Prisoners of War will conform to the actual situation on the spot (the type of work, the relative difficulty of the work, the urgency of the labor, the season of the year, the health of the prisoners and the working hours of local laborers) and you will direct the commander, POW camps, to decide or change these hours . . . and thus maintain elasticity . . . of the working hours of Prisoners of War. Notified by order."[7]

The only trouble with this plan was that bringing prisoners, in unmarked ships, to the Japanese home islands as forced laborers to further Japan's war production effort violated several provisions of international law, which Japan had pledged to observe. As far back as 1907 the leading nations of the world, including Japan, had agreed in writing that enemy prisoners could be made to do hard labor, such as road or farmwork—but they were not to be used in any industry involved in war production. Moreover, the Hague Conventions stipulated that prisoners were to be paid for their work.

When updated conventions were adopted in 1929 at Geneva, Article 31 of the new conventions stated explicitly: "Work which a prisoner is called upon to perform shall have no direct connection with the operations of the war." But obviously this convention interfered with Japanese policy. Testimony presented at the Tokyo War Crimes Trials (which ran from June 1946 to November 1948) described an exchange that allegedly took place at a cabinet meeting in Tokyo in May 1942. Former prime minister Suzuki gave a verbal summary of the meeting. He recalled that Mikoi Yamura, chief of the POW Intelligence Bureau stated: "War prisoners who are slated to arrive in Japan in the near future will be treated in conformity with the Geneva Treaty." To which Minister of War Tojo allegedly replied: "Impossible! They must undergo compulsory labor!"[8]

It would have been hard to find a POW company worksite in Japan during World War II that was *not* directly related to war production. All of the POWs sent to the home islands were brought there explicitly for that purpose. Even if they sometimes worked on a dam or road project for a time, all prisoners eventually wound up doing some form of war production, at one of the 94 company POW worksites identified on the map and list supplied to General MacArthur on August 19, 1945, in Manila, as a condition of his

Doc. No. 2700 $\mathcal{E}X2014$ page 1

(Certified as Exhibit "N" in Doc. No. 2687)

TO: Chief of Staff Taiwan Military Jurisdiction

FROM: War Ministry Adjutant
         Riku A Tn #281 Routine
         16 March 1945

NOTIFICATION CONCERNING WORK OF PRISONERS OF WAR

Up to now there have been directives from the Central
Authorities on the duty hours of Prisoners of War each time the
latter were dispatched, but in view of the fact that the demands
of the situation more and more make necessary a display of the
highest degree of efficiency in the prisoners' service, from now
on the duty hours of Prisoners of War will conform to the actual
situation on the spot (the type of work, the relative difficulty
of the work, the urgency of the labor, the season of the year,
the health of the prisoners and the working hours of local
laborers) and you will direct the commander, POW Camps to decide
or change these hours on his own suitable discretion and thus
maintain elasticity in this matter of the working hours of Prisoners of War. Notified by order.

Chopped by: ANDO, HIGUCHI, TANAK., YOKOTO.

- - - - - - - -

I hereby certify that this is a true translation from
Taiwan Army H.Q. Staff Files concerning POW's. Vol. 1, entry 46.

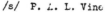

Signed: <u>Stephen H. Green</u>
            STEPHEN H. GREEN

- - - - - - - -

This is Exhibit marked "N", referred to in the Affidavit
of JAMES THOMAS NEHEMIAH CROSS.

Sworn before me this 19th day of September 1946.

/s/ P. A. L. Vine

MAJOR R.M.

*Message sent from the Japanese War Ministry on March 16, 1945, to the chief of staff, Taiwan.
Copies were sent to all POW camp commanders. Message states the need to increase working hours
of POWs in order to meet war production needs.* FILES OF THE INTERNATIONAL PROSECUTION SECTION,
TOKYO WAR CRIMES TRIALS

accepting the surrender by the Japanese government. The list was titled: "Map locating prisoner-of-war camps and places where prisoners are employed." Investigators later identified an additional 33 POW camps, making a total of 127 places where prisoners were "employed," just in the home islands. In all, white prisoners were sent to at least 169 locations in Japanese-occupied territory to do slave labor during the course of the war.[9]

Being forced to work for Japan's war production was one of the most haunting thoughts, psychologically, for Allied prisoners to deal with during their captivity. Fifty-four years later, USS *Houston* survivor Robert O'Brien's voice still shook with anger and emotion when he said at a 1999 news conference in New York City: "You can't imagine what it was like, each day, being made to manufacture weapons of war to be used against your own brothers!" O'Brien had five brothers serving on active military duty while he was a POW in Japan.[10]

When they arrived at existing company facilities in Japan, the POWs could readily see why their services were so "earnestly desired": with nearly all Japanese skilled laborers then serving in the military, the local work pool consisted primarily of elderly men and women, mostly farmers. Not only did they lack industrial skills, but their education was usually quite limited. POWs who sometimes worked alongside Japanese civilians noticed that many, particularly elderly farmers or homemakers, were illiterate. There was no way that they could be expected to read and understand an instruction manual, or easily master the complexities of machinery. So Japan's industrialists had probably been eyeing these thousands of white captives since day one of their captivity under Imperial Japanese forces, knowing that among them were large numbers of trained mechanics, steamfitters, engineers, and shipyard workers.

A monthly report of September 1942, published by Japan's Home Ministry, emphasizes the point exactly:

> As for their wages [at Nippon Transport in Zensuji], the Osaka District Labor Transportation Stevedoring Control Office collects two yen per person per day from the direct employers of the war prisoners. The money is either handed in to the Army, used for the expenses of the POW recreation equipment, or for national defense offerings and general expenses.
>
> The comparatively cheap wage has called the attention of men in the trade to the advantage of using the prisoners of war, and is helping to increase demand for their employment.[11]

Equally illuminating is a report dated October 6, 1942, from Kaitaro Kondo, governor of Kanagawa Prefecture, to the ministers of welfare and home affairs, describing the beneficial effects of POW labor use in the home islands on both the local workforce and the public:

> We have started using prisoner of war labor at Kawasaki and Yokohama . . . the main places of labor are: the Kawasaki Pier of Mitsui Bussan K.K./Mitsui Products Co.; the wharf of the Nippon Ko-Kan/Nippon Steel Tube Mfg. Co.; Nichiman Warehouse Co.; Kawasaki Railway Station; unloading coal and cargo, and lathe-men at factories. At Kawasaki are 1,011 POW; at Yokohama 607 . . . [as] skilled laborers in factories, they are being trained.
>
> In general they are men who have not done any labor for a considerably long time, and it is considered that when they get used to the Japanese workmen their efficiency will increase.
>
> As regards transporting labor at harbors, there had been a shortage of labor and wages were liable to soar with evil effects on getting laborers and on the smooth operation of transportation of goods. It is generally admitted by all the business proprietors alike that the use of POW labor has made the systematic operation of transportation possible for the first time, and has not only produced a great influence in the business circle, but will also contribute greatly to the expansion of production, including munitions of war, and the execution of industry.
>
> Though the public has not been informed of POW labor, those who have guessed about it from seeing them . . . seem to realize with gratitude the glory of the Imperial Throne, seeing before their eyes English and American POWs at their labor . . . [and this] makes them determined not to be defeated.[12]

The Imperial Japanese Army wasted no time in identifying the skills of their new captives. All POWs were required to state their occupation, along with name, rank, and serial number. Otto Schwarz of the USS *Houston* recalls that in the first weeks of their captivity on Java in March 1942, their commander noticed his shipmates who completed the questionnaire, like Bob O'Brien, were immediately singled out and shipped to Japan. So he instructed the men: "From now on, say you were a student." With a bitter laugh, Schwarz recalled: "So *we* got sent to the Burma Railway!"[13]

Edward Jackfert, twice national commander of the American Defenders of Bataan and Corregidor organization, put it this way in a 1998 interview, speaking of his years at Mitsui's Kawasaki stevedoring complex: "*We* were the ones operating the fork lifts, the heavy machinery, and other equipment. And by midsummer 1945, after the bombing raids increased and the Japanese civilians were sent home out of harm's way, we *were* the workforce!"[14]

In order to accommodate the industries' requests, the Japanese government quickly enacted a series of regulations concerning the use of white POWs for labor. On paper, the rules looked good; but they were honored more in the breach than the observance. Their chief purpose seems to have been to provide a frame of reference, to be cited by the companies as they filed the required periodic, but quite misleading, reports of compliance with the government agency. In turn, the official Japanese government report on the wartime treatment and deployment of POWs, released in December 1955, recites all the regulations as if they had been followed to the letter—because on paper the companies apparently said so. To read the report, the prisoners were paid, housing was adequate, medical attention was provided, and food though a tad scarce, was adequate.[15]

The National Information Bureau of Prisoners of War was established on December 27, 1941, just after the civilian and military personnel were taken prisoner on Guam and Wake Islands. In rapid succession during the first few months of 1942, regulations, instructions, and ordinances were issued setting standards for the treatment of prisoners, camp equipment, pay allowances, a scale of labor wages, deployment, as well as the transportation, mail, and relief supplies for POWs. But while the world and occasional Swiss inspectors were being told one thing, prisoners were experiencing quite another.

For example, on February 24, 1942, the Japanese government pledged: "POW shall not be forced to perform labor against their will." Ex-POWs repeatedly mentioned being told by their captors: "No work, no eat." In a 1998 interview, Edward Jackfert was asked what would happen if a POW refused to work. His response was delivered like a machine gun: "You would immediately be put to death. If you had a negative attitude, you would be severely punished."[16] So much for the "no war work" provision in Article 31 of the Geneva Conventions.

Article 31 also stipulated that prisoners were to be paid at the same rate as the detaining nation's workers doing similar tasks. But in February 1942, Japan's POW Management Bureau decreed that prisoners were to be paid according to their rank in the Japanese Army, and that is the rate continually quoted in official records and responses to inquiries on the Allies' behalf, by the Swiss government.

The Japanese government circumvented the thorny provisions of the Geneva Conventions by classifying POW officers as "volunteers" when assigning them work. As mentioned earlier, the Geneva Conventions stipulate that POW officers should not do manual labor. The director of the POW Management Bureau requested that companies using POW labor pay the government thirty yen per month for the use of a field officer, and twenty-seven yen per month for a junior officer. The POW officers were then to be "encouraged" to do voluntary labor, such as be "Supervisor of forced labor, war history records, propaganda activities and other appropriate works," according to records cited in the 1955 Japanese government report.[17] All the POW officers who were forced to do heavy labor for the Japanese might be surprised to learn that they were volunteers.

The same report lists the following wages as having been paid daily to POWs: twenty-five sen for a warrant officer; fourteen sen for a noncommissioned officer (such as a sergeant); and ten sen for a private. In prewar Japan, the official rate of exchange was 345 sen to the U.S. dollar—meaning that the average POW doing forced labor was supposedly being paid a little less than three cents a day. Ex-POWs would also be surprised to know that they supposedly received extra wages, up to thirty-five sen per day, according to their skills or the type of work they were doing.

But it is hard to find an ex-POW who came home with any money from his nightmare experience as an unwilling guest of the emperor. (Some Japanese camp commanders were fond of reminding prisoners that they were guests of the emperor.) In fact, as a result of interviews with several hundred ex-POWs, it is apparent that their experiences varied widely as to how much pay they ever saw, or whether the subject was even mentioned at any of the places they worked.

Alvin Silver's memory was crystal clear on the subject of pay from the Japanese. When the ex-POW was asked if pay was ever discussed by the management at Kumagai Engineering Company, which operated the electrical plant at Mitsushima, or by Showa Denko at its carbide plant in Kanose, Silver vigorously shook his head and exclaimed: "Never!" Were you ever paid? he was then asked. Once again, the nearly shouted response came: "Never!"[18]

At some worksites operated by Mitsui, the largest user of white POW labor in the home islands, the subject of POW pay was, in fact, discussed. POWs were told that they would be paid according to the official scale (listed above), but that most of their pay would be deposited in Postal Savings accounts, and distributed when the war was over. Melvin Routt, a machinist's mate (equivalent to sergeant) on the USS *Canopus*, worked for over two years at Mitsui's Fukuoka Camp No. 17, its giant Miike coal mine at Omuta. He remembered going through a pay line there just once. "I was topside, not down in the mine, because I was recovering from a foot injury," Mel Routt recalled. "I heard they were handing out pay, so I got on line. The Mitsui man, wearing a company uniform, was sitting at a little table. He spoke very good English. When my turn came, he said they owed me 100 sen, but then he showed me how much they were deducting for soy bean milk, cigarettes, clothing—which we didn't get—and living quarters. So all that was left was ten sen."[19] No doubt Routt would have been surprised to know that under

POW Regulation 8, enacted February 20, 1942, a government pay allowance of three yen per month was supposed to be set aside for a POW of his rank, to cover "daily necessities" such as those being deducted by the Mitsui employee that day in the pay line at Omuta.[20]

Geoffrey Pharoah Adams, an Australian who was also a POW at Omuta, described an experience similar to Routt's. In his memoir, he wrote that officers had to sign a pay sheet saying they had received a monthly "salary," from which items not received, like mosquito netting and extra food, had been deducted. He also noted that "Any balance was invested in Japanese Savings Bonds, which were occasionally allowed to be 'cashed' to pay for POW's spectacles or dentures supplied by a local civilian source. [On one occasion] bonds were signed away to pay for a table tennis table which when it arrived was stamped 'American Red Cross/YMCA for use of POW.' It disappeared shortly afterwards."[21]

There are other scattered reports of sporadic pay to some POWs at certain locations. "But then it stopped" is the evidence heard over and over again, followed by: "There was nothing to spend it on anyway." But according to the official 1955 report, canteens and medical dispensaries were set up in every working POW facility; moreover, the Japanese government assured the Swiss minister in response to a 1944 inquiry, that the facilities were well stocked.[22]

Vernon La Heist, who was a POW along with Ken Towery and 1,485 other Americans at Mitsubishi's vast factory complex in Mukden, Manchuria, described his brief experience with pay there:

> The Japanese decided to start paying us for our work and set rate at 20 sen per day for a 10 hour day and 25 sen if you worked overtime. They even paid us in cash one pay day, but when there was nothing to spend our money on, gambling became a problem. As a result the Japanese quit paying, but made us sign the payroll each payday and said the money would be put in a savings account in our name and we would get the money after the war. After a while there was no more signing and we assumed they just stopped paying. In any event, we never saw any more of the money.[23]

Another Mukden POW, Leon Elliott, said he was "Forced to sign a pay roll without getting any money" from Mitsubishi.[24] But apparently Mitsui, Mitsubishi, and all the other companies turned in pay sheets to the Japanese government showing that the POWs had been paid. And since the pay sheets were written in Japanese, POWs usually had no idea how much pay their "employers" claimed to be giving them. Samuel Moody, a Bataan survivor who testified at the Tokyo War Crimes Trials, signed an affidavit on December 12, 1946, demanding the inflated amount of pay the Tobashima

Construction Company claimed it had paid him while he was at Camp O'Donnell in the Philippine Islands. His statement reads in part: "On the first of May [1942] I was sent along with other Prisoners of War to a bridge reconstruction detail in charge of the Tobashima Coy Construction Company of Japan. This lasted until the end of July, at which time I became too ill to work. . . . I was paid four and one-half pesos [yen]. I have since learned that I signed the payroll for 100 times that amount. Therefore, the Tobashima Coy Construction Company of Japan owes me the remaining sum of 9,450 pesos [yen]." Moody died in 1999, still waiting for his back pay from Tobashima, which is still in business.

In a 1997 interview Moody, a founder of the American Defenders of Bataan and Corregidor, said: "*All* of the Bataan survivors were sent to do slave labor in Japan, except a few hundred who stayed behind at Cabanatuan, because they were too sick to travel." Eventually, even the sick prisoners—those who were still alive—were also shipped to the home islands, even though they all arrived half-dead after enduring dreadful voyages aboard merchant ships that the POWs called, simply, "hellships."

Chapter 4

Voyages in Hell

WHEN JAPAN'S TRANSPORTATION CHIEF RADIOED THE SHIPPING TRANSPORT Command in September 1942 to send white prisoners of war by "every returning ship," he meant it. Whatever else the merchant captains might be bringing to the home islands—troops, munitions, or supplies—they were now ordered to cram as many white prisoners as possible into the filthy holds. POWs were so tightly packed aboard that they had no place to sit or lie down, except by some makeshift rotation.

On one trip in October 1944, the Mitsubishi-built *Haruna Maru* sailed from Manila to Formosa (Taiwan), with 1,100 American POWs stuffed in the holds, which were already partially filled: one with horse manure, the other with coal. The lucky prisoners got to sit on top of the coal. Sixty men died en route; prisoners said the stench in the sealed holds was unbearable.

Official Japanese government shipping lists identify forty-eight separate merchant ships that safely transported POWs to Formosa, China, and the home islands between 1942 and 1945. The destination of 90 percent of those vessels was Japan.[1] According to Japanese records, an additional twenty-one merchant ships were torpedoed at sea. All were unmarked.

It is a wonder any of the prisoners survived their voyages in what they said seemed like hell itself. Many did not; thousands died at sea, either from the conditions aboard or by drowning. Official Japanese records tell a grim story: of 55,279 Allied POWs transported by sea, 10,853 drowned, including 3,632 Americans. At least 500 perished at sea from disease and thirst.[2] The Japanese recorded all the deceased as "shipwrecked" without acknowledging the number of prisoners who were simply unable to survive the horrendous travel conditions. And the most striking fact about those conditions is that they were always the same, aboard each of the transports. Every survivor's account reads or sounds alike: men already sick with dysentery, malaria, and malnutrition were jammed down ladders into the dark, filthy holds of the ships: 2,200 on one; 1,800 on the next; 700 or fewer only if the ship were under 300 tons in size. And then, in an act of uniform cruelty, the hatches were always sealed, and the sick men, already packed like sardines, had no fresh air to breathe during most of the voyage. Here is medical orderly Harry Menozzi's description of his voyage from Manila to Japan aboard the Kawasaki-built *Nagato Maru*, in November 1942:

> At the time the men were suffering from loss of weight, dysentery, malaria, beri beri and other diseases endemic to the tropics. The extreme heat from the over-crowded area was unbearable and some men even were on the verge of suffocation and the thoughts of suicide. We had no count of the number that died during our journey. Our latrine facilities consisted of two five-gallon oil cans in the center of our hold. With about 400 men in this hold and most with a diarrhea condition these cans were always full and overflowing. The Japs would permit us to empty the cans only twice per day. This sanitation condition could only be described as horrendous. Our food and water supply was lowered in the same area. To add more to our misery we were infested with millions of lice, and it was not long before we were being eaten alive by these miserable bugs.[3]

The first group of Americans transported for slave labor from Wake Island left on January 12, 1942, aboard the Mitsubishi-built *Nitta Maru*, bound for China via Yokohama with 1,235 men aboard. But first, before embarking, they were required to read preboarding instructions from the "Commander of the Prisoner Escort, Navy of the Great Japanese Empire," which were posted, in English, in a prominent place. The instructions, titled "Japanese Naval Regulations for Prisoners of War," read as follows:

> 1. The prisoners disobeying the following orders will be punished with immediate death:
>   a. Those disobeying orders and instructions.
>   b. Those showing a motion of antagonism and raising a sign of opposition.
>   c. Those disordering the regulations by individualism, egoism, thinking only about yourself, rushing for your own goods.
>   d. Those talking without permission and raising loud voices.
>   e. Those walking and moving without order.
>   f. Those carrying unnecessary baggage in embarking.
>   g. Those resisting mutually.

American prisoners lining up to board the Japanese merchant ship Nitta Maru *at Wake Island, January 12, 1942, bound for Yokohama, Japan, and Woosung, China. 1,235 men were crammed into the hold of the ship.* SKETCH BY JOSEPH ASTARITA

    h. Those touching the boat's materials, wires, electric lights, tools, switches, etc.

    i. Those climbing ladder without order.

    j. Those showing action of running away from the room or boat.

    k. Those trying to take more meal than give to them.

    l. Those using more than two blankets.

2. Since the boat is not well equipped and inside being narrow, food being scarce and poor you'll feel uncomfortable during the short time on the boat. Those losing patients [*sic*] and disobeying the regulation will be heavily punished for the reason of not being [illegible].

3. Be sure to finish your "Nature's Call," evacuate the bowels and urine before embarking.

4. Meals will be given twice a day. One plate only to one prisoner. The prisoners called by the guard will give out the meal quick as possible and honestly. The remaining prisoners will stay in their places quietly and wait for your plate. Those moving from their places reaching for your plate without order will be heavily punished. Same orders will be applied in handling plates after meal.

5. Toilet will be fixed at the four corners of the room. The buckets and cans will be placed. When filled up a guard will appoint a prisoner. The prisoner called will take the buckets to the center

of the room. The buckets will be pulled up by the derrick and
be thrown away. Toilet papers will be given. Everyone must
cooperate to make the room sanitary. Those being careless will
be punished.

6. Navy of the Great Japanese Empire will not try to punish you
all with death. Those obeying all the rules and regulations, and
believing the action and purpose of the Japanese Navy, cooper-
ating with Japan in constructing the "New order of the Great
Asia" which lead to the world's peace will be well treated.

The End

And indeed, the voyage was the end for five prisoners who were
beheaded for "misbehaving." The other prisoners were brought up to the
deck and made to watch the punishment, which was carried out by a Japanese Navy officer who was accompanying the POWs on this merchant ship as
an escort. Many other POWs died belowdecks before the *Nitta Maru* reached
its destination at Woosung, China.

POW Joe Astarita, an accomplished artist, was able to get some paper,
pen, and ink in Woosung, the first of several camps to which he was sent.
While the images were still fresh in his mind, Astarita made some sketches of
what life was like belowdecks on a hellship. He rolled the drawings up and
placed them in an empty metal tube that once held tooth powder. Somehow,
Joe Astarita's remarkable drawings survived the war.

A fellow Wake Island survivor, J. O. Young, was one of forty POWs
stuffed into the narrow bow hold of the *Nitta Maru*. In a few short sentences,
he showed that the promised accommodations did not quite materialize:

> It was crowded and hot . . . two five gallon cans were used for
> latrines. Fellows were sea sick. The air was bad . . . the further
> north we got the colder it got. We were issued one blanket that did
> not keep us warm. Four of us decided to bunch up together . . .
> but the guards put a stop to it at once. . . . The latrines were car-
> ried up and dumped once a day. Our food was what would prob-
> ably be not over a tablespoon of dry barley . . . A drink of water
> once a day. . . . We stopped at Yokohama . . . I guess we spent
> two days in port . . . we were not allowed to go on deck.[4]

In his account of a July 1944 voyage as one of 1,500 POWs aboard the
Mitsubishi-built *Nissyo Maru*, Robert Dow described how universal the
nightmare was:

> Those in the hold were obviously very frightened as they were
> being crammed in. . . . As more and more of us were forced down

Wake Island prisoner being beaten by Japanese crew member aboard the Nitta Maru. *Prisoners said they were beaten at random, for the amusement of the crew.*
SKETCH BY JOSEPH ASTARITA

into the hold, many of the men passed out and were trampled by others. We were required to throw everything we had, except for the clothes we wore, through an opening in the hatch boards into the lower part of the hold. That was the last we saw of them. Soon the hatch opening was covered as more men were forced into the hold. It became almost impossible to breathe and panic reigned. Men were screaming, fainting and dying. . . . We soon anchored for seven days . . . men had to be bound and gagged when they went mad for want of water . . . if you weren't in the general area of where the [water] bucket was lowered, you got much less than a cup and sometimes none at all. . . . When we entered the China Sea we came into rough waters and many of the men became seasick. Their vomit, added to the human waste in the cans, soon became mixed and flowed all over the deck and us . . . we had it all over us. . . . Words can never accurately describe what went on in the hold of that ship. The dead would be passed to the after end of the hold where the Japs would let them lay until they were allowed to be passed to the top deck where they were dumped over the side.[5]

But the episode that epitomized what these voyages in hell were all about, and which many ex-POWs cite—if indeed they can speak about the experience at all—occurred when a priest, the Reverend Bill Cummings, was trying to lift the spirits of his fellow prisoners by reciting the Lord's Prayer. As he spoke the words: "Give us this day . . . ," Father Cummings expired. No one aboard the *Brasil Maru* ever forgot that moment.[6]

The Japanese merchant ship Brazil (Brasil) Maru, *one of at least sixty-nine Japanese vessels used to transport POWs. None were marked as POW transports, as required by international law.* COLLECTION OF EDWARD JACKFERT

That any prisoners arrived alive at their destinations is a testament to their remarkable courage. But despite the appalling conditions on board every hellship, many more POWs would have survived the voyage if their vessels had been marked as POW transports, as demanded in the statutes of international law. As far back as the Hague Conventions of 1907, it was established that vehicles or ships transporting wounded soldiers, Red Cross or medical supplies, and prisoners of war should be clearly identified, so that their need for safe passage could be recognized.

During World War II, the Germans marked vehicles transporting POWs with the letters "KG" *(Krieg Gefanginer,* or War Prisoners). Since the Japanese did not mark any vessels transporting prisoners, it is not known what symbols they may have had in mind. What we do know is that although merchant ships often travelled as part of a convoy, which included oil tankers, freighters, and sometimes navy destroyers, the ships carrying POWs usually rode at the outside of the convoy, where they were easy pickings for American submarines and aircraft, whose missions were to disrupt supply lines to Japan as much as possible.[7]

By an irony of history, two incidents in which U.S. Navy ships sank Japanese hospital or relief supply ships may have considerably hardened Japan's resolve not to bother with ship markings. The first such incident occurred in January 1944, at the beginning of the peak year for POW transport by sea. Of thirty-three merchant ships carrying prisoners toward the home islands that year, fifteen were sunk and eighteen arrived safely. So the fact that the year opened with the sinking of a Japanese hospital ship just about guaranteed that no prisoner transport would be marked.

In January 1944, the *Buenos Aires Maru* was sunk by an American submarine. The Japanese government not only demanded an apology, but pointed out that no fewer than seventeen Japanese hospital ships had been attacked by American planes or ships. Not only did the U.S. government refuse to apologize for this apparently obvious violation of international law; but no apology from Washington was forthcoming when an even worse transgression took place the following year.

In March 1945, the United States agreed to give safe passage to the Japanese merchant ship *Awa Maru,* which was said to be carrying Red Cross relief supplies from Moji, Japan, to Southeast Asia, destined for POWs in Malaya and the Dutch East Indies. No one mentioned that the *Awa Maru* had just arrived in Moji from Singapore with 525 POWs in its hold, allocated to do slave labor in the many mines of Fukuoka Prefecture. So the *Awa Maru* was not a marked hospital ship, but because of its special mission this merchant vessel had been promised safe passage by the U.S. government. The timing and route of *Awa Maru,* its cargo of relief supplies, and its guaranteed right to safe passage had been communicated to all American submarine commanders operating in the area. However, Comdr. Charles Laughlin, captain of the submarine *Queenfish,* mistook the *Awa Maru's* radar image for a Japanese destroyer, and ordered four torpedoes fired, which sank her.

Despite a Navy court-martial and reprimand for the submarine's skipper, the U.S. government refused to apologize to the government of Japan.[8] So in a twist of fate, it is possible to argue that the attitude of the United States had a direct bearing on Japan's continued refusal to abide by international rules about prisoner ship identification.

The government of Japan may have failed to order its POW transports marked for a variety of reasons, but its failure to notify the International Committee of the Red Cross or Allied governments when large numbers of prisoners of war were lost at sea was truly inexcusable, because the Japanese kept a complete roster with the name and nationality of every man who boarded one of these ships. Repeated inquiries by the Swiss on behalf of the United States and British Commonwealth nations brought no response from Japan; despite the fact that in some sinkings, such as Mitsubishi's *Rakuyu Maru* in September 1944, a handful of survivors were rescued by the same American submarines that had torpedoed the ship. So the Allies occasionally had firsthand information that large numbers of prisoners had been lost at sea. For the *Rakuyu Maru* the tally was awesome: 1,317 POWs aboard; 1,181 perished, according to official Japanese records.

The worst single disaster involving American POWs was the sinking of the *Arisan Maru,* built by Mitsui. It was torpedoed on October 24, 1944, with 1,782 American POWs aboard, bound for Japan. Just eight men survived.

Perhaps the worst disaster in maritime history occurred the previous month, when the *Junyo Maru* sailed from Batavia, Java [Indonesia], with 2,200 white POWs aboard, including 14 Americans, 4,320 Javanese conscript laborers, and 506 Asian POWs. The ship was torpedoed in the Java Sea and 5,640 men perished.

But the sinking of the POW transport that became a focal point of the Tokyo War Crimes Trials was that of Mitsubishi's *Montevideo Maru,* which sailed on June 22, 1942, from Rabaul with 1,053 Australian POWs and civilian internees, as well as 63 crewmen aboard. The unescorted ship was torpedoed off the Philippine island of Luzon; Japanese records list no survivors. But three Japanese crewmen did survive, and they reported the ship's loss to the Japanese Army authorities, who in turn notified the ship's owner and the Japanese government's Prisoner of War Information Bureau, which was provided with a list of everyone on board. Despite repeated inquiries over the next three years from the British and Australian governments via the Swiss and the International Red Cross, the Prisoner of War Information Bureau not only withheld information on the names of POWs and internees who had perished, but the agency continued to accept mail addressed to the drowned prisoners—even forwarding letters to the POW mail sorting center at Omori camp in Japan. So for over three years, families continued to write to their loved ones, believing the prisoners were still alive. It was not until after the war that an Australian investigator uncovered the truth, and the families were finally notified.[9]

It is hard to imagine what it is like to be sealed in the hold of a ship when a torpedo strikes. It is harder still to imagine the added terror of being "rescued" by your captors; being sealed in the hold of yet another ship, and enduring more days and nights, as you continue on your way to slave labor in Japan—wondering every minute whether another torpedo will strike. But that is exactly what happened to Australian George Carroll and a few of his fellow POWs who were aboard the *Rakuyu Maru.* Carroll told his story for the first time in a lengthy interview with this writer in Melbourne, Australia, in 1991. He recalled the details of his bizarre odyssey:

> The ship was sunk at 2 A.M. [September 14, 1944]. We jumped overboard, then got back on the ship during the day, till evening when it sank. The torpedo missed the hull. Only one person was killed on the ship. He was a Jap!
>
> We scrounged supplies. The Jap escort vessels came back. The lifeboats were adrift. I was one of the last ones off the ship. There was a small dinghy with two Japs in it. It sank. I and one Jap got back on it. We thought the escort vessel would pick up POWs. By

nightfall we got 14 lifeboats rounded up. There were about 20 to a boat. . . . We tied the boats together. A typhoon came up, and we cut loose. Three boats stayed together, but when we woke up we were all by ourselves. We heard machine gun fire; we thought a Jap sub had surfaced.

We saw ships in the distance; they passed. We thought they were mirages. On the fourth day, we saw three ships. They were Jap cruisers. They picked us up. As each POW climbed aboard, we got a hit in the head or back with a baton or rifle butt, or whatever they had handy. I fell back into the lifeboat from the force of the blow, and had to climb up and get another whack. They put the POWs in front of a double-barreled gun. The captain spoke English. The Japs had no rations, hardly. They gave us broken biscuits soaked in brandy.

We went to a port, Sangai, in Hainan Province, China. We were put on an oil tanker. There was an air raid that night. The bombers missed us—bad shots!

We were on a U.S. whaling vessel which had been captured by the Japs and renamed the *Kibibi Maru*. There were 150 POWs on board. Everyone was packed below deck for three or four days. They were steel hatches. We were being constantly fired upon by Allied ships. On the fourth day we were allowed up for fresh air. We met the commander—he hadn't been home for eight years! He was in charge of troops going to Japan. He improved our conditions.

There were twenty ships in our convoy. When the shooting began, our ship turned to avoid a torpedo, and a boatload of Japanese women and children got the torpedo. Finally, we saw Japan. It was a thrill! We had just half a cup of water and a rice cake per day. As we came into Tokyo Bay, the ship behind us got torpedoed.

By the time we got into Moji, I could hardly stand up. I was half blind, and covered with oil. The Japs gave each of us a small box of rice and a turnip—that was it![10]

Even if they had not been shipwrecked along the way, all the prisoners who arrived at the port cities of Japan stumbled off those transports dazed, disoriented, sick, and very weak. The dubious distinction of being longest at sea goes to Melvin Routt and his 1,000 fellow POWs aboard the *Matu Maru:* they sailed from Manila to Moji, Japan, by way of Saigon, and were sixty-three days at sea.

As they staggered through the streets of Moji shivering, half-clad in what was left of their tropical clothing, sometimes naked, the men were often gawked at, jeered, and spat upon. They became the target of sticks, stones, broken glass, or whatever bits of street debris the local citizens felt like tossing at them—all in violation of international law. Article 2 of the 1929 Geneva Conventions states that prisoners of war, "Must at all times be humanely treated and protected, particularly against acts of violence, insults and public curiosity."[11]

But Robert Dow and his fellow survivors from the *Nissyo Maru* found themselves the instant objects of public humiliation at Moji: "We were greeted with an anal inspection in full view of a crowd of civilians . . . on the way to a warehouse Jap civilians who turned out in large numbers to see us could not stand the sight or the smell of us, and held their noses and turned away."[12]

Tom Woody, a Texan captured on Java, was in one of the first groups of Americans to arrive in Japan for use as slave labor, in December 1942. He arrived on the first anniversary of the attack on Pearl Harbor, December 7, in Nagasaki—the city that would later mark the war's end by being the target of the second atomic bomb. He remembered being scared to death, and not clearly knowing why he had been brought to Japan. But he and his fellow POWs were afraid to show any reaction:

> As we came off the *Kamakura Maru* we were lined up to march, almost as though this were to be a parade. . . . There was no band, but there were lots of people. We started out, passing through rank after rank of laughing, cheering, screaming Japanese who jeered us at every turn. They spit at us, shouted taunts, and did everything but throw things. Now it's easy to describe all this calmly, but I'll tell you that it was not an enjoyable experience. We were scared to death, afraid to react in any way, for we had no idea of why we'd been brought to Japan, what they intended to do with (or to) us, or how to behave. We just marched, trying to duck the insults. . . . We were without food or water, and it was uncomfortably cold. Our clothes were still the summer gear we'd worn when we were imprisoned [in Java], and by now some of the shirts had become tattered and let the wind in.[13]

Despite the ridicule, every man was spoken for. As each ship docked, the prisoners were separated into groups to fill company orders: 800 to Osaka, 200 each to Hokkai and Tokyo. The official Japanese records list destinations for each shipload of POWs. Company bosses had to be prepared for the disappointment of being a little short of their labor quota, depending on the number of prisoners who died en route. But there were always more on the way.

Conditions on the ships were actually of sufficient concern to prompt this secret message on December 10, 1942, from the Japanese vice-minister of war and the vice chief of the Prisoner of War Management Bureau to "Units concerned," intercepted by Allied intelligence:

> Matter Concerning POW Transport to Japan Notification from Vice-Minister and Vice Chief to Units Concerned.
>
> Due to improper treatment on the way of transport of POW who were recently sent to Japan there were a great many of sick people (dead) and many who could not immediately be used for labor work. Further thorough care should be taken as to selection and medical inspection of POW to be sent to Japan, allotment of POW sanitation personnel, necessary medicine on the way of transport, preparation of provisions, supervision on the way of transport, conveniences given at ports of call and supply of clothes.[14]

These instructions were issued a few days after the *Nagato Maru* arrived in Moji in November 1942. Of the POWs aboard 150 were so sick that they were considered useless for work, so they were just left on the dock, and never seen again. Apparently the Prisoner of War Management Bureau, as well as the company bosses, knew the supply of captured white prisoners was virtually unlimited. They were right. Pacific tides continued to bring half-dead prisoners to the home islands in ever-larger numbers, all through the war.

Chapter 5

Mitsui: "We Will Send You to Omuta"

"IF YOU DON'T DO EXACTLY AS YOU ARE TOLD, WE WILL SEND YOU TO Omuta," Japanese guards at Cabanatuan, on the Philippine island of Luzon, would taunt their exhausted American captives, prodding the prisoners to do work they were already too weak from hunger and disease to perform. Most had barely survived the brutal, sixty-five-mile Bataan Death March—nine days of forced marching on empty stomachs with no water and very little rest. The remnants of Gen. Douglas MacArthur's Army of the Pacific mingled with sailors, Marines, and airmen as they stumbled around their second prison camp in the late spring of 1942.

The largest number of survivors were from the 200th Coast Artillery Regiment, a New Mexico–based unit that was the first to fire in World War II, and the last full unit to surrender in the Pacific. They were also the last army cavalry unit to use horses in battle. Fewer than 20 of the 1,800-man unit died in battle, but only half came home alive from Japanese captivity. None of the horses survived; one by one they were slaughtered and consumed for food in the last desperate weeks on Bataan. "We didn't know until after the war that we had eaten our horses," Leo Padilla remarked wistfully.[1]

Most Bataan survivors say theirs was a medical defeat, even more than a strategic one. "We were starved by our own people," is a bitter phrase one still hears at reunions of the American Defenders of Bataan and Corregidor, referring to the supplies that never came as they held out for five months. None had eaten anything close to a decent meal for two weeks when they finally ran out of ammunition too, and were forced to surrender.

So now they were at Cabanatuan, dispirited, sick, and watching comrades die at the rate of 100 a day. As many as 3,000 died at the Cabanatuan camp and "hospital" complex (which the men nicknamed the "Zero Ward" in a grim reflection of the survival rate) while it was the main holding center for American prisoners in 1942. By the time six months had passed, 5,000

Americans had died in Japanese captivity. Everyone at Cabanatuan was sure he would die if he stayed there.

Agapito "Gap" Silva remembered guards at Cabanatuan making the threat about Omuta, and wondering what place could possibly be worse than where they were now, still numb from the long march of death they had just endured, and faced with the daily fear of being summoned for a work detail by the "white angel," a Japanese officer who wore a white uniform. Silva, from the 200th Coast Artillery, seemed to recall each day of captivity as if it were yesterday.

"We called him the 'white angel' because he was like the Angel of Death," Silva explained in a 1998 interview. "Each day we prayed he wouldn't pick us—because no one ever came back from his work details." Could some place called Omuta really be more terrifying than a summons from the "white angel"? Silva wondered. The answer, which their guards knew and many American prisoners would soon discover, was yes.

So when a group of Americans, including Silva, were told in the summer of 1943 that they were going to Japan, they were actually relieved, because by that time they all believed staying at Cabanatuan was a certain death sentence. They had no idea what lay ahead.

Japanese soldiers goading American captives with threats about Omuta knew that their country's largest coal mine, operated by Mitsui Mining

Sketch of American POWs at Cabanatuan, the Philippines. Many were sent to Mitsui's Omuta coal mine from here. POW Agapito Silva is shown in center foreground, standing as he eats. COLLECTION OF AGAPITO SILVA

Company near the town of Omuta in Japan's Fukuoka district, was a hazardous and frightening place to work—even for an experienced miner. This had been especially true since 1923, when a devastating earthquake shifted the bedrock of Japan's home islands, and Mitsui had to seal off some of the deep mine's shafts and tunnels, declaring them too unsafe for anyone to work in. Despite that caution, cave-ins and explosions could happen unexpectedly anywhere in the vast mine, and all the workers knew it. So the threat of being sent to Omuta, used in more than one POW camp to keep prisoners in line, seemed like a strong one to a soldier assigned to guard POWs. There may have been some former Mitsui coal miners among those guards; by 1942, most able-bodied miners, along with factory and shipyard workers, had been conscripted into the Imperial Japanese armed forces.

The Mitsui family is the most powerful dynasty in Japan, outside of the Imperial Palace. Baron Takanaya Mitsui, who headed the vast Mitsui shipping, mining, and heavy industry empire, had studied in the United States; he was a 1915 graduate of Dartmouth College in Hanover, New Hampshire. Two years after his graduation, the family opened its huge coal mining complex, the Miike mine at Omuta. Built by American engineers, it was for many years the largest coal mine in Japan, and operated until 1997. At its peak, the mine had nine levels, and its tunnels extended 700 feet under Omuta Bay.

Since the production of coal was vital to Japan's war effort, Mitsui's urgent request for the use of white prisoners was no doubt given a priority. Sure enough, in August 1943, the first group of 500 American POWs from Cabanatuan, including Gap Silva, arrived at Omuta, not because they had misbehaved, but because skilled workers were desperately needed if monthly production quotas were to be met, and Americans were a likely bunch to have

Sketch of American POWs inside barracks, Cabanatuan, the Philippines, summer 1942.
COLLECTION OF
AGAPITO SILVA

many useful skills. Few, if any, had ever worked in a coal mine, but they had to learn on the job, in the pitch dark, working the already worked-out tunnels, which had been sealed off for the past twenty years. And if one was injured or killed, he could always be replaced. Or so the prevailing philosophy of the POWs' new "employers" seemed to be, judging from the brutal treatment and minimal training and equipment the prisoners were given.

When the first 500 Americans arrived at Mitsui's Omuta coal mine in mid-August 1943, still dazed from their voyage aboard the *Clide Maru* (nicknamed *Benjo* "toilet" *Maru* by the POWs) and a long, stifling ride from the port of Moji crammed into railroad boxcars, the bedraggled prisoners were the first white POWs townsfolk had seen, and their greeting was a barrage of stones and catcalls.

The POWs also got a bittersweet taste of home at Omuta. Army staff sergeant Harold Feiner, a New York electrician by trade, remembered noticing the familiar labels of General Electric, Honeywell, Joy drilling equipment, and Ingersoll-Rand compressors. Mitsui had hired American engineers and purchased almost exclusively American equipment to build its Omuta mine in 1917. Little did those American engineers know that a quarter century later, their fellow American citizens—soldiers and civilians—would be forced to work on American equipment in this now-hostile land with no choice, almost no food, long hours, no pay, no safety gear, and next to no clothing.

The Omuta site had been designated as Fukuoka Camp No. 17, and Mitsui had built flimsy, wooden barracks on company property for the POWs, with no heating. Despite the fact that coal was all around, there was apparently not enough available to warm the prisoners, except for one hour a day. At the end of the hour, a company employee would walk through the long barracks to the small coal stove, open the door, and remove the few warm coals with a small scoop—even on the coldest winter nights.

Soon the barracks were crawling with fleas, lice, and other vermin. Prisoners slept on mats on the bare floor, seven to a chamber. They were separated from one another by a flimsy curtain, which Amado Romero of the 200th Coast Artillery remembered, "Might as well have been electrified . . . prisoners who touched [it] were severely beaten."[2] Blankets were thin and infested with vermin. No one had warm enough clothing; the winter of 1943 to 1944 was the coldest in forty-two years in Japan.

Harold Feiner recalled the irony of being handed woolen uniforms, which had been looted by the Japanese from British supplies in Hong Kong. "But as soon as we got them, we were told to put them on the shelf for 'special occasions.' We were never allowed to wear them, except during a rare visit by a Red Cross inspector." Feiner did not hide the bitterness in his voice, even though he told the story with a little chuckle, when he described one of those rare Red Cross visits. It was Christmas 1944, and the men were told to put on those still freshly creased British uniforms. "By that time we were pretty skinny," Feiner says. "They made us wear scarves so the inspectors wouldn't see how scrawny our necks were." Then, Japanese officers broke open some of the locked-up Red Cross boxes, and placed food in front of each starving man, which he was not allowed to touch. "After the inspectors left, the Japanese took all the food away from us. We never got to eat even one bite!" Feiner exclaimed, shaking his head at the memory.[3]

Dr. Marcel Junod, head of the International Committee of the Red Cross in Tokyo during the latter part of the war, wrote a chilling description of such a visit: "The prisoners, British and American, did not dare to speak, but bowed low to the Japanese, their arms kept tightly to their sides until their heads were almost on a level with their knees."[4]

One ex-POW said he wished the Swiss inspectors could have seen the Japanese guards eating the Red Cross food. Prisoners remembered that when the Red Cross inspectors visited the clinic set up by POW physician Dr. Thomas Hewlett at Omuta, the Mitsui employees put the camp cooks in the beds as patients, and hid the sick men in the mines. So the Red Cross report read: "Sufficient clothing; good medical care."[5]

Perhaps the most bizarre aspect of barracks life for the prisoners was the staff who were in charge of them. "Most of them were wounded or disabled veterans from the China occupation, and the Rape of Nanking," Feiner said. "They must have been driven a little crazy because of what they had seen and done in China," he speculated, "because their behavior was completely unpredictable. One minute they were in their quarters; the next minute they would rush out and start screaming at us or beating us for no reason. Then they would go back to their quarters. It was very nerve-racking!" Some POWs wondered if perhaps their barracks supervisors were listening to radios, and when they heard of yet another Allied victory, they would vent their wrath on the nearest prisoners.

Once the workday started, POWs were completely under the control of Mitsui employees, who arrived at the barracks each morning to escort the prisoners to the mine and order them to meet an impossible quota of output. Some of the most severe beatings any prisoner received were administered on the job, by company employees. If a prisoner was injured while working—a frequent occurrence in such hazardous conditions—the accident would be the excuse for a relentless thrashing. The most brutal beatings were handed out by a company superintendent in charge of explosives, whom the POWs nicknamed the "dynamite man" because he had a temper that matched his specialty. To the great relief of many POWs, the "dynamite man" died in an accident in the mine, when he became caught in a conveyor belt and was crushed.

In fact, the injury rate was so high at Omuta that an investigator for the War Crimes Trials told Mel Routt that Omuta was put at the top of his list, to visit first, for that reason. The investigator, an attorney from Greenville, Kentucky, named Robert Humphrey, Jr., took a series of twenty-four photographs of the POW camp facilities at Omuta, as the company was dismantling the buildings and covering the site with dirt in early 1947. He offered them for sale to ex-POWs who had been at the camp, and Routt purchased the set.

Harold Feiner spent 1,243 days as a prisoner of the Japanese, most of them at Omuta. Even fifty-five years later, when he walks he leans slightly to the left, because he suffered permanent skeletal damage from being forced, day after day, to hoist loads too heavy for his emaciated body to carry. In a room where Feiner's fellow members of the American Defenders of Bataan and Corregidor are gathered, one can almost pick out the ones who toiled at Omuta. Many walk bent slightly forward; for the rest of their lives, these men have been unable to stand fully straight. This is their legacy from Mitsui employees who forced them to work twelve- and fourteen-hour shifts, day after day, in tunnels barely four feet high—or less.

"Sometimes the ceilings were so low, we had to crawl on our bellies like a snake, wearing nothing but a G-string," Frank Bigelow, a sailor from the USS *Canopus* recalled, the disgust plain in his voice as he described wiggling his six-foot-six frame along dank passages. "You had a little rubber band for your head, with a little battery light at the forehead—that was our 'hardhat miner's cap,'" Bigelow sneered. Gap Silva said the prisoners were issued rubber split-toe flip-flops, and when those wore out, no new footwear was issued. Most POWs were forced to work barefoot in the mine.

And always there was the fear. When the POWs discovered that Mitsui was opening tunnels that had been sealed off, and ordering the prisoners to enter those tunnels for the first time in two decades, they were terrified. "You have no idea how scared we were, every day, to go into that mine," Bigelow explained in a 1996 interview.

Mel Routt said the prisoners were given just ten days to learn the names of tools, and the various job assignment orders—in Japanese. But what they needed most, and didn't have, was experience—and the skills needed to do such hazardous work with some degree of safety. Army master sergeant Frank Stecklein recalled: "We rode a cable car down [the shaft]. I felt as though I was going to Hell and prayed all the way down."[6]

"We were 'pulling pillars'—the most dangerous work you can do in a mine," Frank Bigelow remembered. "In this country, a miner would get paid a high premium for doing such work, *if* you could get him to do it. And we were made to do that kind of thing every day. When a tunnel is all worked out, just a thin pillar of coal is left. It's all that's holding up a ceiling. We were

Ex-POW, Sgt. Frank Stecklein, in Mitsui office at Omuta, 1947, with the chief operating officer of the mine. He was the same CEO who had been there when Stecklein was a POW. He is shown presenting a gift kimono to Stecklein, who had returned to Japan to testify at the Tokyo War Crimes Trials, and decided to stop by Omuta for a visit. Stecklein said the POW quarters were being dismantled while he was there. COLLECTION OF FRANK STECKLEIN

supposed to pull down those pillars as we left the tunnel, and the ceiling would collapse behind us."

But one day part of a ceiling fell on Bigelow's leg, because he didn't quite move fast enough. He found himself pinned under a rock, 1,600 feet below the mine's surface. Bigelow wondered how his friends carried him up so many vertical levels to the top of the mine on that awful January day in 1944.

> The Mitsui foreman wouldn't let my buddies carry me to the "hospital." He made them lay me on the stone floor in what we called the "Buddha" room, a small shrine at the entrance to the mine, where we had to go in and bow to Buddha every morning. Then he ordered them back to work, and I lay there in the freezing cold for another five hours, till the work shift was over. Later Dr. Thomas Hewlett, our camp doctor, told me the only thing that kept me from bleeding to death was I got so cold my blood coagulated. He tried to save my leg, but with no medicine, and no anaesthetic, eventually he had to cut it off. I remember asking him, "Doc, you got an aspirin or a shot of whiskey or something you can give me?" He answered, "If I had a shot of whiskey, I'd

take it myself." Then a couple of men held me down while he did the job. But he saved my life![7]

Gap Silva was also made to wait without assistance after the mine ceiling collapsed on him in September 1944, on orders of the Mitsui foreman. Silva suffered four broken ribs, a fractured right pelvis, and two crushed vertebrae on the lower part of his back. "For the first eight weeks I could not walk. Two corpsmen were assigned to help me. I was given massage and hot tubs. Gradually, I was able to walk; gradually I recovered. I was sent back into the mine."

Silva also described injury inflicted by a Mitsui employee, for a minor infraction:

> Another time prior to the mine injury, another POW and I were late in getting in line to go to the mess hall. A Japanese guard caught us, took us to the guard house where he swatted our buttocks with a pole two by two [inches] by six feet. He swung the stick three times like a baseball bat. We cried out each time because the pain was excruciating. Each time we cried he would swat us again. Our buttocks got so swollen we could not sit for three weeks.[8]

Army corporal James Stacy described the daily working conditions at Omuta:

> I worked in water from ankle deep to waist deep. [I] had cold water dripping on my head, back and shoulders all the time. . . . Our labor there was anywhere from ten to fourteen hours daily. . . . I was forced back to the mines to work with [my] left hand swollen up so big I couldn't even bend or move my finger. I was beaten [by a Mitsui employee] with a pick handle and a 2 × 2. This time I had such a beating that my whole buttock was as bloody as a piece of beef steak. I had to be carried to camp. . . . I was beaten on several occasions.[9]

The word "hospital" requires quotation marks when describing what passed for medical facilities at company-owned POW worksites in Japan or, for that matter, any of the 170-odd places where Allied prisoners were held by the Japanese during the war. Despite the dedication and daily miracle-working by POW doctors (when a camp was lucky enough to have a medical doctor or corpsman), the lack of medicine, supplies, and surgical equipment was heartbreaking—especially because Red Cross boxes containing such vital and lifesaving equipment remained locked up in warehouses at just about every place where POWs were confined. Omuta was no exception. In a postwar report, Dr. Hewlett wrote:

> Following the exodus of the [Japanese] guard detail in August
> 1945 . . . we found several warehouses packed with Red Cross
> food and medical supplies. The dates of receipt and storage indi-
> cated that these items had reached Japan prior to August 1943.
> Thus while we suffered from lack of food, essential medicines, sur-
> gical supplies and X-ray equipment, these items, gifts of the Amer-
> ican people, were hoarded in warehouses during our two years in
> Japan. The reason we were denied these essentials remains a top
> secret of the Imperial Japanese Army.[10]

Still, the POWs were lucky to have a multinational team of physicians,
headed by Dr. Hewlett, who credited Baron Mitsui with seeing to it that the
clinic at least had adequate space for beds, even if medicine, equipment, and
supplies were sadly lacking. The company had a fairly well-equipped hospital
on the property, but the prisoners were afraid to be treated by Japanese doctors, and requested their own facility.

If the fear of death from injury was ever-present, the fear of starvation
was a daily reality, as these prisoners felt their bodies gradually weakening.
Once again, the meticulous record kept by Dr. Hewlett tells the grim, graphic
story. Dr. Hewlett notes that the minimum daily caloric requirement, a balance of protein, carbohydrates, fat, and vitamins, is 2,800 calories for a young
male aged twenty to twenty-five doing "moderate labor." But the diet at
Camp No. 17 in Omuta in 1943–44 was 80 percent rice and 20 percent
filler, and amounted to 597 calories for the men being sent out to work, 469
calories for men confined to quarters, and just 341 calories for men in the
camp "hospital." (The Japanese during World War II had a practice of not
feeding sick prisoners at all in most locations; those at Omuta were lucky to
be allocated anything. What they got was usually sneaked in by comrades.)

By 1944–45, the last year of their captivity, Dr. Hewlett's records show
that the food allocation for prisoners had become 60 percent rice and 40 percent filler, with just "traces" of vitamin content; caloric intake for the men
had dropped to under 500 calories for men going to work, 408 calories for
men in quarters, and just 153 calories for men too sick to work.[11]

Little wonder that the average weight loss for prisoners in Japanese captivity was between 70 and 100 pounds; most said they weighed between 80
and 90 pounds when the day of liberation finally came. Their families never
saw these POWs at their worst, because by the time they were transported
from camp, they had been eating air-dropped real food, courtesy of the U.S.
Navy and Air Force, for at least two weeks. But half a century later, their
bodies and eyes are still struggling with the long-term effects of such severe
malnutrition.

An incident referred to by the ex-prisoners as "the truckload of oranges" illustrates just how precarious their nutrition was; as told by Harold Feiner:

> In the summer of 1944 many of us began to go blind. Dr. Hewlett told the camp commander we needed vitamin C. A truckload of small oranges [*mikan*] appeared, and we ate them up, skin and all. And we began to be able to see again!

Harold Feiner also recalled how persistently Dr. Hewlett tried, every day, to pry loose medical supplies and food for his comrades. "Each day, the Mitsui company doctor would accompany Dr. Hewlett on his rounds," Feiner said softly. "Dr. Hewlett would say: 'We need this, we must have that,' and the Japanese doctor would say, 'tomorrow, tomorrow'—always, it was 'tomorrow.' But tomorrow never came," Feiner added, shaking his head as his voice trailed off.

For the survivors of Mitsui's Fukuoka Camp No. 17, their tomorrows began when the emperor of Japan broadcast his message of surrender on August 15, 1945. For many of their comrades, it was already too late. For those who came home, their postwar lives have been marked by the effects of malnutrition, breathing coal dust, and post-traumatic stress. Not one was restored to full health in which to enjoy his hard-won freedom. A total of 1,859 prisoners, including 821 Americans, were sent to Mitsui's Omuta coal mine. Despite the high injury rate, 1,733 survived. Forty-nine Americans died. Fewer than 200 of those Americans who toiled at Omuta were still alive in 1999.

When Gap Silva finally returned home in September 1945, he was met with a painful example of what life over the past three years had been like for families who had received no word from or about their loved ones. When he ran to greet his father, instead of a joyful smile of recognition, the elder Silva traced his fingers over his son's face. Doctors told him that the windy nights he had spent crying for his son as he worked in the rail yard at Gallup, New Mexico, had dried his tear ducts and eye moisture, eventually causing blindness.

"In my whole experience as a prisoner of war, that was the hardest thing to bear," Silva said.

Chapter 6

Mitsui: Hidden Horror, Hidden Treasure

"YOU ARE GOING TO JAPAN. IT DOESN'T GET COLD THERE," WAS THE ANSWER a thousand shivering American prisoners got when they asked for warmer clothing at Pusan, Korea. It was early November 1942; the emaciated and sick survivors of Bataan and Corregidor had just spent a month aboard the *Tottori Maru*, which they bitterly nicknamed the *Torture Maru*—2,000 American prisoners crammed into a filthy cargo space, which might have accommodated 500. The old merchant vessel had been built in Glasgow and sold to a Mitsubishi subsidiary in the 1930s.

Several hundred American POWs were being issued warmer clothing at the Pusan docks that day, because they were headed for Mitsubishi's factory complex in Manchuria. But the POWs bound for the home islands would just have to make do with whatever they happened to be wearing when they surrendered on a hot April day in the Philippines. A few days later, after watching more of their comrades die at sea, the surviving POWs shivered below decks, partly in fear of American torpedoes, partly from cold, as the old merchant ship headed at full steam, in complete blackout at night, at last arriving at Osaka. The men had been forty-one days at sea. Dazed, stumbling, and shivering more than ever, the prisoners were divided into groups of seventy, so their captors could more easily count how many were needed to fill the requests of each company that had contracted with the Japanese government for their services. Then the POWs waited, in their flimsy tropical shorts and shirts, at the windy railroad yards for the train to Yokohama.

"It was the *coldest damn* wait I have ever known," army air force staff sergeant Herbert Zincke noted in his diary. Zincke was somehow able to keep his handwritten daily jottings hidden from his captors. When he got back home, he worked off and on over a period of years to transcribe his notes. Even with the elite-sized typeface of an old manual machine, Zincke's diary runs to 319 pages, double-spaced. It is a remarkably accurate description of exactly what each day was like in Japanese captivity. And those days were marked by watery soybean soup, diminishing portions of rice, no warm water, and constant fear of death.

Zincke was one of nearly 300 Americans in the first group forwarded by train to Kawasaki, where the prisoners got off and walked three miles to the Mitsui Company's vast warehouse-and-rail-shipping Kawasaki stevedoring complex, Mitsui Bushan Kiaka. The company's POW camp was designated as Tokyo POW Branch Camp No. 2, and the exhausted, emaciated, and sick prisoners were greeted with these words from a Japanese interpreter: "You are not prisoners of war, but guests of the Emperor. Do not try to escape, or you will be shotted!"[1]

Each man was assigned a number by Mitsui. If he was sent to the worksite of another company, that company assigned him a new number. Each company kept *exact* records listing every POW's name, branch of service, nationality, job he was doing when captured, military serial number (if he wasn't a civilian), and date of birth. At the Kawasaki camp, a Mitsui supervisor, Private Kondo, ordered army master sergeant John Britton to keep the roster for this camp. Britton meticulously noted who was transferred out or who died, and the date of each man's departure or death.

Eventually the camp population was increased; half the Americans were sent daily to work at the nearby Showa Denko chemical plant, so 133 Java Dutch soldiers and a few British were brought in to keep the workforce quota of POWs at around 350.

TOKIO PRISONERS OF WAR
CAMP NO.2   Page 2

Arm.	No.	Rank	Name	Nat.	Serial No.	Date of Birth	Occupation
A.	66	PFC	O'Brien,Patrick David	A.	6259152	18-7-24	Air-Mechanic
A.	67	Pfc	Paluch,Stanley John	A.	19019871	19-10-13	Truck Driver
A.	68	PFC	Pozzani,Mario	A.	6950024	20-8-28	Air-Mechanic
A.	69	PFC	Price,Orren Glen	A.	19011092	18-6-22	Truck Driver
A.	70	PFC	Quick,Henry Davis	A.	7000775	19-3-9	Air-Mechanic
A.	71	PFC	Ray,George Cheston	A.	6396814	18-9423	Air-Mechanic
A.	72	PFC	Richardson,Raymond C.	A.	19020678	21-1-12	Truck Driver
A.	73	PFC	Riley,James M.	A.	18043083	21-1-20	Air-Mechanic
A.	74	PFC	Wagner,Elmer F.	A.	17021273	19-12-14	Auto-Mechanic
A.	75	PFC	Wantland,Robert E.	A.	19011043	21-6-2	Auto-Mechanic
A.	76	PFC	Warner,Grant T.		6236879	19-7-1	Air-Mechanic
A.	77	PFC	Wilber,Charles Owen	A.	18046031	19-8-2	Truck Driver
A.	78	Pvt	Wiley,Harold Wayhard	A.	6911553	20-11-1	Air-Mechanic
A.	79	PFC	Cavanaugh,James Keevin	A.	33050298	19-4-1	Truck Driver
A.	80	PFC	Graham,Charles Hale	A.	6888431	18-7-28	Air-Mechanic
A.	81	PFC	Gomm,Verl Vogel	A.	6934168	16-5-30	Air-Mechanic
A.	82	PFC	Heimbuch,George R.	A.	14054600	21-3-15	Salesman
A.	83	PFC	Oliver,John Henry	A.	18056307	22-11-26	Elec,Welder
A.	84	PFC	Phillips,Robert W.		6913730	20-8-12	Air-Mechanic
A.	85	Pvt	Didio,Vincent James		19034142	13-3-22	Auto-Mechanic
A.	86	Pvt	Ervin,William Elmer		16040803	19-8-9	Air-Mechanic
A.	87	Pvt	Frank,Elmer L.		19002071	18-3-25	Auto-Mechanic
A.	88	Pvt	Houston,Ralph L.	A.	19056976	18-6-26	Student
A.	89	Pvt	Kendrick,Grant Matthew		19045757	21-5-23	Air-Mechanic
A.	90	Pvt	Manier,Elsworth A.		18061810	22-5-30	Student
A.	91	Pvt	Raymond,Lester James		19018986	22-6-13	Truck Driver
A.	92	Pvt	Silverman,Luis		12033446	20-11-83	Plumbers Helper
A.	93	Pvt	Turner,John Rufus		18029831	16-11-26	Truck Driver
A.	94	Pvt	Wilkens,Joy Edmond		6951476	19-11-19	Welder

Page from the roster kept by M.Sgt. John Britton at Mitsui's Kawasaki stevedoring operation, Mitsui Bushan Kiaka, Tokyo POW Camp No. 2. COLLECTION OF EDWARD JACKFERT

Mitsui converted its office building to living quarters for the prisoners, doing some carpentry to create double-decker sleeping shelves on either side of a central hallway. A crude ladder allowed men to climb to the top shelf, where the headroom was barely three feet.

The company also took individual head-and-shoulder photographs of each prisoner, showing his number written on a piece of paper and pinned to his clothing. A second set of photographs was taken outdoors on November 12, 1943, in front of the new Mitsui office building. The prisoners are grouped in several rows around hired guards and Mitsui employees. These group photos were confiscated by Sgt. John Britton, who spotted them amid Mitsui office papers scattered after an air raid in July 1945.

It was a hazardous worksite for men with no decent shoes, almost no clothing, and no safety equipment, as they tried to step over railroad tracks, yard debris, and rough gravel, or around cranes and forklifts. After many requests, some POWs were given British woolen winter uniforms, along with shoes—if a man was lucky enough to get a pair that fit. When the shoes wore out, they were not replaced. The men were allowed to wear those uniforms to and from work only, in cold weather—and for the group photographs.

Group photo taken November 12, 1943, by Mitsui employee of American POWs and Mitsui company employees, including guards. POW Robert Phillips (1) is identified near center of back row. Mitsui office building (2) is directly in background. Old Mitsui office building, used as barracks for POWs (3) is in background to right. COLLECTION OF EDWARD JACKFERT

Army air corps sergeant David English recalled: "My first detail was on the waterfront shoveling coal from Italian ships. The coal was wet and the work was extremely dirty. The shifts often ran twenty-four hours straight because the ship had to be emptied to meet deadlines. We had few breaks and little or no food. I worked in a crouched position putting long hours of agonizing strain on my knees and legs."[2]

The agony in his knees has been a lifelong trauma for former army private first class Ray Richardson, caused by the cruel impatience of a Mitsui employee. Richardson, a tall, soft-spoken man with a gentle smile, was asked by this writer in a videotaped 1998 interview whether he had ever been injured on the job at the Mitsui complex. "Yes," he answered. "We were on a work detail, going into the hold of a ship unloading iron ore. The guard pushed . . ." His face contorted, and he lost his composure. You could see him reliving the pain of that moment, and the lifelong disability he has suffered because of it. Several of Richardson's fellow ex-POWs were in the room, waiting their turn to be interviewed. Roy Gentry, national commander of the American Defenders of Bataan and Corregidor, who had been at this Mitsui site with Richardson, was taping the interview. He waited silently, the camera whirring. No one said a word. "Excuse me," Richardson whispered, and then he went on. "He pushed me onto the pile of iron ore, and it threw my knee out of whack, and that's still a bad knee. I went up to go to the *benjo* [toilet] and was coming back down the ladder. He pushed me with his rifle butt and I lost my balance and fell."[3]

Former army private first class John Oliver also described working round the clock: "A work day was about ten or eleven hours, and for seven days a week. I also remember on many occasions we worked twenty-four hours on a shift with only a thirty minute break for lunch and dinner. We had another break at midnight for about thirty minutes, with one half of a rice ball lunch with a pickled cherry or *daikon* [a long, hard radish] slice on top."[4] Oliver also kept a small, secret diary, with just four or five well-chosen words under each date. "You had to be careful what you wrote, in case someone discovered your diary'" he said. "The Japanese didn't want us to write anything bad about them." So Oliver's diary is peppered with "Good day" (meaning he didn't get a beating) or "Hard day" (meaning he did).

Regardless of their work detail or health, the prisoners were made very aware that the company's work quota had to be met. And for several months, between their arrival in November 1942 and January 1943, the POWs at Tokyo POW Branch Camp No. 2 had no doctor to intercede for them, or to tell a Mitsui *hancho* (supervisor) that a particular POW was really too sick to work. So it was with a great deal of relief that the prisoners welcomed a British navy captive to their midst, and a surgeon at that: Lt. (jg) Dr. Peter Curtin. He

Page from the secret diary of John Oliver. Notation of "Good day" meant he did not receive a beating that day. COLLECTION OF JOHN OLIVER

had been captured by a German ship in the South Pacific and turned over to the Japanese. Although he was beaten repeatedly by Mitsui personnel, he persisted in his demands and finally, after several months of arguing, was allowed to set up a hospital for the prisoners, and to have the authority to keep men from going on work details. Sometimes Dr. Curtin was successful; sometimes not. All of the men were suffering from diseases brought on by malnutrition, made worse by the fact that Japanese camp staff often helped themselves to the prisoners' ration of rice, leaving the POWs with only barley, which has almost no nutritional value. "They [the Japanese] didn't like barley either," an ex-POW wryly commented. So it became a matter of degree as to how sick or weak a prisoner might be, and whether or not Dr. Curtin could persuade the Mitsui supervisor that it would be worth leaving a particular POW behind that day as he escorted the prisoners from their living quarters to their work details. As for the rest, they faced another day of struggling to avoid beatings, and to do their tasks without injuring their weakened bodies. No prisoner at Tokyo POW Branch Camp No. 2 was really up to the task, and Mitsui executives saw the condition of these prisoners firsthand, on a daily basis.

Charles Graham, a former private first class in the army, gave a graphic description of how impossible those tasks were for starving men. Of somewhat small build even in the best of times, Graham was down to 110 pounds when he was routinely assigned to carry sacks of rice to be stacked in Mitsui's warehouse. The men especially dreaded lifting sacks of Saigon rice, because they weighed up to 220 pounds. It took four emaciated prisoners to lift a sack onto the shoulder of one man. In a 1998 interview, Graham recalled in sparing words: "It was somewhat stressful—you were pushed to keep moving.

Mitsui photo of POW Charles Graham.
COLLECTION OF
CHARLES GRAHAM

Walking up a slanted narrow board [in the warehouse] with a 130-pound sack on your back—it was hazardous," he said with a chuckle of disbelief at the memory.[5] One man sustained a fractured spinal cord trying to perform this task. Artist Joe Astarita sketched this dangerous balancing act of trying to walk the narrow plank with such a heavy burden. It was a common sight at many company locations.

Edward Jackfert remembered the burlap sacks filled with sharp pieces of scrap manganese the men had to carry, with no protective clothing. "The sharp corners often penetrated our skin," he said in a matter-of-fact tone. "You had to be careful." Jackfert recalled one warehouse detail when he and other POWs were assigned to roll out fifty-gallon drums filled with aircraft fuel from a Standard Oil warehouse about a mile from the Mitsui complex. After punching holes in as many drum bottoms as they could, the POWs carefully loaded them bottom side down on a waiting rail freight car, so the fuel would be gone by the time the train reached its destination.

While they were inside the warehouse, the POWs made an interesting discovery: bags and bags of silver coins. "The coins were from Singapore, and Thailand, and all over Asia," Jackfert recalled.[6] Apparently while Japan's leaders were promoting the Greater East Asian Co-Prosperity Sphere, their army and navy were bringing bags of it back home to be stored in company warehouses.

But what Jackfert remembered even more sharply were the daylight air raids, which intensified as 1945 began. B-29 crews targeted many installations in the Yokohama-Tokyo area, unaware that POWs were living and working right in these targets. To their horror, the prisoners realized that they

POW walking on narrow plank over open water, with heavy load, trying not to fall. This sketch was done by Joseph Astarita of the stevedoring operations at Japan Express, Osaka Camp No. 2, but it is typical of the hazards described by Charles Graham and POWs at many stevedoring locations. SKETCH BY JOSEPH ASTARITA

were being forced to continue working through the air raids, with no place to hide. After five months of steadily increasing bombings, the prisoners were allowed to construct air-raid shelters in May 1945. But still they were often made to stay out in the open, while the huge planes dropped their loads of incendiary bombs on Yokohama.

The POWs did not know that a year earlier, the Allies had sent urgent messages to the Swiss government asking the Swiss minister in Tokyo, Camille Gorgé, to protest once again to the Japanese about placing prisoner camps in dangerous areas. One secret message, sent in July 1944 from the Swiss Foreign Ministry of Foreign Affairs, Protecting Power Activities Division, in Bern to Minister Gorgé in Tokyo, was transmitted on behalf of the Canadian Legation. It reads in part:

> With regard to location of prisoner of war camps in dangerous areas, His Majesty's government are not sure whether Minister Gorgé quite understands the nature of their anxiety. They do not demand internment of prisoners of war in open country or in mountains (although of course they would prefer it), but merely their removal from the immediate vicinity of docks, aerodromes, military [installations] and war production factories. . . . His Majesty's government can give formal assurance that no prisoner of war or civilian internment camps for Japanese Nationals . . . are located near such military objectives. . . . If Minister Gorgé really thinks it useless to ask this then at least . . . the Japanese authorities should provide deep shelter trenches and give prisoners of war access to them during raids.[7]

1709

From: Berne (Politique Intérêts)
To: Tokyo
14 July 1944
SZR-SZC

#631

The Canadian Legation wires:

"His Majesty's Government are grateful for the expression of the Swiss Minister's opinion as contained in your 700 to 705[a] and will endeavor to carry out his recommendations as far as possible.

With regard to location of prisoner of war camps in dangerous areas, His Majesty's government are not sure whether Minister GORGÉ quite understands the nature of their anxiety. They do not demand internment of prisoners of war in open country or in mountains (although of course they would prefer it), but merely their removal from the immediate vicinity of docks, aerodromes, military --2U-- and war production factories. As stated in the last part of our 926[b] His Majesty's Government can give formal assurance that no prisoner of war or civilian internment camps for Japanese Nationals in their territories are located near such military objectives and this assurance can be renewed. This is a case

Swiss   #131450
              Page 1

where real reciprocity is possible and its principle could be usefully invoked. But if Minister GORGÉ really thinks it useless to ask this then at least (although His Majesty's Government would regard this as very much less satisfactory) the Japanese authorities should provide deep shelter trenches and give prisoners of war access to them during raids.

His Majesty's Government also inquires whether Minister GORGÉ had any reply to his latest representations (see our #479[a] and #630)[a]. According to a recent I.R.C.C. report camp #1 in Formosa was in June still situated in a dangerous area. No question connected with prisoners of war gives His Majesty's Government greater concern than this question of dangerous location.

--4U-- To the question on the condition of the camps (? please?) do everything in your power to obtain --2U--

a- Available if requested.
b- Not available.

Inter 14 Jul 44   (1)   Swiss   #131450
Rec'd 15 Jul 44   Page 2
Trans 19 Jul 44 (3816,1535-s)

Message from Swiss Foreign Ministry in Bern to its minister in Tokyo, Camille Gorgé, passing on concern expressed by Canadian Legation about POWs being placed too close to industrial air-raid targets. FILES OF THE NATIONAL SECURITY AGENCY

At a September 1999 news conference in New York City, Edward Jackfert shocked a room full of veteran reporters when he told them that he and his fellow prisoners were forced to retrieve the body parts of their comrades after twenty-two were killed by a direct hit on their worksite.

By midsummer 1945, Mitsui had sent all their Japanese employees home, out of harm's way. "They would have had to shut down if we hadn't been there to run the equipment," Jackfert said bitterly in a 1998 interview. "By the summer of 1945, we *were* the work force at Mitsui!"

For Allied prisoners in Japanese custody, there were always two kinds of beatings: mental and physical. And both were applied constantly. In his diary, Herbert Zincke used aviator's terminology to make note of beatings by Mitsui employees: "Saito helped Shiojawa *strafe* the men, and he broke two of Kendrick's ribs when he beat and kicked him while he was on the ground." Zincke and his fellow survivors of this Mitsui worksite were pleased to learn, in a July 1947 letter from Sgt. John Britton, who testified at the Tokyo War Crimes Trials, that Saito was sentenced to thirty years, and Shiozawa to twenty years, for mistreating prisoners. Britton ended his letter with a request: "Please pass this on. The more affidavits we have the surer we will be to get justice."[8]

Unfortunately, the sense of satisfaction ex-prisoners may have felt at seeing justice done was short-lived. Just five years later, when the American occupation of Japan ended in 1952, most Japanese serving sentences in Tokyo's Sugamo Prison were freed. By 1958, all had been released.

One of the most bizarre postwar incidents experienced by survivors of Japanese captivity happened to ex-POWs who had toiled at a Mitsui subsidiary, Electric Chemical Company (Denki Kagaku Kogyo Co., Ltd.) at Aomi, known as Tokyo POW Branch Camp No. 13. According to what the Japanese interpreter there told several POWs, Aomi was the camp where "undesirables, the sick and Jews" were sent. From their descriptions, life at Aomi was extremely harsh and dangerous. The POWs worked in open iron ore pits, and at the smelting furnaces under very hazardous conditions with no safety equipment. And the beatings by company employees were relentless.

Yet the night before the prisoners left the camp, company president Tetsuji Kondoh gave a farewell dinner for the POW officers at his home, in thanks for all their efforts on the company's behalf. British officers attended; American officers refused to do so. POW camp commander Stephen Abbott, who was British, had to remain on duty in the camp, so Mr. Kondoh sent Abbott's dinner to him. The following day, Mr. Kondoh accompanied the ex-prisoners to the railroad station, to say good-bye.

Subsequently, Mr. Kondoh contacted Abbott and asked for the home addresses of all ex-POWs, British and American, who had toiled at Denki Kagaku Kogyo. Abbott, who had allegedly turned in fellow POWs to the Japanese for "stealing" undistributed Red Cross parcels meant for them,[9] sent Mr. Kondoh the information he requested.

Kondoh waited until early July 1947, after the War Crimes Trial prosecutors had made the decision to drop indictments against the heads of major Japanese companies (the *zaibatsu*), including Mitsui. On July 7, he mailed the following letter to each ex-prisoner who had been at his worksite:

> My dear sir:
>
> Two years have passed since I bid farewell at Aomi station. I beg to pay my highest esteem and courtesy for your hard work while you were at Aomi for a long time & at the same time I am anxious to know about your welfare since then.
>
> We Japanese are endeavouring to bring about a spiritual revolution in speeding the establishment of a democratic, peaceloving & cultural nation.
>
> I trust Japan will become a comfortable land in the near future and I hope you will have a good chance to visit Japan to inspect her old customs & manners.
>
> Please give my best regards to your family.
> Believe me,
> Yours sincerely.
> Tetsuji Kondoh [signed]

Denki Kagaku Kogyo is still in business.

The copy of Mr. Kondoh's letter obtained by this writer was addressed to Irving Strobing, who was the Army radio operator at Corregidor. Strobing sent the last desperate messages before this final Philippine outpost surrendered to Japanese forces on May 6, 1942. Strobing's transmissions were released to the public three weeks later, just before Memorial Day. They were broadcast on radio stations and printed in newspapers all across the country, because even in the midst of despair, Strobing's cryptic phrases were laced with humor and hope.

Strobing died in 1997; his reaction on receiving this letter could not be verified. But fellow Aomi survivor Wilburn Snyder said when he opened that same letter, his reaction was a mixture of anger and discomfort at the thought that his former "employer" now knew exactly where he lived.[10]

Tetsuji ·Kondoh

President of Denki Kagaku
Kogyo Co., Ltd.,

♯3, 1-chome, Shintomi-cho,
Chuo-ku, Tokyo

July 07, 1947

Mr. Strobing, Irving

605 Barbey Street

Brooklyn, New York,

U. S. A.

My dear sir;

Two years have passed since I bid farewell at Aomi station.

I beg to pay my highest esteem and courtesy for your hard work while you were at Aomi for a long time & at the same time. I am anxious to know about your welfare since then.

We Japanese are endeavouring to bring about a spiritual revolution in speeding the establishment of a democratic, peaceloving & cultural nation.

I trust Japan will become a comfortable land in the near future. and I hope you will have a good chance to visit Japan to inspect her old customs & manners.

Please give my best regards to your family

Believe me,

Yours sincerely.

Letter sent July 7, 1947, by Tetsuji Kondoh, president of Mitsui subsidiary Denki Kagaku Kogyo, directly to the U.S. homes of former POWs who had worked at his company's mine at Aomi, Japan. Many ex-POWs were disturbed that the Japanese company president had obtained their home addresses from the British POW camp commander.

Chapter 7

Showa Denko:
Daily Dangers

"HAVING EAR TROUBLE DUE TO THE TERRIFIC NOISE OF THE MACHINERY AT the 'copper mill,'" Herbert Zincke wrote in his diary on September 4, 1943. Zincke was one of about 100 American POWs sent on regular work details from the Mitsui POW Branch Camp No. 2 site to the Showa Denko chemical plant nearby, named Kosaka Soko. Prisoners called it the "copper mill" after the copper-green–colored piles of powdered chemicals they had to work around—and inhale the dust from, because they had no face masks or other protection. At the plant this powder was combined with ammonium nitrate to form either fertilizer or explosives. The POWs were told it was fertilizer they were making.

"The machinery was old and rusty, and when they were all operating, the noise was deafening," Zincke (who suffered permanent hearing loss) noted. "The bosses were grumpy old men who were always in a hurry to keep [things] moving."[1] Zincke described having to use long poles to push the piles of powdered chemical through a hole in the floor to a conveyor belt below. But apparently the old machinery couldn't keep up with the old men's pace, either: a prisoner sustained a serious back injury when a conveyor belt snapped and whiplashed him. One day all the machinery broke down.

"Stewart and Moore burnt their legs with nitric acid," Zincke noted. "They were unloading tank cars of nitric acid and it spilled on their legs." (No boots, rubber aprons, or similar protective gear was issued to POWs forced to handle these hazardous materials.) A few weeks later, the same thing happened to Zincke. A leaky valve in the tank car he was unloading splashed nitric acid on his flimsy pants, immediately searing his skin and badly burning his knees. Luckily, there was a drainage ditch nearby filled waist-high with water, into which he quickly jumped. This act allowed him to avoid more severe burns; even so, it was many weeks before he could walk normally again without terrible pain.

Day after day, the prisoners at Showa Denko were exposed to toxic fumes from ammonium nitrate, hydrochloric acid, and sulfuric acid, as well as chemical dust; some said it felt like inhaling poison all the time, which in fact is what they were doing. They all worried about having no protective equipment or clothing. On one occasion, prisoners were invited to fill out forms listing the improvements they would like to see when working at these factories, but nothing came of that exercise. Those who were lucky enough to survive came home with permanent hearing loss and damage to their internal organs, which would gradually manifest into chronic illness.

"If I had known what lay ahead, I would have put a gun to my head, right there on Bataan," Alvin Silver told CBS News in a 1999 interview. In the next breath, he added: "But at the same time, I decided if one man was going to walk out alive, it would be me." That viewpoint served Silver well. He landed at Moji on Thanksgiving Day 1942, aboard the Kawasaki-built *Nagato Maru.*

Silver was taken to an "unlisted" camp, Hiraoka Subcamp No. 3, operated by the Kumagai Engineering Company, at the village of Mitsushima near Nagano in the mountains of northern Honshu.[2] Over the next year and a half, this camp became notorious even by Japanese standards. The death rate from pneumonia, dysentery, starvation, and brutality was so high that the commandant ordered a stop to funeral services because their frequency was demoralizing. Even the POW Management Bureau in Tokyo found the death toll at Mitsushima unacceptable, and the bureau ordered most of the POWs shipped to a new location: Showa Denko's carbide plant at Kanose, also in northern Honshu. The commandant ordered the American POW commander, Maj. Walter Hewitt, and the Canadian commander, Capt. Leslie Chater, to each select fifty of their men to open the new camp in April 1944 at Kanose, designated as Tokyo POW Branch Camp No. 16-D, in the Niigata district. Silver was in this group.

Once again, prisoners found equipment at this Showa Denko plant to be old, badly in need of repair, and very dangerous to work with. Captain Chater noted in his diary: "Furnaces exploding and bursting out sides . . . Lots of explosions from [factory] works last night. They shook our quarters. Seems as if they couldn't tap one furnace all day and at night it broke out of side and when liquid carbide hits water it goes off with a terrific report. Often get these when water jackets burst. Machinery is in bad condition and someone is going to get hurt one day. . . . Concerned re large number of men sick with boils and septic carbide burns."[3]

On March 9, 1945, Chater's worst fears were realized. Three of his men were badly burned when the bottom fell out of a piece of equipment. The entry in his diary for that day is disturbing: "Three moved to [Japanese] hospital.

Funeral service, Mitsushima, 1943. COLLECTION OF LESLIE CHATER

Nurses very good but Doc poor. *The [Japanese] were laughing about it.* "After clinging to life in great pain for several days, all three died. High-level Showa Denko executives attended the funeral.

But production with the hazardous old machinery was stepped up; the POWs were made to extend their periods of work to twelve-hour shifts. At the same time, their food ration was cut in half, prompting Captain Chater to protest to the camp commandant, Lt. Hiroshi Azuma. The solution offered to Chater by the Japanese camp sergeant was to only send half the number of men to work the next day, if they once again were given only half rations. Chater noted that he was also told: "The [Showa Denko] factory representative and the Cook House Honcho [are] always drunk and . . . are trading rice for drink as they don't get much money."

Alvin Silver remembered not so much the broken equipment, but the terrible cold and his broken skull. In the winter of 1944–45, Silver recalled, "The snow was even with the rooftops, and we had to walk to work in our flimsy clothes. The fabric was like rayon, and that was it. We weren't given any warm clothes." And then there was the day the camp interpreter, Heitaro Fukijima, fractured Silver's skull with the *daikon* Silver had stolen from the kitchen. "This large radish can get as long as three feet, and is the size of a baseball bat," Silver said. "It's hard as a rock. The Japanese staff were very single-minded when they did their sudden searches. If they were looking for food and you had a radio, they wouldn't pay any attention to it. That day, they were looking for vegetables. We all had to stand at attention while they searched our belongings. I must have had twelve bags of rice behind the pillow on my bed, and they just moved it aside. Then Fukijima spotted the *daikon* behind my pillow.

Photo of POW Alvin Silver taken by Showa Denko employee at the company's carbide plant, Tokyo POW Branch Camp No. 16-D, Kanose, Japan, April 1944.

COLLECTION OF

ALVIN SILVER

He hit me on the shoulder with it, and I turned to avoid the second blow—exposing my head. So the second time, he hit me on the back of my head with the *daikon*. I still have a lump there. For years I had splitting headaches, very frequently. Now the headaches are less frequent, but I still have them."[4]

Brutal beatings by company employees were a daily occurrence. Some beatings and punishments at Kanose were so extraordinary that they became the subject of testimony at the Tokyo War Crimes Trials. Major Hewitt testified against camp commandant Azuma and several Showa Denko factory employees at the trials. Captain Chater couldn't bring himself to return to Japan to testify, but he did agree to allow his diary to be entered into the record as an exhibit, and to lend his support to Major Hewitt's testimony at Yokohama, where the trials involving mistreatment of prisoners took place. Major Hewitt testified intensively about the hazardous factory working conditions; the forcing of sick prisoners to work; the beatings by factory guards and supervisors; the injuries and deaths of prisoners. According to the daily informational summary of trial proceedings issued by the Legal Section of General MacArthur's headquarters on July 31, 1947:

> Hiroshi Azuma, former Lieutenant in the Japanese Army, was Camp commander of Prisoner of War Camp 16-D, Kanose, Niigata, Japan, from April 1944 until August 1945. He was charged with command responsibility for numerous severe beatings and abuses

American POWs celebrating Christmas at Kanose, 1944. Red Cross parcels had been distributed for the occasion — a rare event. COLLECTION OF ALVIN SILVER

that were administered to prisoners by non-commissioned officers and civilian factory guards under his control. Azuma also personally beat and mistreated American and Allied prisoners held at this camp. He was sentenced to seven years imprisonment at hard labor.

Hisao Kaneyama, former guard at the Kanose Carbon and Carbide Company where the prisoners were compelled to work, was known as one of the worst guards at camp. He was charged with beating and torturing prisoners, sometimes striking, kicking and stomping the victims into a semi-conscious state. On one occasion he beat Major Walter Hewitt . . . who appeared at this trial as the prosecution's chief witness, with such severity that it broke Hewitt's right ear drum. Kaneyama was found guilty of clubbing Fred L. Kolilis . . . and Don A. Martindale . . . after they had been discovered playing cards in the barracks. He then forced the two men to stand at attention holding large cakes of ice in their bare hands until the ice melted. This happened on one of the coldest nights in February and the men were forced to stand this way all night. Kaneyama was sentenced . . . to fourteen years at hard labor.

Tokio Minagawa and Kiyoji Ishibe, civilian guards, were each found guilty of beating and mistreating a British prisoner. Minagawa was sentenced to one year six months, and Ishibe to two years imprisonment.

Kiromitzu Saito, known as "The Bulldog," was sentenced to five years imprisonment after he was found guilty of consistently beating numerous prisoners.

Heitaro Fukijima served as an interpreter at Camp 16-D. He was charged with brutally beating American prisoners with wooden shoes, clubs and other instruments. He was sentenced to seven years imprisonment.[5]

The summary doesn't mention the *daikon* with which Fukijima fractured Alvin Silver's skull; it may have been included in "other instruments."

After the sentences were handed down, Captain Chater received a letter from Burton R. Philips, defense attorney for the Japanese staff at Kanose, not only asking for his reaction to the sentences, but inviting him to consider recommending lighter sentences for the accused, indicating that he was planning to submit a petition for clemency. Philips added: "Your opinion might serve to advance somewhat the cause of democracy we are attempting to teach to the Japanese."[6]

In a March 2000 interview, Chater confirmed that he had indeed sent a letter to the War Crimes Trials Court, recommending a reduction in the sentence of camp commander Azuma, because "He really did the best he could for us, and got us medicines and increased our food supply when he could." Chater let the other sentences stand. But they didn't stand for long. "They were all let off by 1955 or '56," he said.

The name of Showa Denko, the company that owned the property where the prisoners were housed, and owned and operated the factory where they were forced to work, and employed the personnel who abused them, is not mentioned in the transcript of this trial. Robert Donihi, a former prosecutor at the International Prosecution Section Class A Tokyo trial, recollected that he was one of two prosecutors making recommendations to Chief Prosecutor Joseph Keenan about who should be indicted for the trial. The industrialists—the *(zaibatsu)*—were named as suspected war criminals, but at a 1992 symposium on war crimes at St. John's University, Donihi said: "There were no industrialists on trial, distinct from Nuremberg, where industry used slave labor. Despite Soviet pressure, Austin Hauxhurst and I (having been assigned by Mr. Keenan to study the question) recommended against the inclusion of the industrialist *(zaibatsu)* category."[7] However, Donihi later said he believed the industrialists could have and should have been tried separately for their crimes against prisoners of war at the Class B and C trials, which dealt with the treatment of POWs.[8]

Because the *zaibatsu* were not named in the indictment, it became a matter of practice for prosecutors to avoid mentioning the names of the individual companies that operated camps where prisoners were sent to do forced labor. As a result, rarely is a company name to be found in transcripts of the Tokyo War Crimes Trials.[9]

Chapter 8

NKK: Hard Times Everywhere

WHEN 500 SICK AND SHIVERING PRISONERS OF WAR ARRIVED AT NIPPON Ko-Kan's (NKK) Kamaishi Iron Works in the mountains of northern Honshu late in November 1942, they had just survived an arduous trip from Singapore aboard the Mitsubishi-built *Dai Nichi Maru;* they were still in tropical clothes; and it was very cold in those mountains. Ex-POW Robert O'Brien recalled that the temperature was below freezing most of the time, "And we had no warm clothes." (Eventually they were issued coarse woolen pants and jackets, but no underwear.) This would be their home of hardship for nearly the next three years: Sendai POW Branch Camp No. 5, at Ohashi.

Prisoners worked relentlessly long hours in the mines, the separation mill, the welding shop, or on the railroad tracks. They were mining iron ore and cutting up scrap iron (much of it stamped "Made in USA") to create Japan's weapons of war.

Robert O'Brien of the USS *Houston* recalled being given a Japanese bank account book (probably a Postal Service account), into which the money amount he allegedly was being paid would be entered each week. He never saw any money. NKK employees beat O'Brien so severely that they knocked out several of his teeth. And part of his 100 percent disability classification is listed as "bone pain" from all the savage beatings he sustained at Ohashi.[1]

Former army sergeant Jesse Stanbrough of the Texas 131st Field Artillery, captured on Java along with O'Brien, remembered that three or four POWs died each day at Ohashi. It was a grim statistic, which was all too common at other NKK POW camps throughout the home islands.

Nippon Seitetsu (Nippon Iron and Steel, as NKK was called in prewar days) was founded in 1934, and by the time Japan bombed Pearl Harbor, the company had mining operations in Hirohata, Yawata, Kawasaki, and Wanishi, in addition to the Kamaishi Ohashi complex. American POWs were sent in large numbers to nearly all of these locations: 492 to Hirohata; 500 of

Liberated POWs outside barracks at Sendai POW Branch Camp No. 5, operated by Nippon Ko-Kan (NKK) at Ohashi, Japan, late August 1945. COLLECTION OF MRS. JESSE STANBROUGH

1,200 POWs to Yawata; 200 to Kawasaki. Everywhere in NKK's iron empire the work was hard, long, and brutal.

Here is what army technical sergeant Robert Renfro wrote in his diary on November 5, 1944, at NKK's Tokyo POW Detachment No. 5, Kawasaki:

> A few days ago four Americans got beat up on the job by Jap civilians. Then the Japs in charge of this camp went out there and beat the American prisoners some more. The Lieutenant beat them in the guard house also and made them stay three days without any food. Hughes wanted to change the grinding wheel and the Jap would not change it. The Jap hit Hughes over the back with a vise and Cornick, Phillips and Stendament came over to stop it and got beat up also. Lots of protection we have here! Every time it rains the steam goes off and we have no chow. They can't get any vegetables so we have no soup. A three-fourths bowl of maize (chicken feed) and a [small] tangerine is what we have been having for chow. Every day three times a day we eat chicken feed and like it, for two years. How much longer is this going on? . . . I

Photo of POW Robert Renfro taken by NKK employee in July 1943 at Tokyo POW Detachment No. 5, Kawasaki, Japan.

COLLECTION OF ROBERT RENFRO

Photo of POW David English taken by NKK employee on July 16, 1943, at Tokyo POW Detachment No. 5, Kawasaki. The mixture of fear, anger, and hunger on the prisoner's face is unmistakable.

COLLECTION OF DAVID ENGLISH

sometimes wonder if I am going to last this war out. . . . The Japs can't get anything now either and steal anything they can. I can't put in this book the things that are going on here and what the Japs are doing. Boy, what a hell-hole this is.

A couple of months later, in early January 1945, Renfro's diary entry reads:

> They [guards hired by NKK] pulled us out of the barracks one night and made us stand at attention in rows. It was the early part of the year and cold. They would not let us bunch up or try to keep warm. If they thought we were too close together they would hit us with their bayonets. We spent all night there. Some of the POWs who were really sick or pretending to be sick passed out and fell to the ground. To make sure they were really out the Japanese would hit them on the head with the butt of their rifles. Of course that made the rest of us stand at attention.
>
> The next morning we had to go to work without breakfast. . . . That night we did not get a chance to go inside the building. Instead we had to stand at attention all night long. . . . To stand at attention from five o'clock in the afternoon until seven o'clock the next morning without moving a muscle and in very cold weather was the most difficult thing I ever did in my life. This was just one of the things the Japanese inflicted on us. Without the will to live we would have died.[2]

Photo of POW Lloyd Nelson, taken by NKK employee at Osaka POW Camp No. 5. Note number 195 pinned to his tattered shirt.
COLLECTION OF
LLOYD NELSON

Some POWs who survived their years at NKK's Kawasaki site still wonder how certain comrades made it back. His friends watched Wake Island civilian construction worker Joe Goicoechea being beaten so severely by a company guard that he bled from his eyes and ears.

"We felt like rabbits during hunting season." That is how Seaman Edward Settles, a navy gunner, described daily life for prisoners at NKK's Hirohata steel mill, designated as Osaka POW Camp No. 12. Constantly under threat of death, trying to dodge beatings, no place to safely hide—the image is chillingly apt.

"My nickname was Knobby because of so many knots on my head caused by being struck by the [company] guards. . . . I had my right clavicle and shoulder broken but was never released from work detail. . . . There were no medicines available. . . . The windows in our quarters were ordered open in the winter and closed for the summer months. We were told this was for healthful reasons and [the company's] concern for us. I lost eighty-seven pounds. . . . We lost many, many men and as there were no burial spaces open to us the bodies were cremated in a fiery furnace and the ashes discarded."[3]

When Bataan survivor army airman William Milne hurt his back at the mill, NKK employees placed six pieces of punk (molded sticks used to ignite fuses) directly on his flesh and lit them. The scars remained throughout his life. "I saw many men beaten for no good cause," he said.[4]

Some 492 Americans were sent to Hirohata beginning in October 1943, and company managers knew what they were looking for in requesting white

Liberated POWs outside barracks at Osaka POW Camp No. 12B, Hirohata. Japanese were required to supply paint so "PW" could be marked on the roof to aid in airdrops of food and supplies while prisoners awaited rescue. COLLECTION OF STEVEN KRAMERICH

prisoner laborers, especially Americans. Infantrymen were put on the slag pit, yard, iron ore, and ship-unloading details; signals and communications prisoners were assigned to the electrical shop. Prisoners were given company uniforms and thin rubber shoes—both expected to last for two years.

"It seemed like we could always tell something was up [with the progress of the war]," army air corps signalman Stephen Kramerich wrote in his memoir. "The camp guards would take it out on us and a few days later we would find out that such and such a [Japanese-held] place had been bombed [by American planes] a few days ago."[5]

An official report on conditions at Hirohata compiled at war's end by the American POW Information Bureau states: "Had it not been for supplemental food purloined [by POWs unloading rice and other foods] from Japanese ships, it is estimated that the death rate from starvation would have been very high. . . . The most serious detriment to the convalescence of the sick was the attitude of the Japanese enlisted medical corpsman. He had the power to counteract the orders of the American medical officer [Capt. Sidney E. Seid, a child psychiatrist]. He frequently changed diagnoses, would refuse to issue medicine and would force the men with high temperatures to work. At times he would beat the prisoners who answered sick call."[6]

Army Corregidor survivor Joseph Sterner was one of several POWs who had very specific recollections about this Japanese medical corpsman [*segaduchi*]:

> The medic was called "Alice" because he was slightly built and very effeminate. Alice was not soft, or generous, or sympathetic. To the contrary, he was tyrannical, sadistic, and obsessed with authority over us. While he delighted in torturing and beating those prisoners who were held in camp because they were ill, he especially thrilled at beating the bigger and stronger persons in camp. He never used his hands. He always used a heavy stick. Alice needed no excuse to single out a person for punishment. While the prisoners were made to stand at attention, Alice would beat them about the head and across the small of the back with the stick, trying to knock the prisoners down. When they fell, he became infuriated and beat them where they lay. . . . It was common practice for those who were too sick to work to stand at attention from the time the morning work detail left until it returned late in the afternoon. If a prisoner could not stand at attention that long he was beaten. If the American doctor interceded, he was beaten.[7]

Pvt. John Aldrich, a Bataan survivor, had an unprintable nickname for this particular medical corpsman. His recollections show why:

He derived the most joy when he could order us to stand at attention in an absolute naked condition. . . . In one instance, during the winter, he ordered us outside, without clothing. He walked up and down the assembled ranks and he had a pair of forceps in his hand. If any of our men impressed him as being generously endowed, it was common for him to apply his forceps to the penis of his victim and delight in waving and gesticulating. . . .

An outright criminal act was perpetuated by this "sack of s—t" when he decided to give us some sort of injections which we were led to believe were either vitamins or protein shots. The same hypodermic was used on American after American without evidence of any type of sterilization. Also, the Japanese injected the "medicine" in the soft portion of flesh above the breasts of each man; one shot above each of the breasts and additional shots in the soft flesh of the upper arms. Whatever transferrable disease any one may have had was thusly transmitted to all men who followed.[8]

Paul Reuter, a fellow airman and close friend of Aldrich, still talked with pride about how he was relieved of his job in the company machine shop after he was finally caught performing one of many acts of sabotage. Sitting side by side over a half-century later, the two lifelong friends remembered minute details of their two years in "that hellhole called Hirohata," as Reuter put it. What one man would begin to say, the other could finish. Each incident was that fresh in both minds. Even when being tortured, Aldrich maintained his sense of humor—or defiance:

I was reported for stealing [food] on board ship and was punished. We had huge concrete "fire barrels" outside each barracks. It was mid-January and there was a layer of ice on top of the water. My punishment was to climb into the barrel and stay until ordered to come out. After about twenty minutes or so, one of the guards came by and asked me if I wanted anything and I replied, "Yes, a cake of soap." For that remark, I was confined an additional portion of time. I came out of that barrel a beautiful hue of blue and it took my buddies the better part of a couple of hours to thaw me out.[9]

A final irony for the prisoners at Hirohata came in the form of a farewell memorandum posted by camp interpreter S. Tahara on the day they were leaving, September 9, 1945. POW John Zubay removed it from the barracks wall on his way out the door. It is addressed "To all Men":

Flag-raising ceremony at Hirohata on day surrender was signed, September 2, 1945. POW Frank Muther said that for several weeks, a machine gun had been mounted just behind the flagpole, pointing directly at the POW parade ground. COLLECTION OF STEVEN KRAMERICH

Surely you have gained some valuable experience and learned some of life's lessons while in P.O.W. Camp.

Perseverance is not only one of the important things in life, but life always offers problems that can not be avoided and which you can overcome if you have perseverance.

You should gain a sense of personal satisfaction for having proved your worth. Think carefully over the things you have learned—do not throw away the knowledge and experience you have gained.

When you return, apply what you have learned in your new life for a new future. Strive to contribute to human welfare and fulfill a great mission with all your mental and material powers.

I appreciate the fact that I cannot fully and properly express my sincere feelings because of my limited knowledge of your language.

May God be with you always.

BON VOYAGE, S. Tahara [signed]

So many POWs died each day at NKK's Yawata Iron Works, designated as Fukuoka POW Branch Camp No. 3, that the Japanese staff poked fun, literally, at the dying prisoners.

"Japanese soldiers [part of the NKK hired staff] would go to the sick room and poke the dying men with sticks," Jack Burton, a Wake Island civilian, remembered:

> Telling them they would die, making all kinds of gestures showing them how they would die . . . When our boys would die, the Japs would put them in pine boxes, and place them by the entrance to the building, so the men going to work would have to pass and see their dead comrades. . . . We looked like the picture [skull and bones] on a strychnine bottle. . . . The Jap doctor told me how sick I looked. 'Very soon we will send you out in a box to join your friends. . . . You will never leave here.'
>
> When they buried [a POW] . . . I thought: if this should happen to me my fervent wish would be for them to cremate me. I couldn't stand the thought of being buried in Japan . . . that God-forsaken country.[10]

The building entrance mentioned by Jack Burton, where dead POWs were displayed for their comrades to see, was the camp hospital. The facility was classed in a postwar U.S. government report as "a good building . . . steam pipes were installed, but the Japanese camp commander would not allow the heat to be turned on, except late at night during the winter." Sick prisoners had to wear whatever overcoats or clothing they had in an effort to keep warm. There was no hot water; the running water was contaminated.

Approximately 1,300 boxes of Red Cross supplies delivered to the camp, containing medicine, surgical supplies, clothing, and food, were used by the Japanese staff but withheld from the prisoners, except for a brief time around Christmas 1944. The government report notes: "After a bombing raid in 1945, two American doctors performed an arm amputation with a hacksaw, two old scalpels and few hemostats, although there was a complete chest of Red Cross surgical equipment unopened in the camp"—a fact discovered just days later when the Japanese surrender was announced.[11] NKK company doctor Hata, the same one who had mocked Jack Burton's condition, was later deemed personally responsible for withholding medical supplies, contributing to the extremely high death rate of nearly 50 percent at this camp. Each day, between one and five POWs died, depending on the weather and time of year.

The constant deaths, and erasure by cremation, finally prompted one very brave Marine to do something about it. Cpl. Terence Kirk was captured in North China before sunset on the day Pearl Harbor was attacked. He had been at Yawata since mid-November 1942, transferring to the company's new barracks at nearby Kokura about a month later. Kirk decided somebody had to find a way to record what was happening to these men—and why. "I had been thinking for months [to] get some pictures of the sick and dying prisoners, so that some day all Americans could see how the Japanese treated American prisoners of war."[12]

In the spring of 1945, Kirk enlisted the aid of an equally brave *nisei* interpreter, who had grown up in San Francisco and been duped into returning to Tokyo late in 1940 by a bogus telegram from his "dying" grandmother. When he arrived, he told Kirk, he was met at the docks by officers of the Imperial Japanese Army and conscripted as an interpreter. Like Kirk, this interpreter risked his life to acquire X-ray plates from the nearby hospital, while Kirk found a couple of cardboard boxes and made a pinhole camera, the way he remembered building one with his brother at the age of twelve.

"These prisoners who are dying are not ordinary men," Kirk told the interpreter. "When they were captured, they were perfect physical specimens . . . and I think someone should be held accountable. . . . It's impossible to look into a crock of ashes and say this guy died of starvation, beriberi or some other disease. [A photograph] will be indisputable proof."[13]

Kirk asked Dr. Markowitz, a navy surgeon, to select five of the sickest men in his clinic, and stand with them outdoors in the bright sunshine while Kirk took five remarkably clear photographs of the dying men. Three were so weak they could not stand unassisted, so navy corpsmen stood behind each one, propping him up long enough to be photographed. All but one were Americans, and according to Kirk, all died at Kokura or within six months of returning home at war's end.

For his darkroom, Kirk used the space under the Japanese staff's bathtub. Terence Kirk's extraordinary photographs are the only ones known to have been taken by a captive prisoner of war in Japan. (Some photos were taken secretly by Australians on the Burma Railway in Thailand, because a few had tiny cameras among their personal belongings when captured.) Although a number of newly freed POWs were photographed in Japan either by liberating troops or with cameras they had commandeered from their former captors, only Kirk succeeded in taking such pictures, developing them on-site, and leaving camp with them in his possession.

With the interpreter's help, Kirk had several sets of prints made for distribution to intelligence personnel and, he hoped, for use as evidence in the War Crimes Trials he was sure would occur. Kirk even obtained written permission from the POW camp commander, Maj. William O. Dorris, to distribute and publish the photographs.

Three photographs taken by POW Terence Kirk with a homemade cardboard-box camera, showing POWs dying of malnutrition at NKK's Fukuoka POW Camp No. 3, Kokura, Japan, in May 1945.

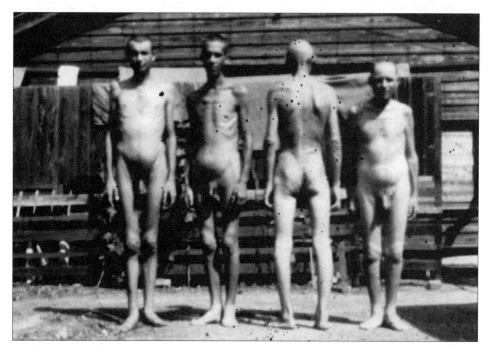

POWs, all Americans, near death from malnutrition. All died in captivity or within six months of release, according to photographer Kirk. COLLECTION OF TERENCE KIRK

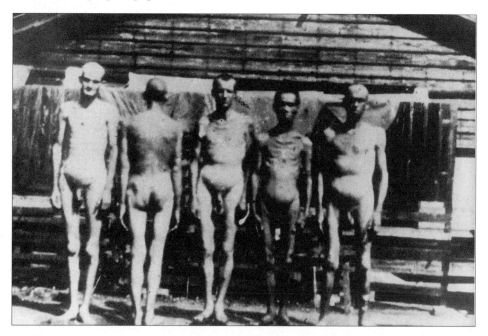

Man in middle, a Sikh guard captured in China, cannot stand unaided. He is being held up by a medical corpsman standing just behind him. He died the next day. The other two, Americans, died within the next two months. COLLECTION OF TERENCE KIRK

But that wasn't good enough for the military and civilian intelligence personnel who interviewed Kirk on his way home. On orders from Washington for reasons that have infuriated him for the rest of his life, Kirk was told, in his words, to "Take these photographs home, put them away, and do not show them to anyone."[14] Verbally, he was cautioned that if he disobeyed this order, he would face court-martial. He was then ordered to sign a statement saying he would not discuss his experience as a captive of the Japanese without prior clearance from the military. (See page 146 for a copy of the order Kirk signed.)

It took thirty-eight years for Kirk to get up the courage to self-publish his memoir, in a limited first edition of 1,000 copies, and to use his photos in the book. "Finally, I said to hell with it—this story needs to be told," Kirk said.

But the question lingers: If Terence Kirk's story and photographs had been more widely circulated half a century ago, would the picture of Japanese corporate responsibility have been clearer at the Tokyo War Crimes Trials?

Chapter 9

Mitsubishi: Empire of Exploitation

MITSUBISHI OCCUPIES A UNIQUE PLACE IN THE HISTORY OF CORPORATE Japan's use of POW slave labor during World War II. This company built, owned, and operated at least seventeen of the merchant "hellships," that transported prisoners to their assigned destinations; and this company profited from prisoner labor over a larger range of territory than any other. From the mountains of northern Honshu to the jungles of Thailand and the outer reaches of Manchuria, Mitsubishi made money from the use of Allied prisoners of war.

According to official Japanese government records, thousands of American prisoners were requisitioned by Mitsubishi over the course of the war, to work at its ancient copper mine at Hanawa; its mines at Hosokura, Kozukura, and Ikuno; its airplane factory at Nagoya; its shipyard at Nagasaki; its steel mill at nearby Zosenjo; and the complex of factories in Manchuria that the company took over in the 1930s: the huge machine tool factory at Mukden; and the Manshu leather and textile factories nearby at Hoten.

Mitsubishi also supplied the wooden crossties for the 225-mile Burma-Siam Railway, which was built between Thanbyuzayat, Burma, and Kanchanaburi, Thailand, at such a great cost in prisoner lives. In all, some 668 Americans toiled on the railway's construction.

The Osarizawa Copper Mine at Hanawa has been in continuous operation for 1,300 years; and some of the 503 Americans forced to work there for Mitsubishi during the war claimed mining methods were as primitive in the 1940s as they had been centuries earlier. The company's POW camp at Hanawa, in the mountains of northern Honshu, was designated as Sendai POW Camp No. 5. Americans destined for Hanawa were among 1,035 prisoners crammed aboard the *Noto Maru*, built, owned, and operated by Mitsubishi, which arrived in Japan from Manila in September 1944. (The company also used its merchant ship *Haru (Haruna) Maru*, which the POWs nicknamed the *Horror Maru,* to bring 1,100 POWs to Japan for work in its Hosokura mine and elsewhere, a few weeks later.)

"The mine was cold and damp and had icicles hanging from the ceiling," Kenneth Calvit recalled. The prisoners had to walk over two miles up a steep mountain road to get to the mine. "On one stretch of the road there was a cut in the mountain where the wind and snow were blinding, so we used a rope and would go hand by hand to keep from getting lost,"[1] Calvit said. During the few months when snow wasn't on the ground, the POWs would try to catch grasshoppers along the way, in a desperate search for protein to add to their watery soup. They had no midday meal from the company. Calvit also remembered the time ammonia leaked from pipes in the company's refrigeration plant into the vat of soup—which was served to the POWs anyway.

But what the prisoners remembered most was the terrible cold, how they were only allowed two hours of heat per day, and how, when they tried to bring a few scrap timbers from the mine to put in the little barracks stove, the company guards would take them from them. "At times I thought I was going to freeze to death," David Summons said.[2]

"We weren't even expected to live," Robert Johnston stated bitterly. "Today I'm totally disabled thanks to the Japs and especially Mitsubishi. It was a terrible three and a half years. I can't describe it fully and I know most people can't imagine it."[3]

The prisoners at Hanawa were so incensed by their brutal treatment, the primitive mine conditions, their constant exposure to cold, the high death rate just from pneumonia, and their constant hunger—that the minute they learned the war had ended, they seized the camp commander, Lt. Toshinori Asaka, placed him under arrest, brought him with them to Yokohama, and turned him over to the Shore Patrol of the U.S. Navy.[4]

Things weren't any better for the 250 American prisoners at Sendai POW Camp No. 3, Mitsubishi's Hosokura mine not far from Hanawa. John Boswell got pneumonia there, and was unconscious for two weeks. Company employees insisted he go back to work in the mine a few days after he had regained consciousness. "I was too weak to walk to and from the mine, so other prisoners would carry me," he said. "We called our barracks 'the ice box' because it was so cold. We burned our wooden pillows for heat. There was no soap, no toilet paper, no toothbrushes or toothpaste."[5]

On August 10, 1945, a Swiss Red Cross representative arrived in the camp and told the POWs about the dropping of atom bombs on Hiroshima and Nagasaki earlier that week. Boswell recalled that the company guards immediately disappeared and "The Japanese commandant gave orders for all of us to gain weight!" When B-29s tried to drop oil drums full of food and supplies, the topography made accuracy difficult. Three newly freed prisoners were killed by falling supply drums. It took nearly a month for liberating troops to reach the camp and set the POWs free.

Prisoners in camps of the Mitsubishi factory complex at Mukden, Manchuria, had the distinction of being set free not by American troops, but by the Russians; and the newly liberated POWs had the satisfaction of watching a team of Russian workers, mostly women, strip the factory bare of the machinery the prisoners had spent so much time sabotaging to slow Japan's war production.

But the Mukden POW camps designated as POW Branch No. 1, Manshu Machinery Manufacturing Company; POW Detachment No. 1, Manshu Leather; and POW Detachment No. 2, Manshu Tent—have another, more sinister distinction because of their proximity to the infamous Unit 731, officially designated the Anti-Epidemic Water Supply and Purification Bureau building in nearby Harbin, where medical experiments took place. Much has been written and filmed about the secret work that went on at Unit 731. And a certain ambivalence has prevailed, until very recently, about whether Allied prisoners were included in these experiments.

After interviewing dozens of ex-POWs from the Mukden complex, it seems apparent to this writer that on several occasions, medical personnel from elsewhere were allowed to visit the POW hospital and some barracks at the Mitsubishi Mukden camps, and that after they left, a certain number of POWs became very ill or subsequently died in a short time. It is equally apparent that many ex-POWs who were at Mukden were not aware of, or suspicious about, unusual medical activity, but this is not surprising. The Japanese doctors had a lot of subjects to choose from: Mitsubishi brought over 2,000 Allied prisoners to its base camp at Mukden of whom the majority, 1,485, were Americans.

The company was so eager to have as many prisoners as they could get to this large complex of factories that the first group of POWs who arrived in November 1942 found that no accommodation had been prepared for them. In Manchuria, where the temperature hovers around forty degrees below zero in the long winters, lack of shelter can be life-threatening. And winter had already arrived.

Nearly 2,000 American prisoners sailed from Manila to Pusan, Korea, aboard the *Tottori Maru:* a vessel built in Glasgow, captured in Singapore, and renamed by her new owner, Mitsubishi. On arrival 1,500 POWs, many of them barefoot, stepped onto the Pusan docks in three inches of snow. They were given scratchy new woolen uniforms and put on a train, with the shades drawn, for the three-day ride to Mukden. At least the POWs weren't still wearing tropical clothes when they entered their temporary living quarters:

old Chinese Army earthen huts, half above ground, with sod roofs and brick floors below ground level. The prisoners were cold all the time.

"When we got up in the morning, the frost on the bricks looked like it had snowed," Gene Wooten recalled.[6] Then they had to walk five miles each way to work. Three hundred prisoners perished at Mukden that first winter of 1942–43.

Housing improved considerably the following June, when a two-story brick barracks for the POWs was completed. Even the food improved somewhat, but the beatings and daily abuse never stopped. The weather was as much their enemy as their captors; being forced to stand at attention, naked, outdoors for long periods of time was a ritual that went on all year long, even in subzero temperatures.

The MKK (Mitsubishi Ko-Kan) Machine and Tool Factory wasn't ready, either, so the POWs had to spend the next five months setting it up, pouring the concrete floor and bolting the American-made machinery in place. Anything they could do to slow or interfere with production, the prisoners did. There are more sabotage stories from Mukden than almost any other facility.

"Every time we poured concrete, we buried as many tools as we could," Leo Padilla remembered with a proud, mischievous grin. "We must have buried 100 shovels under that factory floor."[7] And somehow, the machinery kept breaking down.

Over at the textile factory, where the prisoners were supposed to be making tents for the Japanese Army as well as bolts of heavy-duty fabric, some learned to move a lever when the company guards weren't looking, and all of a sudden they were weaving something that looked like cheesecloth. Wesley Davis showed his fellow POW how to pull the levers all at once and bend the framework of the machines. "The Japanese transferred me to warehouse work," he dryly remarked.[8]

The worst offenders—over 150 of them, all Americans—were sent to Mitsui's lead mine at Kamioka, Japan, as punishment in June 1944. Bob Dow was among those transferred out of Mukden. "We had to wear red armbands the whole time we worked at Kamioka."[9]

Even with the worst saboteurs supposedly weeded out, there were still about 1,100 Americans remaining at Mukden, forever finding ways to disrupt Japan's war production. The prisoners were aware that they were making parts for field artillery and aircraft at the MKK factory, so the incentive was very high to turn out a weapon that might jam when fired. POWs tried to make sure that on their shifts, no product left the MKK Machine and Tool factory in good condition.

One POW did create something useful at the factory, but it wasn't intended for the Japanese. Vernon La Heist invented a combination padlock for his toolbox, because the night shift of Chinese and Japanese workers were stealing his tools. He made several more for his friends. The next thing he knew, Mitsubishi executives were admiring his padlock and wishing they had the materials for him to make 1,000 more. Several years after the war, La Heist was walking by a locksmith shop in Tokyo. There, in the window, was one of his padlocks for sale. "Did you buy one?" he was asked. "No." There were too many memories attached to the item.[10]

Air raids, especially when the awesome B-29s appeared overhead, were thrilling and terrifying at the same time for the prisoners, because the factories at Mukden city were a primary target. On December 7, 1944 (a date no doubt selected on purpose), two B-29 bombs struck within the camp. The prisoners had spread out, lying down, on the parade ground, because until that time they had been forbidden to build any sort of air-raid shelters. Nineteen POWs were killed and thirty-five were wounded. Prisoners immediately began digging slit trenches, without waiting for permission.[11]

The Japanese wasted no time in making propaganda advantage of this incident. Five days later, the vice-chief, General Staff, sent a secret message to the attaché, in Budapest, titled "Part 1, Propaganda Notice No. 103." It read: "On the 7th in the Mukden raid by B-29's the prisoner of war shelter was hit, causing about 4 deaths. In the future please propagandize the fact that such indiscriminant bombing will result in self-destruction of the enemy."[12] The discrepancies contained in this cable are worth noting.

Some of the most frightening time for prisoners at Mukden was at night. That was when Japanese medical personnel would enter the barracks while the men were sleeping to conduct their medical experiments. Wilson Bridges told his wife that three prisoners would move their cots together, trying to keep warm. He was the one in the middle, and credited that fact with his survival. Many nights, he said, he would see a Japanese approach and give shots to the two men on the outside cots. When Bridges awoke the next morning, his two buddies would be dead.[13]

W. Wesley Davis also spoke of nighttime disturbances by Japanese medics:

> I was asleep on a straw mat on the platform (our beds) in our barracks. At about 4 A.M. I was awakened by a tickling sensation. I awoke with a start to see the face of a Japanese unfamiliar to me [i.e., not one of the Mitsubishi company employees or guards he knew by sight], holding a feather under my nose. When I awoke, he quickly said "excuse me" and moved away, before I could ask what he was doing.
>
> Later, the men compared notes and we found similar experiences had happened to others: awaking in the middle of the night to find

an unfamiliar Japanese face moving among us, sometimes with the feathers, at other times tying a tag with a number on it on a man's toe. In each instance, when the Japanese saw that we had awakened, he would say "excuse me" and move on, before we could ask questions. We all believed they were trying to take us by surprise, and do things to us while we were asleep.[14]

Davis also said his full service records were never released. He believed this is because the U.S. Army knew of the experiments at Mukden. Without his full records, Davis has been unable to show the possible cause of his lifelong illnesses and disabilities. "I lost ninety-two pounds in captivity and weighed eighty pounds when I was liberated," he said.

Navy seaman Peter Locarnini told of all the injections he was given, supposedly vaccines against cholera—but he didn't believe it.[15]

Army Bataan survivor Frank James remembered being sprayed in the face by Japanese doctors, in addition to receiving numerous injections. "Everybody had six or seven blood samples taken," he said, adding that he believed, "All of us at Mukden were directly or indirectly used for experiments. I had constant diarrhea. Medical data was being constantly taken [on POWs] by Japanese doctors."[16]

Army airman Robert Brown was a medical technician in the POW camp hospital at Mukden. He recalled that during the winter of 1942–43, a team of Japanese medical personnel arrived on a truck, wearing white smocks and masks. They gave injections to some of the prisoners, who subsequently became sick. When a prisoner died, he could not be buried until the Japanese doctor had performed an autopsy, according to Brown. When asked if the Japanese medical team came from Unit 731, Brown replied: "I don't know what medical facility they came from. There was also a hospital nearby in Mukden. All I know is they arrived by truck, they were in medical garb, they were not part of the Japanese medical staff at our POW camp, and they visited our facility several times."[17]

On one of those occasions, fellow Bataan survivor Art Campbell recalled:

A crew of Japanese we hadn't seen before lined us up. They were dressed in white and gave each of us half an orange. Two or three days later, everybody was very sick. I had a high fever. Later, we figured out the oranges must have been doctored with something. I know I'd have eaten it anyway because I had scurvy so bad.

They took nine of us and put us in a special ward. They tested our blood, everything. They started giving us shots regularly, 500cc's at a time, and said it was horse urine and would be good for us because it had vitamin C in it.[18]

As mentioned earlier, there are many Mukden survivors who disclaim any firsthand knowledge of medical experimentation at the camp. It was a very large facility; there were nineteen barracks units at the base camp. Incidents occurring at some locations would not necessarily be common knowledge, especially among a population of 2,000 men. And there are some former officers at Mukden who rather strongly dispute the medical experimentation stories, saying they would have surely known of them. But the officers were billeted separately from the enlisted men, and the contact was not that close, most of the time.

For this writer, the journalist's rule of thumb applies: if several sources, *independent of one another,* tell the same story, it holds a certain amount of credibility, especially if the individuals are not interviewed at the same time or at the same gathering. Several of the men who told of medical experiments, or what they surely believed to be medical experimentation forced on them at Mukden, did not know one another. On many occasions they volunteered the information as part of a lengthy, wide-ranging interview. And it was always as part of their personal experience.

Although there appeared to be an unusually high level of Japanese medical activity at the Mukden POW camp, incidents of Japanese medical personnel giving injections to POWs in an unusual way at several locations in the home islands have already been cited. Just as John Aldrich mentioned the Japanese medic at Hirohata using one needle on a large number of prisoners, Sidney Farmer said that at his camp in Taihoku, Formosa (Taiwan), "We were given three inoculations for cholera and typhoid, and two smallpox vaccinations, or so we were told. The Japanese [medics] used three needles for 450 men."[19]

Army Corregidor survivor Floyd Smith said he was given a shot in the chest at the Electric-Chemical Co. POW camp at Aomi. Shortly afterwards: "A Japanese guard came for me. He gave me an outfit of Japanese Army pants, an English shirt, a Japanese Army overcoat, an Australian hat and a mask over my mouth and nose, so I would not be recognized as an American. He took me on a train. We arrived at 2 A.M. at the Shinagawa Hospital in Tokyo."[20] After the war, Smith spent thirteen months in a U.S. hospital. At least four American POWs were taken to Shinagawa from Aomi for medical experiments, according to other POWs at the camp.

Gleneth Berry was selected from the ranks of POWs at the Kawaminami Shipyard POW Camp No. 2, Fukuoka, and sent to the Shinagawa Hospital. "My three months of time there is a complete blank. I was quite ill," Berry said. From Shinagawa, he was sent to the Hidachi Manufacturing Company at Jinsen (Inchon), Korea, where he spent the rest of the war sewing buttons on hospital garments—hardly a typical POW work assignment.[21]

As in the Mukden interviews, the incidents just discussed were mentioned by ex-POWs who contacted the author to relate other, specific details about their slave-labor work at a number of Japanese company worksites. They were not sought out because of this writer's prior knowledge about their role in medical experiments as prisoners of war. Despite the frequency of anecdotes from other locations, the impression remains that the Mitsubishi facility at Mukden was the site of the most frequent and systematic incidents of medical experimentation on American prisoners of war.

One of the POW hospitals at Mukden was the site of the only visit the camp ever received from a delegate of the International Committee of the Red Cross (ICRC), and it occurred less than two weeks before the war ended. Dr. Marcel Junod had been newly appointed as the ICRC head delegate to Tokyo, and on his way there via the Soviet Union and Manchuria, Dr. Junod was determined to visit the Mukden prisoner camp, as well as the undisclosed site where Gen. Jonathan Wainwright, last commander of Bataan, and Britain's highest-ranking prisoner, Gen. A. E. Percival, Singapore's former commander, were being held.

After much red tape and delay, Dr. Junod arrived at Mukden on August 5, 1945. No words more graphically describe the humiliation and complete subjugation to which Allied POWs were subjected by their Japanese captors than Dr. Junod's narrative of that day. Dr. Junod, a physician, was accompanied by Colonel Matsuda, the commander of all prisoner of war camps in Manchuria. Dr. Junod could hardly control his anger:

> At the top of the steps stood four men in shirts and shorts at attention. They were the first prisoners of war I had seen in Manchuria. As our procession mounted the steps after [Colonel Matsuda] the four men bowed low, their arms kept tightly to their sides, until their heads were almost on a level with their knees.
>
> In a low voice, and making an effort not to show the indignation which was boiling up in me, I said: "That's not the manner in which soldiers of an occidental army salute."
>
> "No, it's the Japanese manner," replied Colonel Matsuda.
>
> We were taken along a corridor with sick-rooms on either side. Standing by the wall near each door were three or four sick prisoners, all of whom bowed low as we approached. Those prisoners who were unable to arise were seated [cross-legged] on their beds, their arms crossed on their chests, and they too bowed as low as their bandages, wounds or mutilations would permit. When the last Japanese officer had passed they resumed the upright position, their eyes raised fixedly on the ceiling. Never once did their eyes meet ours. . . . This was indescribably horrible. Matsuda tried to lead us on but I stopped before a group of four prisoners, three British and an American.

"Is there a doctor amongst you?" I asked, trying to keep my voice firm and not betray the emotion I felt. No one answered, and the Japanese behind me kept silent. I stood directly in front of a big fellow who towered above me. I could see only his chin and his stretched neck as he looked up at the ceiling. Not a muscle stirred and I repeated my question. There was still no reply and I turned grimly to Matsuda.

"Why doesn't he reply?" I asked. "Isn't he allowed to?"

The Japanese were stupefied at my audacity, but Matsuda was evidently unwilling to risk an unpleasant incident and he indicated one of the men standing against the wall with the others. "This Australian is a doctor," he said.

I went towards my Australian colleague with outstretched hand. I had to overcome a lump in my throat to get out the banal words: "How do you do?"

The man lowered his eyes, but not to me. It was at Matsuda he looked. It was the colonel's permission he sought. After several seconds which seemed incredibly long his hand slowly rose to mine. I took it and shook it warmly, trying to convey to him all the emotion and sympathy I felt and hoping he would afterwards communicate them to his comrades.

I told him as briefly as possible who I was and why I had come, and I tried to get into conversation with him. He replied slowly and in monosyllables and each time before he spoke I could see that he silently sought the approval of Matsuda over my head.

"Will you accompany me on a tour of the wards?" I asked finally. This time Matsuda intervened. "No," he said. "A Japanese doctor will accompany you."

I felt it was impossible to insist any further and I let go the man's trembling hand which stiffened back to the attention against his sides whilst his eyes rose again to the ceiling.[22]

Dr. Junod was equally appalled when he was taken to Seihan, where the "important prisoners" were held. He had insisted upon being allowed to speak to General Wainwright:

> I had difficulty in realizing that I was about to come face to face with the hero of Corregidor, the defender of Singapore, the Governor of the Dutch East Indies and twelve other soldiers of high rank whose armies were still fighting everywhere in the Pacific. And suddenly a disturbing sight presented itself.

There they stood upright and motionless in the middle of the room. I should not have been able to distinguish their faces even if I had not involuntarily turned my head away because they bowed low, their arms close to their bodies, as soon as the sabre of Matsuda tapped on the floor. The last man in the row refused to submit to the humiliation and remained upright.

"General Wainwright." My emotion was so great that I could hardly utter the words I had to speak. He maintained an icy reserve towards the Japanese around me. Nothing, it seemed, had broken his spirit. His voice was still vibrant as he replied to the pitiful and absurdly abrupt questions which were all I was allowed to ask him . . .

"Have you any request to make?"

"Certainly. Can I make it now?"

"No," put in Matsuda at once. "It will have to be made in writing to Tokyo."

The ghost of a skeptical smile passed over General Wainwright's lips.[23]

The date of this brief interview was August 6, 1945. None of the parties involved were aware that 1,000 miles away, the atom bomb was being dropped on Hiroshima. Three weeks later, General Wainwright, in full uniform, greeted Dr. Junod in Tokyo with these words: "Now we can talk in peace."

But Junod's visit to Mukden haunted him. In 1951, writing his memoir, he said: "I can still see the camp at Mukden with the bowed backs of its slaves."

Mitsubishi also profited from prisoner labor as a contractor supplying materials for the Burma-Siam Railway, a project that might never have been undertaken had the Imperial Japanese Army not found itself with an expendable labor force of 61,000 Allied prisoners of war, including an entire Australian engineering battalion captured on Java (Indonesia). British engineers had considered constructing a railroad along this same route in 1936, but abandoned the idea as not feasible—too much dense jungle; too much risk of malaria and other diseases. But the Japanese considered no such impediments. So 13,708 POWs died building the railway and "Bridge on the River Kwai," including 133 of the 668 Americans who toiled there.

As previously mentioned, Mitsubishi supplied the heavy wooden crossties, or sleepers, which were laid along the 225-mile route, profiting handsomely from the lucrative contract. Otto Schwarz, a sailor off the USS *Houston* who swam ashore to captivity on Java when his ship was sunk offshore early in 1942, remembered how heavy and sharp those beams were.

POWs working on the Burma-Siam Railway, Thailand, laying wooden crossties supplied by Mitsubishi. Photo taken by Japanese engineer. COLLECTION OF OTTO SCHWARZ

Unlike the tree trunks the prisoners used for bridge work, Mitsubishi's crossties were "Very well made, perfectly cut at the ends [by sawmill equipment], and very sharp. We used to try and find rags to put on our naked bodies, so we wouldn't cut ourselves so badly lifting those heavy pieces of lumber." Schwarz said he believed there was no equipment along the railway that could have manufactured those sleepers. "They had to have been brought in from somewhere else."[24]

Takashi Nagase, a Japanese interpreter who was part of the military police *(kempei tai)* unit supervising all the Imperial Japanese Army discipline, criminal investigations, and anti-espionage operations along the railway throughout the war, confirmed that Mitsubishi supplied not only the railway lumber, but also foodstuffs to the Japanese staff there. The company had personnel stationed at the town of Kanchanaburi, where the construction base was located, to keep track of supply needs and deliveries for the company. Nagase recalled that he was told several years before by an aide to the commanding officer of the 4th Battalion, 5th Railway Regiment, in charge of collecting materials for the project, that the aide had on one occasion overheard the major shouting at a Mitsubishi clerk in a rage at the exorbitant price the company was charging the army for its crossties.[25]

From slave-ship transports to slave-labor projects, Mitsubishi seemed ready to provide goods and services, for a handsome profit, during World War II.

Chapter 10

Kawasaki:
From Slave Laborers
to Subway Riders

OF ALL THE JAPANESE COMPANIES DOING BUSINESS IN THE UNITED STATES, Kawasaki Heavy Industries may have gained the most from hiding its past as a user of American POW slave labor, because so much of its business has been with state and municipal agencies subsidized by the American taxpayer. One of the most lucrative lines in Kawasaki's 1998 balance sheet was its $190 million contract with the New York State Metropolitan Transportation Authority to provide 100 new subway cars for the New York City Transit Authority. In June 1999 the company announced further multimillion dollar contracts with New York's MTA and other state transportation departments to build at least 180 double-decker rail cars for the Long Island Railroad and transit systems in Maryland and Massachusetts.[1] In 1999, Kawasaki delivered several new railcars and diesel engines for the Long Island Railroad, and the first new subway cars for New York City were delivered in July 2000.

When a company is contracting with state or municipal agencies, the company must affirm that it now complies and will continue to comply with the existing labor laws. Until recently, the fact that so many Japanese companies arranged to use thousands of American prisoners for their wartime workforce had not been clearly established. So the question would not have been likely to come up during Kawasaki's bidding processes over the years since World War II.

Kawasaki's shipyard at Kobe was founded in 1886, and the location is still the company's world headquarters. The company requested its first group of skilled American prisoner laborers early in 1942, shortly after most of the 1,216 newly captured civilians and over 300 Marines had been transported from Wake and Guam Islands to China aboard the *Nitta Maru*. Kawasaki built at least seven of the merchant ships used to transport prisoners to Japan: the *Brasil Maru; England Maru; Hohuku Maru; Nagato Maru; Singapore Maru; Thames Maru;* and *Umeda Maru*. Some of these vessels were also operated by Kawasaki.[2]

The Kawasaki Dockyard Co. (the company's name from 1939 to 1968) was probably one of the first industries in the home islands to put in a bid for the use of these particular American prisoners, already skilled in shipyard and air base construction—civilians who, under international law, should have been sent back to the United States. Early in 1942, about 300 Wake Island workers found themselves at Osaka POW Detachment No. 5, near the shipyard at Kobe operated by Kawasaki.

About 700 POWs were in this camp, and every morning the *hanchos* (foremen) from Kawasaki's shipyard would arrive at the camp and select their work detail for the day. The prisoners walked about a half hour to the shipyard, to begin a grueling twelve- or fourteen-hour day of very heavy labor for such malnourished bodies. It took six prisoners to lift the huge five-by-twelve-foot iron plates, which had to be heated and beaten with a sledgehammer to shape them for a ship's hull.

No safety equipment of any kind was issued to these ill-clad men. Jack Hoskins, a Wake Island worker, lived with severe hearing loss since his time at the shipyard, becoming nearly deaf in both ears because of the hours he spent riveting in Kawasaki's facility with no protection for his ears.[3]

Prisoners from Wake Island were aware that they were being forced to help build warships for the Imperial Japanese Navy, whose officers had dealt with them so brutally and contemptuously in their first weeks of captivity.

"Lots of times the men heating the rivets would just burn them up," Frank Mace remembered. "As long as they were hot you could batter a head on them. When they got cold, they were covered with red lead, then painted. They looked good, but we knew they would not hold for long. We did this to a lot of outside plates and also on the inside water-tight compartments."[4]

One Wake Island civilian remembered a bright spot in his long days at the Kawasaki shipyard, recalling one good *hancho* who would give the men food and who tried to protect them from the guards, who were relentless in their cruelty.[5]

Frank Mace described a common torment:

> For punishment the Japanese would take a piece of bamboo about three inches wide and four feet long with quarter-inch holes drilled in it, make us stand at attention and then beat us over the back with the bamboo stick. When it hit our backs it would pop holes in the skin, so we had running sores most of the time. They would never get a chance to heal before we would get another beating. Since the only clothing we wore was a breech cloth these beatings were extraordinarily cruel.[6]

Korean conscript workers, who were housed nearby in Kobe, would work the shipyard shifts after the Americans had left for the day. The Koreans had a unique way of protesting their assignment, especially on weekends. When the Americans returned on Monday morning, there would be human feces on the workbenches.

Most of the ex-POWs who did slave labor for Kawasaki in World War II live on the West Coast in California, Oregon, or Washington. Unless they come to New York City as visitors, they won't ride New York's subways or take commuter trains along the East Coast, so they aren't likely to see the shiny steel plate that reads: "Mfg. by Kawasaki Rail Car, Inc."

It was difficult for this writer to locate survivors of the Kawasaki Kobe shipyard POW labor force for interviews. Those few who could be reached said that most of their fellow ex-POWs have died. The majority of Kawasaki POW laborers were civilian construction workers captured on Wake Island. Why the attrition rate has been so high among this group of ex-POWs remains an unanswered question.

Chapter 11

Double-Crossed Relief

ON NOVEMBER 11, 1943, LT. COL. J. M. WILLIAMS, THE AUSTRALIAN OFFICER commanding Allied POWs of No. One Mobile Force on the Burma-Thailand Railway, made a stark entry in his secret diary: "We are completely out of foodstuffs. No meals can be served today." Several thousand starving, diseased, threadbare, and exhausted American, Australian, British, Canadian, Dutch, and Malay men under the colonel's charge had nearly completed their task of building a supply railway for the Japanese through the forbidding jungles of Thailand and Burma. But on this day, the most vital supply allocated to the prisoners—food—had dwindled to absolutely zero.

Colonel Williams seethed with the knowledge that one of his senior officers reported spotting Red Cross parcels containing urgently needed supplies such as medicines, food, clothing, and boots, stockpiled in a warehouse near the Japanese commandant's headquarters. And he watched his men trade their last shreds of personal identity—watches, penknives, wedding rings—to natives for an occasional piece of fruit or, if they were really lucky, some powdered quinine to ease a comrade's malaria. The death toll mounted daily, and in the records he as commanding officer was allowed to keep openly, Colonel Williams carefully noted exactly the cause of each man's death. Mostly, it was malnutrition, which allowed every infection or tropical parasite to become a killer.

A total of 668 Americans toiled on the Burma-Thailand Railway, some of them working as part of the advance unit under Colonel Williams's command. Most were part of a Texas field artillery unit captured on Java (Indonesia) in March 1942, or survivors of the USS *Houston,* sunk in the Java Sea on March 1 of that year.

Like the Australian battalion Colonel Williams commanded, the Americans had been forced to surrender when the Dutch decided to give up Java to the Japanese. In all, 61,000 prisoners of war were thrown together to build this railway through nearly impenetrable jungles. Their saga was popularized, and highly fictionalized, in the 1957 film *The Bridge on the River Kwai.* Before the war ended, 13,708 Allied prisoners would perish along its route, including 133 Americans.[1] Theirs was a desperate situation from the day of capture until they were released, three and a half long years later. These prisoners were in such a remote location that they felt totally isolated, and at the mercy of their captors. But almost from the time of their arrival, friendly eyes were watching and sending back word of their plight.

Some of the same Thai natives who traded food for POW trinkets were also part of an excellent intelligence network, centered in a group of forty young Thai men who had been trained by the U.S. Office of Strategic Services (OSS) with the help of the prime minister of Thailand, who also happened to head his country's resistance movement. When the United States declared war on Japan on December 8, 1941, the Thai ambassador in Washington contacted all the young Thai students he could find, and sent them to the Massachusetts Institute of Technology in Cambridge, where OSS operatives spent several months giving the students a new education in the techniques of how to be clandestine operatives within their own country.[2]

The trainees returned secretly to Thailand, and positioned themselves near camps where POWs were being held. Soon they were relaying disturbing stories of Red Cross workers being turned away from the gates of POW

Prisoners of all nationalities lining up at the canteen, Kanchanaburi, Thailand, early 1944. No new clothes were issued during the three and a half years of their captivity, despite the presence of undistributed Red Cross parcels in the camps. COLLECTION OF THE AUTHOR

camps; of relief packages being delivered but promptly locked up in the commandant's headquarters, or piled at the foot of a Japanese soldier's bed; of round-the-clock forced labor; of brutal beatings and beheadings; of pitiful daily processions by ragged prisoners to makeshift burial spots in the jungle.

An October 1943 entry in Colonel Williams's diary reads: "The sick boys, who worked 18 hours, were not allowed to eat the meal taken out to them . . . the night shift returned to camp at 1330 hours after completing 31 hours straight. The day workers are still out and no one has any idea when they will be back. No instructions to send a meal, or meals, out to them. . . ." And in early December 1943, the colonel made this stark entry in his diary: "No food at all delivered to camp today."

As Allied intelligence units received word about the increasingly desperate situation of prisoners building the Burma Railway, a series of urgent communications crackled between Washington and London. By early 1944, the U.S. and British Commonwealth governments agreed on a plan: they would each sell monetary gold in Switzerland, convert the proceeds to Swiss francs, and turn the money over to the International Committee of the Red Cross (ICRC), with specific instructions that the funds be used for the immediate relief of American and British Commonwealth POWs on the Burma Railway. (Later, the Dutch government contributed to the fund through its diplomatic representative, Sweden.) By directly transmitting the money to bank accounts it maintained at Swiss National Bank branches in Bangkok and Saigon, the ICRC hoped to enable their officials to purchase supplies locally for speedy packaging and delivery to the Saigon docks, where supplies were gathered for transport to prison camps in the region.

But the Japanese derailed this plan by announcing that beginning in January 1944, relief funds from all sources, designated for prisoners of war and civilian internees in Japanese-occupied territory, would first have to be cleared through Tokyo and deposited in Japan's official government bank, the Yokohama Specie Bank, at a conversion rate arbitrarily set by the Japanese government. Thus, by decree, the Japanese took control of several million dollars of international humanitarian aid money, and it soon became apparent that they were in no hurry to part with it. Brazenly, the Japanese government agreed to an elaborate clearing agreement for the disbursement of relief funds, and then spent the rest of the war interfering with it.

On April 20, 1944, the U.S. Treasury Department opened a special dollar account, designated "Banque Nationale Suisse Special Account T" in the Swiss National Bank's account at the Federal Reserve Bank in New York. Correspondingly, the Swiss National Bank opened a Swiss franc account designated "Federal Reserve Bank of New York Account Number 4."[3] But despite the urgency of the prisoners' plight, it would be several months before money was deposited into these accounts.

Just after the accounts were opened, the Swiss government infuriated Secretary of State Cordell Hull by attempting to use humanitarian aid fund availability as a lever in negotiations concerning America's ongoing blockade of Indochina (Vietnam, Cambodia, and Laos), then controlled by the pro-Nazi French Vichy regime and garrisoned by Japanese troops. In a July 21, 1944, telegram to American ambassador Leland Harrison in Bern, Hull thundered: "It is inconceivable to us that the Swiss should take such a position or should attempt to use humanitarian activities as a bargaining point in their negotiations concerning the blockade."[4]

Meanwhile, on May 24, 1944, Japan's ambassador to Berlin, Lt. Gen. Hiroshi Baron Oshima sent a top secret message to the Foreign Office in Tokyo, acknowledging the delay in implementing the U.S.-British Burma Railway funds: "The Australian Government considers this matter to be one that bears upon the question of monetary aid to prisoners in Thailand in accordance with principles professed [the 1929 Geneva Conventions regarding treatment of military POWs, which Japan had not ratified but pledged to honor; and the Red Cross Conventions, which Japan did ratify]. It is difficult for the Japanese Home Office . . . to recognize this matter so long as it does not feel the urgency of [relief supplies] with regard to Australian prisoners. . . . If a compromise can be seen . . . that will be a preliminary settlement."[5]

A week later, the Foreign Office in Tokyo, responding to Oshima's concerns, replied that, "The Imperial Government consents to the use of the relief funds of the English Government. . . . The gist of the above has been wired to the Swiss Consul at Sydney. Please request . . . that relief be effected for Japanese."

This latter sentence highlights a striking fact: as mentioned earlier, in a 1948 postwar report, the International Committee of the Red Cross noted: "No remittance of funds was made by the Japanese to the ICRC for the relief of prisoners of war held by the Allied [nations]. The Japanese took no interest whatever in their nationals who were taken prisoner, since the Japanese code of honor looked upon these men as a disgrace to their country and their families."[6] Aware of this, the Australian government, which had custody of most Japanese POWs, offered to use its own funds for the relief of Japanese prisoners as a way to get the Japanese to release the Burma Railway relief money.

By the time these messages were being exchanged in the spring of 1944, thousands of Allied prisoners had already been buried in the huge POW cemetery near Kanchanaburi, Thailand, which can be visited today. Almost as many Japanese as Allied Pacific War veterans visit the cemetery each year, standing silently and watching as figures move between the endless rows of white crosses to pause at the marker for a friend or relative.

By mid-1944, Swiss diplomats, serving as intermediaries among the Japanese, U.S., and British governments, were becoming increasingly frustrated at their inability to get the relief plan funded. On July 5, the Swiss

Foreign Office answered a plea from its vexed consul in Bangkok: "Concerning the refusal of Japanese officers to authorize Hirsbrunner [the Swedish consul in Saigon, representing the Netherlands] to send some additional shipments to Camp Docks in Saigon . . . Try to obtain for Hirsbrunner through the Japanese embassy in Bangkok the authorization to proceed with the relief shipments in kind and in cash. . . . If the results of your [efforts] are negative notify [Swiss minister in Tokyo Camille] Gorgé, whom I am informing of this affair. Inform Hirsbrunner that the British Government thanks him for the very valuable information concerning Camp Docks in Saigon."

In a move that even the Nazis didn't have the nerve to make, the Japanese cut off communications between International Red Cross headquarters in Geneva and its officials in Asia. As a result, no one knew for sure until after the war how few relief supplies intended for POWs actually reached them, while the ICRC did not know how or where its delegates were. Otto Schwarz, a sailor from the USS *Houston* who survived the building of the Burma Railway, remembers the Saigon Camp Docks very well; he spent the latter part of his captivity there, loading and unloading supplies, including many Red Cross parcels. One day, Schwarz recalled, the POWs off-loaded several Red Cross boxes filled with medicine and surgical instruments destined for the Railway POW camps. "When the Japanese discovered the contents of these boxes," Schwarz said, "they laughed and joked how they must thank the Americans for supplying these scarce items to the Imperial Japanese Army."

According to Article 29 of the Geneva Conventions, each prisoner was to be allowed one Red Cross package *per week*. But Schwarz remembered just one occasion in Saigon, when the Japanese officer in charge offered to let Schwarz and another American POW share a parcel clearly marked from the American Red Cross. Schwarz protested, arguing that POWs of other nationalities should have some boxes, too. Finally, the Japanese officer relented—and seven POWs got to share the original box. "It was the only Red Cross box I had in three and a half years," Schwarz noted in a 1997 interview.

Kyle Thompson, a member of the Texas 131st Field Artillery Unit captured on Java in March 1942 and put to work on the Burma Railway, remembers how the hungry, exhausted POWs had to step aside on jungle trails to let freshly supplied Japanese combat troops hurry through on their way to Burma: "Often, we would see a Red Cross box strapped to a soldier's backpack," Thompson recalled. With the perspective that only a half-century of separation from such events can bring, Thompson observed: "I suppose if you are uncertain what lies ahead, it's understandable that you'll take whatever supplies you can get your hands on."[7]

So prisoners of the Japanese continued to grow weaker, and to die by the day, while diplomats pleaded for action. On August 1, 1944, the Siamese

(Thai) chargé d'affaires in Bern queried the Foreign Office in Bangkok: "Unofficially I have learnt that a clearing agreement, based on funds supplied to English and American prisoners, has recently been concluded between Japan and Switzerland, details of which are not yet available. . . . I would be obliged if you would let me know. . . . May I, however, once more confirm the fact that the matter is really urgent."

There is a special irony in the date of this particular transmission: August 1, 1944, was also the day that Allied intelligence intercepted a general order from the War Ministry in Japan, circulated to all civilian and military prison camp commandants, instructing that ultimately all prisoners were to be executed: "In any case the aim is to annihilate them all, and not to leave any traces." Did this order affect the attitude of the Japanese government officials and military commanders about relief supplies? One has to wonder.

As the summer of 1944 dragged on, the U.S. government's urgent request for four million Swiss francs—about 900,000 1944 dollars, worth over $5 million today—had to await the return from summer vacation of two key members of the Swiss Federal Council. In an August 11, 1944, telegram U.S. consul Harrison in Bern told Secretary of State Hull: "Today I was assured by Mr. Pilet-Golaz [head of the Swiss Ministry of Foreign Affairs], that he would take up our request . . . at the first meeting of the Federal Council when he expected both Mr. Stampfli and Mr. Nobbs to have returned from vacation."[8]

Finally, on August 17, 1944, a clearing agreement was settled among the governments of the United States, Britain, Sweden (representing the Netherlands), Switzerland, and Japan. The initial deposit of U.S. dollars for the relief of prisoners on the Burma Railway was made the following day into the Swiss National Bank's Special Account T. In all, the United States contributed 2.8 million Swiss francs, or about 6.2 million 1944 dollars, to the relief fund—worth over $55 million today. With contributions from Britain and the Netherlands, the fund eventually totalled 98.5 million Swiss francs, or about $197 million today.

These arrangements were so secret that the Treasury Department in Washington did not even supply the Federal Reserve with copies of the U.S. transactions for this account.

A conspicuous gap exists between July and December 1944—just the time frame when deposits would have been made into Special Account T. In fact, the transactions were so secret that when the Swiss National Bank's New York representative, Mr. Pfenniger, sent a Christmas 1944 greeting to Federal Reserve chairman Allan Sproull—thanking "You and your collaborators for the constant support you have extended to me in the fulfillment of my work"—a perplexed Chairman Sproull penned a note to his secretary asking who and what Mr. Pfenniger was talking about! The handwritten reply reads:

From: Tokyo
To: Shanghai*
21 August 1944

M-1357

The following measures regarding the sending
of expenses needed by Switzerland for her work in representing the interests of enemy countries in East
Asia (including relief funds) and expenses for the
International Red Cross Commission, were adopted through
an interchange of official notes on 17 August between
the Foreign Ministry and the Swiss Minister at Tokyo.

1. Switzerland will send these expenses
through the Yokohama Specie Bank to its Tokyo branch.

2. The forwarding of these funds from Tokyo
to the East Asia area will follow the fixed procedure
used by U.A. in handling exchange.

3. The funds which have been forwarded according to this procedure are to be paid into a special
account, under the name of "SWISS EXCHANGE", in the
branches of the Yokohama Specie Bank in the Chinese

Japanese   #144734
            Page 1

areas to which the funds are sent; the funds will be
converted at the revised exchange rate.

4. We shall provide a supplement to the special
account, under the name of the Swiss Consul-general,
in the Shanghai branch of the Yokohama Specie Bank,
which will be in Central Reserve Notes equivalent in
amount to the funds remitted to the Swiss Consul-general
at Shanghai, at the revised exchange conversion rate.
It has been decided also, more or less out of consideration
for the position of the Swiss, not to have the Bank
reduce the Central Reserve Note conversion rate. We
are firmly maintaining the exchange price, but, as a
special and very secret measure, we intend to supply
special funds.

The implications of this matter, as seen in
4 above, create a very delicate problem. No announcement of this plan is being made inside this country, and
therefore particular care must be exercised not to let
the truth of the matter leak out past the quarters
immediately concerned --2G--   --26 11 MG--
* Also to Nanking, Canton, Head of Embassy Office in Peking.
a - YOKOHAMA SHOKIN GINKO.
b - CHOBIKEN.

Inter   21 Aug 44 (2)   Japanese   #144734
Rec'd   21   Page 2
Trans 1657 1

Secret message from Japanese foreign minister Shigemitsu in Tokyo to the ministry in Shanghai, August 21, 1944, describing the existence of the secret Allied relief funds. FILES OF THE NATIONAL SECURITY AGENCY

"The problem of getting the leasing [agreement] and all the Swiss francs it needs for government and [humanitarian] purposes."[9]

Not only did Allied POWs receive little benefit from these efforts on their behalf, but the U.S. Treasury never saw the money again. Some of it rapidly became part of the Japanese war effort —Japan ordered 17 million francs' worth of artillery from the Swiss,[10] though the war ended before the order could be shipped. Some of the relief money—about 2 million Swiss francs, according to the International Committee of the Red Cross—is still unaccounted for. But most of the relief funds just sat in Tokyo and accrued interest at the Yokohama Specie Bank, on instructions from the Japanese government.

Diplomats and Red Cross officials constantly tried to pry the funds loose. Intercepted diplomatic messages reveal how increasingly frustrated relief workers kept begging their governments to prod the Japanese into honoring the agreement. On September 9, 1944, the Swiss chargé d' affaires in Bangkok, Mr. Siegenthaler, sent an urgent message to the Foreign Ministry in Bern, which reads in part: "Maize deteriorated because the Japanese postponed unloading the shipment." A few weeks later, on October 6, Mr. Siegenthaler sent a cryptic message to Bern: "Funds are exhausted. Please speed up remittance. [Today] I cabled [Swiss ambassador to Tokyo Camille] Gorgé: 'On 19 September the Department authorized a transfer of 500,000 [Swiss francs] for me via Tokyo for the relief program for war prisoners. Because of exhausted cash funds I have to discontinue the program. I therefore request intercession with Japanese authorities so that transfer will be speeded up.'"

Four days later, on October 10, the home office relayed to Siegenthaler a top secret message from the Canadian Consulate in Bern: "[first word garbled] recent refusal to allow relief to prisoners in Northern Siam does not enable the British Government to feel sure that you will seize any opportunity to send relief to prisoners in Burma and Northern Siam." The Swiss Foreign Minister adds: "I shall let you, considering the attitude of Japanese authorities on this matter, decide what can be done for these prisoners."

Three long months later, and after repeated inquiries, the elaborate plan to transfer relief money, worked out at the highest level of both the Japanese and Swiss governments, was spelled out on November 13, 1944, in a top secret, detailed message from Japan's foreign minister Mamoru Shigemitsu in Tokyo to the Japanese Minister in Saigon:

> According to the agreement between this bank [the Yokohama Specie Bank] and the Banque Nationale Suisse.
>
> (i). The Swiss Minister will open a Swiss Minister's Special Account at the Tokyo Branch of our bank. Our bank will open a Yokohama Specie Bank Special Account at the Banque Nationale Suisse [Swiss National Bank], Zurich.

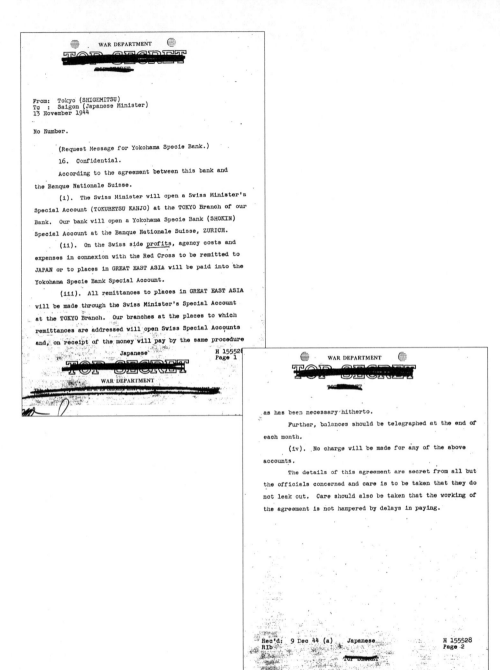

From: Tokyo (SHIGEMITSU)
To : Saigon (Japanese Minister)
13 November 1944

No Number.

(Request Message for Yokohama Specie Bank.)

16. Confidential.

According to the agreement between this bank and
the Banque Nationale Suisse.

(i). The Swiss Minister will open a Swiss Minister's
Special Account (TOKUBETSU KANJO) at the TOKYO Branch of our
Bank. Our bank will open a Yokohama Specie Bank (SHOKIN)
Special Account at the Banque Nationale Suisse, ZURICH.

(ii). On the Swiss side _profits_, agency costs and
expenses in connexion with the Red Cross to be remitted to
JAPAN or to places in GREAT EAST ASIA will be paid into the
Yokohama Specie Bank Special Account.

(iii). All remittances to places in GREAT EAST ASIA
will be made through the Swiss Minister's Special Account
at the TOKYO Branch. Our branches at the places to which
remittances are addressed will open Swiss Special Accounts
and, on receipt of the money will pay by the same procedure

Japanese   H 155528
Page 1

TOP SECRET
WAR DEPARTMENT

WAR DEPARTMENT

TOP SECRET

as has been necessary hitherto.

Further, balances should be telegraphed at the end of
each month.

(iv). No charge will be made for any of the above
accounts.

The details of this agreement are secret from all but
the officials concerned and care is to be taken that they do
not leak out. Care should also be taken that the working of
the agreement is not hampered by delays in paying.

Rec'd: 9 Dec 44 (a)   Japanese   H 155528
RIb   Page 2

TOP SECRET
WAR DEPARTMENT

*Secret message of November 13, 1944, from Japanese foreign minister Shigemitsu to the Japanese
minister in Saigon, describing how the secret Allied relief funds were to be administered.* FILES OF THE
NATIONAL SECURITY AGENCY

(ii). On the Swiss side profits, agency costs and expenses in connection with the Red Cross to be remitted to Japan or to places in Great East Asia will be paid into the Yokohama Specie Bank Special Account.

(iii). All remittances to places in Great East Asia will be made through the Swiss Minister's Special Account at the Tokyo Branch. Our branches at the places to which remittances are addressed will open Swiss Special Accounts and, on receipt of the money will pay by the same procedure as has been necessary hitherto.

Further, balances should be telegraphed at the end of each month.

(iv). No charge will be made for any of the above accounts.

The details of this agreement are secret from all but the officials concerned and care is to be taken that they do not leak out. Care should also be taken that the working of this agreement is not hampered by delays in paying.

But it was hampered. In early 1945, a series of diplomatic maneuvers regarding possible postwar reparations so angered the Japanese that they stopped disbursing the relief funds altogether for the remainder of the war—condemning many men, women, and children from several Allied nations to painful and slow deaths, and the survivors to a lifetime of health problems.

In the first week of February 1945, President Roosevelt sent his special assistant, Lauchlin Currie (later unmasked as a Soviet spy), to Switzerland with a request: that Axis assets in Switzerland be frozen upon capitulation, so funds would be available for postwar reparations payments. The Swiss agreed, and the Japanese were infuriated. In retaliation the Japanese decided, according to a February 17, 1945, cable from Shunichi Kase, the Japanese minister in Bern to the Foreign Ministry in Tokyo, which read in part: "If the Anglo-Americans persist in these demands, it will be possible for Japan to threaten Switzerland and England and America with discontinuance of provision of goods to English and American prisoners in East Asia."

Later that day, Kase sent a second message to Tokyo, pointing out that the agreement to freeze Japanese funds in Switzerland "Is clearly . . . in contravention of the terms of the Japanese-Swiss [neutrality] agreement . . . if we do not achieve our purpose, we shall inform the Anglo-Americans that we cannot continue payments in behalf of the prisoners."

This fateful decision explains why the special relief accounts in the Yokohama Specie Bank doubled between January and August 1945, from 30 to 60 million Swiss francs—a little over 13.5 million 1945 dollars, worth over $81 million today. By now these accounts contained relief money from all sources

From: Bern(KASE)
To: Tokyo
17 February 1945

159

Priority.

With regard to remittances from here in the
past to Sweden, Iberia, etc, the banks were occasionally
reluctant to undertake them, and the recent remittance
to Portugal (the 1,000,000 (?francs?) to Sweden was already
sent) was heard of/by the Anglo-Americans and was categorically
refused on the demand of the Swiss Foreign Office on the
16th, quite separately from the matter of blocking --IG--
funds, by reason of the pressure of the United Nations
economic committee, as stated in YOKOHAMA SPECIE BANK wires
#50ᵃ through #52ᵃ. Thus while I intend to lodge a protest
pretty much on the following lines (I shall try for the
present to settle it within the scope of (1) in order not
to make the matter take on too large proportions), I
should like to have your views in advance when you have
conferred with the Finance Ministry.

Japanese   H 168286
                        Page 1

---

(1). While Switzerland allows this out of
political considerations as a policy of the Swiss Central
Bank, this is certainly unjust and clearly in contravention
of the terms of the Japanese-Swiss agreement (Article VIII).
Therefore, I shall urge the Swiss Government to reconsider
and to get the consent of the Anglo-Americans. (If by
any chance the situation of Switzerland does not permit this,
the Swiss Government should permit facilities, etc., to
take the place of this remittance.)
                                    the Japanese-
(2). Although with regard to/Swiss treaty, we
have always given the greatest consideration to the expansion of Swiss interests out of consideration for the
interests of both countries, if the Swiss Government is
unable to comply with (1) above, we must give concrete
consideration to that fact.

(3). If we do not achieve our purpose by either
of the above points, we shall inform the Anglo-Americans
that we cannot continue payments in behalf of prisoners in
return for funds which cannot be used in support of

Japanese   H 168286
                        Page 2

Japanese diplomatic establishments.

This wire is --2G-- (?from SHIMAMOTO?). Please
transmit it as Bern #20 to KUBO, the head of the Finance
Ministry Foreign Funds Bureau.

a- Not identified.

Inter 17 Feb 45   (1)   Japanese   H 168286
Rec'd 19 Feb 45   Page 3
Trans 22 Feb 45   (2149-s)

Secret cable from Japanese foreign minister Kase in Bern to the Foreign Ministry in Tokyo, advocating discontinuing all distribution of the Allied relief funds. FILES OF THE NATIONAL SECURITY AGENCY

for several POW locations in Asia, not just the Burma-Siam Railway. *Everyone* held captive by the Japanese was directly affected. So the money piled up in the Yokohama Specie Bank, and the Red Cross boxes containing food, medicine, and clothing piled up in prison camp warehouses, or in Japanese soldiers' quarters, all over the Japanese home islands and throughout occupied territory wherever prisoners were held.

One of the most chilling revelations has been to hear, consistently, from both military and civilian prisoners in Asia during World War II, that they only received *one* Red Cross parcel (frequently to share with others) during their entire three and a half years in Japanese hands —usually it seems to have come at Christmas 1943. Dr. Marcel Junod of the International Committee of the Red Cross saw piles of undistributed Red Cross boxes at the Mukden, Manchuria, POW camp in August 1945. When he asked Colonel Matsuda, the commanding officer of POW camps in the region why the parcels had not been distributed, Matsuda answered: "I am saving them up for later. . . . The prisoners will be much better pleased to get their parcels at Christmas than now."[11]

One camp of mostly Dutch women and children in Sumatra finally got their single shipment of Red Cross boxes in October 1945, three months after the war ended. They were still awaiting rescue at that late date, and many had already died from starvation.[12]

Barely a month before the Pacific War ended, on July 3, 1945, the Japanese Naval attaché in Switzerland suggested to Tokyo: "I think it would now be a very opportune move in order to further Japan's war aims if we were to contribute under some pretext or other some of our foreign funds (no matter how much), as one means of conciliating the Red Cross."

The Japanese had reason to be conciliatory to the Red Cross. Not only did the Japanese military cut off communication between Swiss Red Cross delegates in Asia and their home office in Geneva, but they mistreated, jailed, and even murdered Swiss nationals. Japanese diplomats seemed unable to control their military, or to successfully remind the commanders of the Imperial Japanese Army and Navy that Red Cross workers had an internationally recognized mission in combat zones and occupied territory, and that Swiss businessmen and missionaries were from a neutral country with which Japan had a treaty. The military began looking upon Red Cross workers and other Swiss nationals as spies for the enemy. A Swiss businessman was jailed in Yokohama as a spy in December 1944. Other Swiss nationals were jailed in Japan; one woman died in custody. At least sixteen Swiss nationals were slaughtered by rampaging Japanese soldiers and sailors in Manila as American troops were advancing in February 1945, in what became known as the Sack of Manila. And in the most severe incident of all, the Swiss Red Cross delegate to Borneo, Dr. Matthäus Vischer and his wife were arrested, tortured, tried by a Japanese Navy tribunal, and beheaded in December 1943. Several missionaries Dr. Vischer was trying to protect, in line with his duties, were also killed. The Swiss government had been unable to learn what had happened to their people, or to receive cooperation from the Japanese in evacuating them, despite repeated requests.

Even a stern warning sent February 10, 1945, from Japan's ambassador in Berlin, General Oshima, to high-ranking Navy personnel in Tokyo had little effect. Oshima cautioned: "There is a need, in the present European situation, for securing as far as possible the neutral nations like Switzerland and Sweden to our side in order to make use of them for acquiring information, securing material and funds for war purposes, disseminating propaganda abroad, etc."

A month later, another secret message came from Germany to army and navy chiefs in Tokyo, insisting that the military release Swiss nationals in custody. And by late May 1945, after the surrender of Germany, Japan's Naval attaché in Switzerland was urging the chief of the Bureau of Military Affairs in Tokyo "To present in the spirit of 'bushido' a considerable sum of money in sympathy for the Swiss who died in the havoc of war."

Indeed, by the time the Pacific War had ended in August 1945, the Swiss felt as if their nationals had become every bit as helpless and vulnerable as the Allied prisoners they had been sent to protect. So it is not surprising that on August 12, 1945, three days before Japan's emperor broadcast his radio message of surrender, Minister for Foreign Affairs Shigenori Togo sent a letter to the newly arrived Tokyo Red Cross head delegate, Dr. Junod, saying that the Japanese government "Proposed to make a considerable contribution to the International Committee of the Red Cross."[13] As if the unspent Allied relief money would be a "gift" from the Japanese government!

When the war formally ended three weeks later, the tug-of-war for the millions in unspent relief money began. It went on for ten years. Japanese assets on deposit in the Yokohama Specie Bank, including the relief money, were gradually disbursed by a liquidator hired by the bank, under the watchful eyes of Allied officials. In June 1949, 10 million of the 60 million Swiss francs in the special POW relief accounts were transferred to the International Committee of the Red Cross in Geneva.

In September 1951, the Dutch government got 11 million guilders (the equivalent of $3 million) from the fund, disbursing around $70 to each Dutch military ex-POW.[14]

In July 1952, ten months after the signing of the Peace Treaty with Japan, the British government got 4.3 million Swiss francs of its POW relief money back, as Article 16 of the peace treaty specified. Apparently the funds were returned to the British Treasury.

But amazingly the U.S. government didn't ask for any of its share. What little compensation U.S. military POWs got for their suffering at the hands of the Japanese—$1 a day for missed meals and $1.50 a day for "Forced . . . labor and inhumane treatment"—was paid by the government from Japanese assets frozen in the United States. It worked out to about $3,000 to $3,500 per man, depending on how many days one counted in captivity and the degree of permanent injuries sustained. But the thousands of POWs who had been forced to work as unpaid laborers for Japanese companies got absolutely nothing for their toils, a state of affairs that continues to exist to this day.

Civilians weren't even allowed to apply for compensation, on recommendation of the ICRC, and by decision of an executive committee on which the United States chose not to be represented, since the U.S. government had declined to accept any further share of reparations from Japan. The ICRC reasoning, which the committee accepted, was that civilians, unlike military personnel, have no verifiable identification or serial number, and might apply for compensation under different names.[15]

Ten years after the war ended, the 60 million Swiss francs of unspent POW relief money had dwindled to 46 million. In March 1955, the Swiss government, which had not contributed to the relief fund, but possibly believed that its nationals had been victimized just as much as those of Allied nations held captive in Asia, insisted on keeping 13.5 million Swiss francs for its own claims against Japan, and signed a separate treaty with Japan to this effect. This was a very generous amount to divide among just 186 claimants. Swiss nationals and businesses in Asia received the equivalent of $6,000 to $7,000 each, including compensation for automobiles and furniture, which amounted to several times what claimants from other nations received. Although this disparity in compensation placed Japan in the position of breaching the terms of the Treaty of Peace it had signed with Allied nations, Britain and the United States chose to look the other way, and not to exercise their options to receive the same favorable terms when Japan concluded this and subsequent more favorable treaties with other nations.

In May 1955, the International Committee of the Red Cross in Geneva at last received the remaining 33 million Swiss francs from the Yokohama Specie Bank, which included $7,542,500 in U.S. dollars worth nearly $45 million today. The money, including the U.S. government's original $6.2 million contribution, was sent to fourteen beneficiary nations for distribution to military personnel who had been POWs.[16] The United States of America was not included on this list.

The final irony is that Japan, with the consent of the Allies, was allowed to use relief money contributed by its wartime enemies, rather than funds from its own treasury, to settle some of its postwar claims.

The story of secret Allied wartime relief funds might have remained obscured, had this writer not discovered, in early 1997, Japanese foreign minister Shigemitsu's message of November 1944. After news accounts of the revelation appeared in the international press between February and March 1997, the Swiss government asked its leading World War II historian, Michele Coduri, to research the matter. Coduri's report enabled the Swiss National Bank to give this writer a full accounting of the relief funds. The Swiss bank's accounting was later confirmed by the Bank of Tokyo–Mitsubishi, which absorbed the assets of the Yokohama Specie Bank following its postwar liquidation.

But news accounts failed to place the blame for witholding the funds where it rested, in Tokyo. Instead, the greatest furor came from British ex-POWs who demanded to know why their treasury had not disbursed its recovered funds to military ex-prisoners for their postwar comfort, as the 1951 Peace Treaty had stipulated.

Since the relief story has come to light, the Canadian and Dutch Governments have arranged to compensate their citizens who had suffered wartime captivity. At this writing the British government was reportedly considering a similar compensation. Although the U.S. government has continued to maintain that its 1948 and 1952 payments to military ex-POWs were sufficient, by mid-2000, measures were under way in Congress to match the Canadian and Dutch gestures to ex-POWs.

Now that American victims of Japanese captivity have at last learned how hard their government tried to help them during their ordeal, they are calling for a more meaningful postwar gesture, however belated it may be.

Chapter 12

"Not to Leave Any Traces"

For thousands of World War II veterans, Christmas 1945 was their first holiday at home in years—a time to savor the joys of meals and reunions they had dreamed of so often in hostile, strange, and dangerous places. But for British Army signals sergeant Jack Edwards, who had just weeks earlier returned from the Kinkaseki copper mine, Prisoner of War Branch Camp No. 1, Formosa (Taiwan), Christmas in England was hard going.

It had been barely three months since an American sailor cradled the emaciated Edwards in his arms like a baby, and carried him aboard the hospital ship USS *Block Island* in Keelung (Taipei) Harbor, whispering: "God—what did they do to you?"

And because the Japanese had rarely distributed mail addressed to the prisoners, or allowed them to send a preprinted postcard home, it had been just weeks since a Red Cross worker gently told Edwards that his mother had died during his captivity, never knowing whether her son was dead or alive.

"'Missing, believed killed' for nearly five years meant that I was a ghost to many people," Edwards wrote. "I found it difficult to talk or eat with people. I sweated easily and could not control my emotions, crying if I went to a cinema or heard certain music."[1] When a POW friend came looking for Edwards, the two fled to a seaside resort. For two weeks, the ex-prisoners shared feelings neither could express to their families, and wondered how they would get through the holidays.

When Edwards finally returned to his worried family on Christmas Eve, he found a letter waiting from his commanding officer, Maj. J. F. Crossley, saying that the major had been ordered back to the Far East to help with war crimes investigations. Could Edwards send him a list of Japanese and Formosans he thought should be prosecuted—and could Edwards possibly see his way clear to joining the investigating team?

Edwards remembered that just holding the letter brought him a sense of relief. "I jumped at the chance to get away again," Edwards said. The thought of bringing justice to a few of the captors who had caused so many of his friends to die from beating, starvation, and disease (some expired as they were being carried down mountain paths on stretchers to freedom); and perhaps to give testimony at the War Crimes Trials—made Edwards suddenly eager to return to the one spot on earth he thought he'd never want to see again. Now it all made sense to him.

"My own family thought I was crazy, volunteering to go back," Edwards observed in his memoir. "I am certain we were not normal or rational, but were any of us who came back from that? Could anyone be?"

But the trip had its price. "It was ghastly," Edwards said in a 1995 interview. "It didn't do me any good, mentally or physically. It nearly finished me. I had terrible nightmares after that. I still suffer."

Decades later, Edwards could still describe in precise detail exactly what the POW campsite near the Kinkaseki copper mine looked like in January 1946, just four months after he and 1,200 ex-POWs had been liberated from their nightmare:

> The camp was in ruins; the huts where we had spent so many miserable nights were stripped bare. The commandant's headquarters had been completely burned to the ground. I started to poke around with a stick in the charred rubble where his office had been.
>
> "Don't waste your time there, Jack," the major called over to me. "You won't find anything there we can use." How wrong he was!
>
> "Ah well, I just might find a souvenir or two," I called back, and poked a little deeper with my stick. Then I spotted it: the corner of a page, still readable. Someone had made a major mistake in trying to burn all the camp records. He didn't burn them thoroughly enough.[2]

What Edwards and his British and American investigating team found on Formosa that January day in 1946 would be the only complete recovered file, fifteen documents in all, which provided clear, sequential, written proof that the Japanese had developed a policy to publicly mistreat and humiliate Allied POWs, to use them as slave labor throughout Japanese-occupied territory, and then to kill them all. The documents, handwritten recordings of radio messages from command headquarters in Tokyo, were dated from April 1942 to August 20, 1945—five days after the emperor had announced the surrender. Edwards described hearing what the orders said:

American cryptologist Stephen Green, a member of our team, translated each document, one by one, word for word. They went back to 1942, and it was all there—each terrible thing that happened to us was all part of the plan. We were absolutely stunned when, at about two o'clock in the morning, he read us the execution order. We had heard about it from a friendly Formosan, Yue Ten Eki, we called "Big Head." He told Captain M. Brown, who informed Major Crossley. Also, a young Formosan servant had overheard the commandant and officers saying: "If the Americans land here, we must kill all the prisoners." When our translator got to the line: "In any case it is the aim not to allow the escape of a single one, to annihilate them all, and not to leave any traces"— we all just froze. No one said a word.[3]

The words that left Edwards and his team speechless are indeed chilling to read. The order was actually a clarification of a long-standing policy put in place by the highest level of Japanese command in the early months of the war: that no prisoners—or civilian internees—were to be retrieved by the enemy. If a POW camp commandant believed that his location might fall to the enemy, he was to kill all the POWs first. The order that Edwards retrieved was in response to a query from the chief of staff of the 11th Unit on Formosa, who was in charge of all POW administration in his region. He wanted to know under what circumstances he could act on his own, without waiting for orders from his superiors. The reply he received from the vice-minister of war in Tokyo on August 1, 1944, was also sent to the commanding general, the commanding general of Military Police *[kempei tai]*, and all POW camp commanders in the occupied territories and home islands. It reads as follows:

The following answer about the extreme measures for POW's:

Under the present situation if there were a mere explosion or fire a shelter for the time being could be had in nearby buildings such as the school, a warehouse, or the like. However, at such time as the situation became urgent and it be extremely important, the POW's will be concentrated and confined in their present location and under heavy guard the preparation for the final disposition will be made.

The time and method of this disposition are as follows:

(1) The Time.

Although the basic aim is to act under superior orders, individual disposition may be made in the following circumstances:

(a) When an uprising of large numbers cannot be suppressed without the use of firearms.

(b) When escapees from the camp may turn into a hostile fighting force.

(2) The Methods.

(a) Whether they are destroyed individually or in groups, or however it is done, with mass bombing, poisonous smoke, poisons, drowning, decapitation, or what, dispose of them as the situation dictates.

(b) In any case it is the aim not to allow the escape of a single one, to annihilate them all, and not to leave any traces.

While they were still prisoners, Edwards and his superior officers had heard rumors that such an order existed, but what they did not know was that the orders had been systematically carried out as Allied forces regained control of Pacific territories; and that when this clarification was issued, Allied intelligence intercepted it. Plans were put in place to make sure that POW camps would be located and liberated as quickly as possible. But sometimes, camp commanders had taken matters into their own hands when they anticipated attack even if it didn't happen.

For example, the commanding officer on Wake Island, Rear Adm. Shigematsu Sakaibara, was sure the Americans were about to repossess the territory in October 1943, as U.S. forces began heavily bombing the airstrip. So on October 7, he told the remaining ninety-eight civilian construction workers that at last they were going home, that an American submarine was coming to pick them up. The hopeful prisoners were marched down to the lagoon, while the admiral watched from his bunker. But as they were made to kneel facing the water, and as their hands were tied behind them, the awful truth became apparent. Two escaped, briefly; they were caught and beheaded later. The remaining ninety-six were blindfolded and shot in the back. Their bodies were buried in the sand. American forces never did retake Wake Island; Admiral Sakaibara ceremoniously handed it back to the U.S. Navy command on September 4, 1945, two days after the formal surrender was signed.

In December 1944, the commanding officer on Palawan Island was sure General MacArthur would occupy Palawan on his way to the Philippines. So he faked an air raid by sounding the siren, ordered 157 Marine POWs into the air-raid shelter, had gasoline poured into both entrances and ignited, torching the prisoners. Eleven survived. But instead of stopping at Palawan, MacArthur headed straight for Luzon.

A couple of months later, as MacArthur's forces were rolling into Manila, the commandant where nearly 3,500 American civilians, including men,

The "98 Rock" on Wake Island: a message desperately chiseled on May 10, 1943, by a civilian POW hoping for rescue. All 98 prisoners remaining on the island were executed on October 7, 1943, because the Japanese commanding officer feared U.S. forces were about to retake the island. He was incorrect. COLLECTION OF WILLIAM TAYLOR

women, and children were confined on the campus of Santo Tomas University, ordered his troops not to yield their captives, and a three-day pitched battle took place before American tanks finally crashed through the university walls and rescued them. At nearby Los Banos, paratroops rescued 2,146 civilians before Japanese troops could gun them down. Meanwhile 1,100 military personnel and civilians were rescued at Bilibid, together with another 250 scattered at Pasai, Fort Santiago, and Bagio prisons. From the camps in and around Manila, some 7,000 white men, women, and children, mostly Americans, were rescued by liberating troops. But the Japanese didn't give them up easily.

In June 1945, as Allied forces approached Borneo, the commandant at Sandakan ordered 2,000 Australian POWs marched from the beach to the mountains with sacks of rice on their backs. When this proved insufficient to kill them all, he ordered the survivors to march back. Soon just six were left, but friendly natives spirited them into the jungle, and they lived to tell the tale.

As July 1945 drew to a close, the POW officers in Nakom Paton and Nakom Nayok, two of the large camps in Thailand, were quietly making defense preparations because clandestine radios had received a BBC broadcast beamed to the Far East (in hopes that some radios were still operating), warning of the August 1944 execution order.

Sometimes, POWs heard news of their impending fate directly from guards. At Nakom Nayok, guards called the prisoners outside one evening to say that an Allied invasion was expected any day; and when it happened, they would all be shot. At Nakom Paton, the prisoners planned to break out on the night of August 15, but the emperor's broadcast earlier that day made their effort unnecessary.

Kempei tai interpreter Nagase confirmed that "If the day August 22nd, 1945 [the date Japanese intelligence expected British and Commonwealth troops to invade Burma] were the day of invasion really, I was forced to kill the POWs by gun . . . then, by emperor's order, we all soldiers along the Railway were forced to annihilate all the POWs. I happened to see the top-secret documents concerning the annihilation operation at the Bang Pong M.P. [military police] office just before the end of the war."[4]

Luckily for the prisoners along the Burma Railway, Japanese commanders obeyed the emperor's order not to harm the prisoners—a condition set by General MacArthur for accepting the surrender.

Another condition General MacArthur insisted be met before he would accept surrender was that he be given a map and key list of every location in the home islands and throughout Asia where POWs were held. A map and key were delivered to the general's headquarters in Manila on August 19, 1945, by the Japanese Mission to Negotiate Surrender, but it only showed 102 of the 169 POW camp locations. So it was still a race against time, and all Allied forces knew it.

Fearing that word of the surrender might not reach remote Manchuria, a team of six OSS agents parachuted into the huge POW camp at Mukden on August 16 to protect the 1,660 prisoners. They were correct; the Japanese commander hadn't yet received word. He had the OSS agents stripped and disarmed; a few tense hours passed before he could be persuaded to contact Tokyo and learn that now *he* was a prisoner.

As the formal surrender was being signed on the deck of the USS *Missouri* in Tokyo Bay on September 2, preparations were being made to rush ashore and rescue POWs at Omori in Tokyo, where aviators were being held; on Formosa where Jack Edwards and thousands of other POWs were in several camps; while U.S. Navy pilots were ordered to fly low over the civilian camps in Shanghai to "show the flag" and warn Japanese not to harm their captives.

It was the quick work and cool navigation skills of a U.S. Navy lieutenant, Henry Taylor, on the destroyer escort *Thomas J. Gary* that not only allowed Jack Edwards and his comrades an early release, but caused the Japanese commandant to leave so hastily that his files didn't completely burn. Lieutenant Taylor made the Japanese harbormaster come aboard the *Thomas J. Gary* on September 5,

1945, with a map showing the mine locations in Keelung (Taipei) harbor, so that he could get ashore as quickly as possible, jump in a 1937 Buick with his commodore and a Japanese driver, and rush up to Edwards's camp to begin immediate evacuation. Taylor wasn't told why, but he knew the mission was urgent. In an October 1996 interview, Taylor recalled: "Prior to the war's end, I never heard directly that the POW were to be executed . . . our orders changed to go to Formosa, contact the Japanese and liberate the 1,200 POW there. We had no idea of the threats to the POW."

"My assignment back on ship was to stay down below and help the weakened POW in case they needed anything . . . they had to climb a ladder—I can still see one man, asking me for help. As I put out my hand to steady him, I was afraid I'd push right through his skin and break his ribs . . . I'll never forget those men."[5]

With all the eyewitness testimony about the liberated prisoners' condition; and with so many surviving POW depositions and personal accounts at the Tokyo trials, it seems strange that the documented proof discovered by Edwards and his team about their deliberate mistreatment and near annihilation was apparently downplayed at the trials—especially since Edwards's group of investigators made a second important discovery after Edwards found the camp commander's files. Edwards recalled the second discovery:

POWs having their first hot meal in camp near Kinkaseki mine, Taihoku, Taiwan, September 5, 1945. Photo by Lt. Henry Taylor, USN. COLLECTION OF FREDERICK TAYLOR

POWs preparing to leave mountain camp, Taihoku, Taiwan, September 5, 1945. Photo by Lt. Henry Taylor, USN. COLLECTION OF FREDERICK TAYLOR

POW being carried aboard hospital ship USS Block Island *by two American sailors, September 5, 1945. Photo by Lt. Henry Taylor, USN.* COLLECTION OF FREDERICK TAYLOR

We were astonished to learn that the Japanese governor-general, Richiki Ando, was still living in Taipei, in his . . . house, surrounded by his servants and guards—can you believe it? After top-level negotiations we found a second copy of the execution order in his headquarters nearby. Then we knew it was authentic. That clinched it, finding the governor-general's official copy, all hand-written in beautiful calligraphy on rice paper.

What we couldn't figure out was why the general who was then Governor of Taiwan was letting Governor-General Ando stay there—why he hadn't arrested him right away. We had a terrible time getting Generalissimo Chiang Kai-shek to sign the arrest order. We had to get British General Carton de Wyatt to intervene, and he got Chiang to chop the order. Finally the governor-general was arrested and sent to Shanghai prison. We were terribly disappointed to learn that he was somehow allowed to commit suicide. His chief of staff, Isayama, committed suicide, too. So neither one ever stood trial.[6]

Edwards and his teammates were not told that there was indeed a reason why Governor-General Ando had been allowed to remain in his home: he was an Allied agent. His file was deliberately kept intact, waiting to be

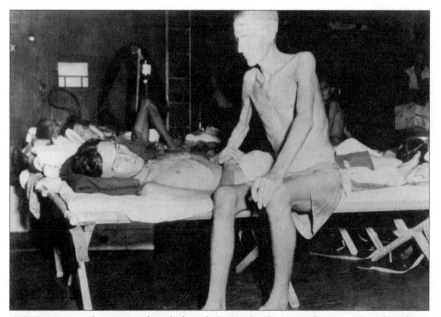

POW sitting with comatose friend aboard Block Island, *September 5, 1945. Photo by Lt. Henry Taylor, USN.* COLLECTION OF FREDERICK TAYLOR

retrieved by Allied forces. And when he was at last brought to the jail in Shanghai, the guards on "suicide watch" were told to look the other way. For Ando, ending his life was preferable to admitting his dual role to his superiors, or testifying at a war crimes trial.[7]

Edwards knew that Stephen Green's translations of his fifteen-document file, along with the governor-general's elegant copy of the crucial order, were turned over to General MacArthur's staff on September 19, 1946—in plenty of time for the upcoming trials. So it is understandable that Edwards, who testified and sat through much of the proceedings, nearly shouted in sheer frustration: "Not one of the documents I retrieved was used at any of the War Crimes trials!"[8]

Edwards's recollection is backed up by Arnold Brackman, a correspondent for United Press who covered the Class A trials in Tokyo of onetime prime minister, minister of war, and minister without portfolio Hideki Tojo, the most powerful member of the Japanese Cabinet, together with those of other top policy makers. Brackman wrote:

> Repeatedly during the trial camp survivors testified that camp commandants had told them that they would be killed if Japan was invaded. No documents were introduced to support these charges; the supposition was that the secret directives relating to the disposal of POWs had been destroyed in the pyres ignited after Japan's surrender.[9]

Not only was Brackman unaware that such documentation existed, but neither he nor Edwards was apparently aware that the execution order was, indeed, introduced as an exhibit on January 9, 1947, but it was *not mentioned in open court.* The prosecutor presented "Document 2701"; the chief judge replied: "Admitted on the usual terms"; the clerk announced: "Document 2701 will be received as Exhibit 2015." That was the extent of reference to this document. No one sitting in the courtroom, including Brackman or Edwards, could have known that Exhibit 2015 was the POW execution directive.

It has actually taken more than fifty years for this fact to emerge, and it is due mainly to the personal efforts of the senior archivist at the National Archives, John E. Taylor, that it has now come to light. Taylor shared this writer's curiosity that the execution order had an exhibit number handwritten at the top of Green's translated copy. Taylor knew the document *had* to have been made part of the trial transcript if it was given an exhibit number. Working with the trial transcript index, and assisted by Mia Waller, a seasoned researcher at the archives, Taylor was able to confirm in April 2000 the January 1947 date on which Exhibit 2015 was presented at the War Crimes Trial proceedings. He then searched the verbatim transcript until he found the courtroom dialogue mentioned above.[10]

Document No. 2701
(Certified as Exhibit "O" in Doc. No. 2687)

Page 1

From the Journal of the Taiwan POW Camp H.Q. in Taihoku,
entry 1 August 1944.

1. (entries about money, promotions of Formosans at Branch camps, including promotion of Yo Yu-toku to 1st Cl Keibiin - 5 entries)

2. The following answer about the extreme measures for POW's was sent to the Chief of Staff of the 11th Unit (Formosa POW Security No. 10).

   "Under the present situation if there were a more explosion or fire a shelter for the time being could be had in nearby buildings such as the school, a warehouse, or the like. However, at such time as the situation become urgent and it be extremely important, the POW's will be concentrated and confined in their present location and under heavy guard the preparation for the final disposition will be made.

   The time and method of this disposition are as follows:

   (1) The Time.

      Although the basic aim is to act under superior orders, individual disposition may be made in the following circumstances:

      (a) When an uprising of large numbers cannot be suppressed without the use of firearms.

      (b) When escapees from the camp may turn into a hostile fighting force.

   (2) The Methods.

      (a) Whether they are destroyed individually or in groups, or however it is done, with mass bombing, poisonous smoke, poisons, drowning, decapitation, or what, dispose of them as the situation dictates.

      (b) In any case it is the aim not to allow the escape of a single one, to annihilate them all, and not to leave any traces.

   (3) To: The Commanding General
          The Commanding General of Military Police

      Reported matters conferred on with the 11th Unit, the Kiirun Fortified Area H.Q., and each prefecture concerning the extreme s

3. (The next entry concerns the

Document No. 2701
(Certified as Exhibit "O" in Doc. No. 2687)

Page 2

I hereby certify that this is a true translation from the Journal of the Taiwan POW H.Q. in Taiwan, entry 1 August 1944.

Signed: Stephen H. Green
         STEPHEN H. GREEN

— — — — — — —

This is Exhibit marked "O" referred to in the Affidavit of JAMES THOMAS NEHEMIAH CROSS,

Sworn before me this 19th day of September 1946.

/s/ P. A. L. Vine

MAJOR R. M.

Execution order issued by Japanese War Ministry on August 1, 1944. Japanese-language original and English translation are shown. Both documents were entered into the record of the Tokyo War Crimes Trials as Exhibit No. 2015, January 9, 1947. INTERNATIONAL MILITARY TRIBUNAL OF THE FAR EAST
TRANSCRIPTS, NATIONAL ARCHIVES

So the mystery remains: why wasn't such a key supporting document given more prominence at the Tokyo trials? Possibly because it was issued by the office of the minister of war, the only member of the cabinet who had direct access to Emperor Hirohito and had private conversations with him. The one firm instruction from Washington as the trials got under way was that under no circumstances would the emperor be implicated or be called as a witness. Also, all important orders were issued *in the name of the emperor.* On November 25, 1947, the Japanese press reported that Chief Prosecutor Joseph Keenan met privately with the emperor the previous day, just to make sure he would not inadvertently implicate the emperor during the trial proceedings.[11] The manner in which Exhibit 2015 was handled at the trials suggests that Keenan did indeed downplay evidence that might have had a result he was under strict orders to avoid.

After the trials, General MacArthur shipped some 7,000 Japanese government papers to army headquarters in the United States, along with all the transcripts for the War Crimes Trials, International Prosecution Section (IPS). By the mid-1950s, all captured Japanese documents were returned to Japan, at the request of the Japanese government and with the approval of the U.S. Congress. But the IPS files and the prewar and wartime treaties Japan had made with other nations, which were exhibits in the War Crimes Trials, were retained, according to Senior Archivist Taylor.

When members of the Japanese Diet library staff came to the National Archives, beginning in the 1970s, to microfilm their government documents that remained there, they were not allowed access to the IPS files. So they paid for the film and for the labor of National Archives staff members to do the job for them. In September 1992 the microfilm containing the execution order was shipped to Tokyo; it has been on file at the Japanese Diet Library since that time.[12]

In June 1995, this writer convened a panel discussion at the Overseas Press Club in New York City, after rediscovering Edwards's full file at the National Archives, with the aid of Senior Archivist Taylor. Included on the panel were an ex-prisoner of war; a deputy from the Japanese Consulate; and a former Marine Intelligence officer who spent twenty years as a postwar Tokyo correspondent.

We discussed the POW execution orders, and whether they might have influenced the timing of the war's end. The ex-POW said he knew the A-bomb had saved his life; the Japanese consul had never heard of the execution order; and the former Tokyo correspondent didn't recollect hearing the order mentioned at the War Crimes Trials.

The Overseas Press Club event was covered by NTV, Japan's largest commercial television network. The NTV crew went to Washington and filmed the governor-general's rice paper original of the execution order; traveled to Taiwan and filmed the Kinkaseki mine and POW campsite; and broadcast a seven-minute news feature, scanning the words of the execution order as the correspondent spoke them. It was aired as part of the Sunday evening network news in Tokyo on June 25, 1995.

One is left to ponder: what would have happened if Jack Edwards's file, and especially the POW execution instructions, had been more prominently displayed fifty years ago? Would the Japanese possibly have developed a little of the collective guilt so prevalent in Germany? Would more Americans have understood that the war's abrupt, atomic end saved the lives of 200,000 helpless military and civilian men, women, and children? Would apologies have been more likely from Japan's government?

What went wrong at the Tokyo trials?

Chapter 13

Tokyo Trials: The Dog That Did Not Bark

"THE DOG THAT DID NOT BARK." THAT IS HOW FORMER STATE DEPARTMENT spokesman Hodding Carter III characterized the 1946–48 Tokyo War Crimes Trials, in opening a 1996 symposium at the National Museum of the Pacific War (Admiral Nimitz Museum) in Fredericksburg, Texas, fifty years after the trials began in the capital of a vanquished nation.

Carter's phrase resonated with the audience of World War II veterans, ex-prisoners of war, historians, war crimes prosecutors with experience from Tokyo to My Lai to Bosnia, and journalists who had covered those events. Half a century later, the Tokyo trials are remembered more for who was *not* put on trial than for the relatively few whose deeds were showcased and punished.

Historians are still examining the long-term consequences of Washington's ironclad instructions to the tribunal's convener, Gen. Douglas MacArthur, that under no circumstances was Emperor Hirohito to be put on trial or even implicated in the proceedings. The sense of national exoneration, lack of guilt, and collective amnesia—which developed among Japan's leaders and people as a result of their ruler being excused from responsibility—will continue to be a subject of debate and reflection until a full-scale, broad-based apology is issued from the very highest levels of Japan's government.

But for thousands of Allied prisoners of war who stumbled home from the mines, steel mills, shipyards, and factories of Japan's industries, the larger oversight was that not one of the industrial executives who ordered them to work every day, and who profited so greatly from their unpaid labor, was ever held accountable, and rarely were their names even mentioned during the entire two years of war crimes testimony. For the ex-POWs, that silence has been deafening.

The list of indicted Class A war criminals was released on April 29, 1946; but the decision to omit Japan's leading industrialists, or *zaibatsu,* from that list may have been sealed six weeks earlier, on February 12, over lunch with the State Department's political adviser to General MacArthur. The lunch was hosted by members of the family who happened to control the biggest Japanese conglomerate of all: the Mitsui industrial empire. The informal luncheon took place in the executive dining room of the Mitsui Main Bank building in Tokyo.

MacArthur's political adviser, William Sebald, had recently arrived in Tokyo to take up his new post from his predecessor, George Atcheson, Jr., who had been killed in a plane crash shortly after publicly stating that the emperor should be put on trial.[1] Sebald was an easy mark for the Mitsui executives. Like nearly all the aides and advisers who were assigned to Japan during the 1945 to 1952 occupation, Sebald had no expertise in the Japanese language, history, or culture. And judging by his reaction to the Mitsui executives' remarks, Sebald was apparently unaware that he was having lunch with CEOs who among them had asked for the use of more American POW labor than any other conglomerate, or that thousands of Americans had been starved and beaten by Mitsui employees, or that hundreds of POWs had died on Mitsui property.

Fifty-four years after that meeting took place, this writer gained access to Sebald's memorandum about it, under the Freedom of Information Act. Sebald's hosts that February day were Taknatsu Mitsui, partner of Mitsui Holding Company; Kiyoshi Miyazaki, president, Mitsui Trading Company; Kisashi Matsumoto, managing director, Mitsui Head Office; Shiro Sasaki, president, Mitsui Real Estate Company; Shinji Okada, president, Sanki Kogyo Ko-Kan; and Katsunobu Kabuda, president, Taiwan Sugar Company.

The Mitsui executives knew all the right buttons to push. They expressed the *expectation* that part of their capital would be frozen to help pay war reparations. Sebald wrote: "The so-called *zaibatsu* is not concerned that a certain portion of its heavy industry is to be taken for reparations." Their concern, according to Sebald, was the delay. They seemed eager to pay up, move on, get their capital unfrozen, and be allowed to use their leadership in rebuilding Japan. They expressed bafflement and frustration at having all their good ideas turned down by MacArthur and his staff.

"The large business interests in Japan have always been pro-American in their sentiments," Sebald said he was told. But the executives hinted that their "good will" toward America was eroding; and that if they did not get clear guidance and assistance soon from the United States, they might be forced to look for help from "non-American [read Soviet] quarters." Surely, they pointed out to their guest, any American would admit that the profit motive is all-important, and bigness is not a bad thing—just look at AT&T, General Motors, U.S. Steel, Du Pont, and Ford. Sebald wrote: "As Japanese companies, under the lash of the military, it is hardly reasonable to expect the large

Japanese combines to do otherwise than carry out the instructions of the government during the war."

The Mitsui executives warned Sebald that if the *zaibatsu* were disintegrated too rapidly, Japan will be ripe for communism—just the words a State Department official did not want to hear at the beginning of the Cold War, with the Communist Party gaining strength among Japanese workers.

Sebald hardly got a word in edgewise during this power lunch. Or, as he put it in diplomat-speak: "Mr. Sebald found the Japanese so eager to present their views that it was generally unnecessary for him to offer direct comment or to actively enter the discussion which was in both Japanese and English. He confined himself to occasional general questions designed to elicit their views on certain aspects of the situation."[2]

Sebald's memorandum reinforced the viewpoint of Secretary of War Henry Stimson and his deputy, John J. McCloy, who had drafted a policy guideline for the occupation of Japan six months earlier in July 1945. McCloy later explained that the dissolution of the *zaibatsu* "Was not primarily intended as a punitive measure in connection with responsibility for war guilt, since there was considerable doubt, at least in the mind of Mr. Stimson, that *zaibatsu* elements had actively supported the war policy in Japan."[3]

Despite Stimson's viewpoint, instructions radioed from Washington to General MacArthur on September 24, 1945, contained this directive: "In the absence of evidence to the contrary, you will assume that any persons who have held key positions of high responsibility since 1937, in industry, finance, commerce or agriculture have been active exponents of militant nationalism and aggression."[4]

Investigators for the War Crimes Trials had just a few months to try and gather enough evidence to dislodge the prevailing wisdom in Washington, and to their regret, they were unable to do so. Unlike German industrialists, who had left a clear paper trail of their deep involvement in the planning and financing of the war, easily retrieved by swiftly advancing Allied forces, Japanese industrialists successfully concealed their similar involvement until all danger of prosecution was past—or burned retrievable papers in the ample time afforded them (nearly three weeks) between the announcement of surrender and the occupation of Japan by American forces.

As mentioned earlier, one of Chief Prosecutor Joseph Keenan's investigators, Robert Donihi, recommended to him that charges pending against the *zaibatsu* heads should be dropped, because the *zaibatsu* did not appear to be policy makers. And whatever conclusions the Americans reached would prevail at the trials, which were billed as the International Military Tribunal for the Far East, but which were controlled by Washington through General MacArthur. Like the staff with which he surrounded himself, MacArthur had very little direct knowledge about Japan, and made no apparent effort to find out.[5] It is said that he took no trips to the countryside, or anywhere else, except from his hotel to his headquarters.

Unlike most of the other Allied nations, which sent their top, most seasoned prosecutors to the tribunal, the United States sent a flamboyant gangbuster; a Washington insider who had been part of President Franklin D. Roosevelt's inner circle. Despite the fact that he was a good organizer and listener, with a degree from Harvard Law School, even some of his own staff did not think Joseph Keenan was up to the job. Arnold Brackman, who covered the Class A Tokyo Trials for United Press, said Keenan's knowledge of Asian affairs "[d]id not extend beyond chow mein."[6] By contrast, the chief justice for the tribunal, Sir William Webb of Australia, spoke fluent Japanese and had just presided over the War Crimes Trials at Singapore.

Like many others who arrived in Tokyo in late 1945, Keenan thought the trials would last six months, at the most. He was stunned to learn that MacArthur's General Headquarters had discovered almost no records that would help them determine who planned and initiated the war. Postsurrender Tokyo was an investigator's nightmare.

When announcement of the indictments was made on April 29, 1946, the absence of any *zaibatsu* from the list infuriated many of America's wartime allies, including some who had come to assist in the tribunal. Associate Prosecutor S. A. Golunsky fumed in Moscow's *New Times:* "The big [Japanese] capitalist concerns exercised a very great influence on the entire political life of Japan. It was they that were the mainsprings of piratical aggression. Wherever the Japanese armies appeared, the great monopoly octopuses stretched their tentacles."[7]

Golunsky had a point. As mentioned earlier, when Imperial Japanese Army engineers decided to build a railway through the jungles of Burma and Thailand, Mitsubishi was ready to profit from the venture, supplying foodstuffs to the army and 650,000 wooden crossties for the railway—at very inflated prices.

As the trials inched through 1948, a commentary over the airwaves by the Soviet Far East Service, transmitted in Japanese, reflected growing frustration at decisions by the American-controlled tribunals, which seemed to contradict the approach agreed to by the Soviet Union, United States, and Great Britain at the Potsdam Conference. That wartime agreement, the Soviet commentator observed:

> Includes the bankers and industrialists who supplied money for Japan's aggressive war. . . . Those who planned, supported and protected Japan's aggressive war are, on the contrary, being protected by the American military courts. . . . Do the American officials

doubt the crimes of the Japanese generals, admirals, bankers and industrialists who killed thousands of American officers and men? It may be that some groups in the United States do not want to set an example by punishing, through international law, those who brought about the war.[8]

Once charges against the *zaibatsu* were dropped, it became a matter of policy not to mention a Japanese company by name, according to Robert Donihi, who had the distinction of being a prosecutor at both the Nuremberg and Tokyo trials.[9] Even when a company employee was being tried for mistreating prisoners, he was usually referred to as a "civilian guard," and the name of the company was rarely mentioned.

The only time the *zaibatsu* were prominently mentioned during the trials was in connection with the Manchukuo (Manchuria) opium trade in occupied China during the 1930s. The *Ko-a-In* (China Affairs Board) was alleged to have been financed by Mitsubishi, Mitsui, Kawasaki, Yasuda, and Sumitomo banks. The organization was headed by the emperor's uncle, Prince Fumimaro Konoe, and its vice presidents were the ministers of war, navy, finance, and foreign affairs. Prosecutors showed that Mitsubishi controlled the trade in the Manchukuo area, while Mitsui controlled central and south China, and these same two giants shared north China.[10] It was alleged that the opium trade was set up to generate revenue for Japan's military aggression.

But what the International Prosecution Section did not discuss in its proceedings was how MacArthur's staff had apparently thwarted the next revenue opportunity for Mitsubishi, Mitsui, and others: the U.S. occupation forces. In China and other occupied territory, as well as in the home islands, Japanese nationals were strictly forbidden to use narcotics. So when MacArthur learned in September 1945 from his counterespionage unit that a tremendous amount of opium had been shipped back to Japan and hidden in the mountains, he felt an urgent need to locate it in order to protect the thousands of Americans expected to be stationed in Japan.

MacArthur contacted Gen. Sherman Hasbrouck, commander of the artillery units of the 97th Infantry Division, which had just arrived from Germany to take up its position as the occupation force for northern Honshu. General Hasbrouck appointed Maj. John F. Kelly, M.D., the unit's medical officer, to be in charge of the Special 106th Military Government Company Occupation Unit, which MacArthur had hastily formed. Dr. Kelly was to head the newly created Japanese Health Department. His mission was to find and confiscate the cache of narcotics, which was believed to be in locations within the Nagano Prefecture.

By mid-September, Dr. Kelly, who had become fairly fluent in Japanese, was studying a Japanese map of the region, and adopting a strategy that would be repeated dozens of times over the next several months. An interpreter, a young woman from a prominent Japanese family, accompanied him, along with a driver, an army corporal with the unlikely name of Admiral Nelson Peckham. The interpreter would telephone ahead to the local police station in a town. Dr. Kelly instructed her to say the two would be arriving to retrieve whatever narcotics they had in the area. They would arrive at the police station, and after a half hour of polite conversation and tea, the interpreter would turn to Dr. Kelly and say: "I think we had better come back tomorrow." The next morning, Dr. Kelly would receive a phone call; the interpreter would take the call and begin to write down road directions. They would drive along a winding mountain road, and there, behind a barn or alongside the road, would be a few boxes.

"That's what you are looking for," the interpreter would say, and sure enough, it was.

"By the end of October, I had confiscated four and a half tons of opium," Dr. Kelly said in an interview in April 2000. Two Japanese soldiers had been put at his disposal; one of the assignments Dr. Kelly gave them was to guard the growing stacks of boxes. If any were missing, he told the soldiers, they would be court-martialed and shot.

"We got snowed in during the winter, but by March 1946, I had confiscated another three and a half tons of opium, and four tons of crystalline cocaine."

It was all very polite and discreet. The overnight retrievals ensured that American authorities never knew exactly in which company's warehouse or mine, or in which individual's home, the contraband had been stored. Dr. Kelly just let it be known that he expected each police department to locate whatever narcotics there were in a particular town, and to turn them over to him. The operation was a success.

Dr. Kelly said the cache also yielded "Hundreds of microscopes, and a large quantity of quinine. These were medical supplies, which I made sure were handed over to local hospitals and clinics."[11]

Dr. Kelly's trove of contraband made the front page of *Stars and Stripes,* as well as his hometown paper, the *Brooklyn Eagle,* in which he was quoted as saying that the opium would be worth $4 million [1945] dollars on the legal market, and $50 million on the black market in the United States. And that was only half the cache. By April 1946 those amounts would double.

As he was leaving Nagano to return to Tokyo, Dr. Kelly received a sincere letter of thanks from Monobe Kunro, governor of the Nagano Prefecture. Dated March 27, 1946, Governor Kunro's letter reads:

Maj. John F. Kelly, M.D., with interpreter and driver, at Nagano, Japan, October 1945, as they set out to search for the cache of opium in the mountain province. COLLECTION OF JOHN F. KELLY, M.D.

Major Kelly, standing, with interpreter and driver, checking the growing pile of confiscated opium in boxes, late October 1945. COLLECTION OF JOHN F. KELLY, M.D.

Dear Sir,

During the past six months since your arrival in the Nagano Prefecture in October 1945 as commander of the Medical Section, your efforts as to the returning of former military medical supplies and installations, and your valuable instructions in sanitation and prevention of plague, are deeply appreciated by the people of our prefecture.

Upon learning of your departure from us, we wish to present to you a painting by Kosui Sano as a souvenir of our heartfelt gratification and respect.

Governor of the Nagano Prefecture, Kunro Monobe [signed]

The governor also may have been grateful that Dr. Kelly had prevented Nagano Prefecture from becoming the new cocaine and opium distribution center in postwar Asia.

Dr. Kelly was a lot more successful than most of the investigators sent by the IPS to visit sites where prisoner of war camps were known to have been located. Investigator William Gill, an army lieutenant, recalled the frustration of going to known company POW sites and being told, repeatedly, that all records had been burned. "We searched in vain for records that could have been helpful to the prosecution," Gill wrote in a 1995 memoir. At one site in Hokkaido, Gill described an encounter with a factory supervisor who began the conversation by announcing that he had been an Olympic hammer thrower. When Gill asked about the records concerning the POWs, "He merely said that he had burned them. We pressed the issue that he may have missed some and that they were to be found; he firmly said that he was told to destroy the records and that he did a good job at what he was told to do."[12]

"We knew they were lying, but what could we do?" Gill said in a 1999 interview. "We had to turn and walk away empty-handed." Sometimes, Gill said, records were found hidden in shrines. And he recalled that interpreters eavesdropping on suspected war criminals awaiting trial at Sugamo prison occasionally overheard prisoners discussing plots to maintain secrecy, or ways to destroy or hide evidence.

One of the most notorious acts of falsification took place on Wake Island, where Admiral Sakaibara decided to make his murder of ninety-eight POWs in October 1943 look as if it had occurred as the result of an American naval bombardment. He ordered the POW remains exhumed and spread for a couple of days on a beach, which had earlier been shelled by U.S. Navy ships. Then he transmitted an "official" report to Tokyo saying this was how the prisoners had died.[13]

Capt. John D. Murphy, USN, director of War Crimes Investigations in the Pacific, stated at the trials: "All records concerning POW captured by the Japanese in the Pacific Ocean areas were destroyed by the Japanese authorities and in every instance investigators were confronted with false information by the Japanese commanding officers as well as the deliberate intention on the part of the Japanese to conceal any and all information concerning persons who were known to have been captured alive."[14]

Yet as soon as the War Crimes Trials were concluded, it was possible for Japanese officials to begin compiling the very detailed *Furyo Joho Kyoku,* Summary Record of Treatment of Prisoners of War, which was published in 1955. It included the Collected Documents of National Legislation Concerning Prisoners of War, which was completed in December 1946. Both documents give precise information about how many prisoners were sent to each company location, what the housing and pay arrangements were, when each camp was opened and closed, which company operated each site—everything a war crimes investigator might find useful. So the information was there; it just wasn't made available at the time it was being requested.

One ex-POW told about visiting the Mitsui Company Kawasaki stevedoring complex in 1987. When he introduced himself at the office, a Mitsui manager greeted him cordially, then opened a file drawer and pulled out one of the group POW photos Mitsui had taken of this man and his friends in 1943!

When this and other photographs and documents were shown to former prosecutor Robert Donihi in a 1998 visit, he exclaimed: "If only we had this evidence in 1946, we might have been able to indict the *zaibatsu.*"

Chapter 14

What is a Lifetime Worth?

FOR YEARS, ROBERT ALDRICH WOULD SIT ON THE PORCH OF HIS RETIREMENT home in the port city of St. Augustine, Florida, and watch the ships come in and out of the harbor. But he would seethe when a big cargo container ship appeared with three wavy lines on its smokestack. That was the Mitsui logo, the same wavy lines he remembered seeing every day for over two years at Mitsui Mining Company's Miike coal mining complex at Omuta, as Aldrich was being pushed and shoved into another exhausting day's work in the mine.

"Those SOBs," Aldrich would mutter quietly to his attorney, forty years later. "They still owe me money." In 1987 Aldrich, a member of the New Mexico 200th Coast Artillery and a survivor of the Bataan Death March, filed a claim for unpaid labor against Mitsui & Co. (U.S.A.) in Florida State Circuit Court. He didn't get very far, partly because Bob Aldrich was about twelve years ahead of his time. He died suddenly on Memorial Day 1988, without having told some of his closest friends about his lawsuit against Mitsui.

The judge hearing Aldrich's complaint dismissed it, citing sections of the 1951 Treaty of Peace between Japan and the Allied nations, signed on September 8, 1951, in San Francisco. The same sections of that treaty have been quoted again and again over the years by State Department officials, members of Congress, attorneys, Japanese diplomats, and just about everyone else ex-POWs have turned to in their quest for some sort of direct compensation from the Japanese organizations that exploited and abused them.

The section of the Peace Treaty most often cited is Article 14, which acknowledges that Japan should pay reparations, but "It is also recognized that the resources of Japan are not presently sufficient" to do so. Paragraph (V) (b) states:

> Except as otherwise provided in the present Treaty, the Allied
> Powers waive all reparations claims of the Allied Powers, other

claims of the Allied Powers and their nationals arising out of any actions taken by Japan and its nationals in the course of the prosecution of the war, and claims of the Allied Powers for direct military costs of occupation.[1]

Article 16 of the treaty is also frequently cited, as proof that Japanese funds were already used to compensate Allied military POWs who "Suffered undue hardships while prisoners of war of Japan." It is true that Japanese assets frozen in the United States at the outbreak of the war were used to pay military ex-POWs under the War Claims Acts of 1948 and 1952, but the POWs maintain that $1 a day for "missed meals" hardly made up for the lifelong effects of malnutrition, and $1.50 "For each day they were forced to perform labor and/or were subjected to inhumane treatment"[2] was not sufficient. Most ex-POWs received just under the $1,300 maximum allotment in the first payment, and around $1,800 in the second payment, depending on how many days they spent in captivity. The 1952 payment was authorized by Congress after the U.S. government had waived its rights to collect direct payment from Japan on behalf of its POWs.

Article 16 of the Peace Treaty called for Japan to:

> Transfer its assets and those of its nationals in countries which were neutral during the war, or which were at war with any of the Allied Powers, or at its option, the equivalent of such assets, to the International Committee of the Red Cross which shall liquidate such assets and distribute the resultant fund to appropriate national agencies, for the benefit of former prisoners of war and their families on such basis as it may determine to be equitable.[3]

But in a statement to the ICRC Conference, "The United States waived its claim to the benefit due it under the terms of Article 16."[4] The United States was the only Allied nation to do so.

Consistently overlooked by the many agencies, jurists, attorneys, and politicians discussing the 1951 Peace Treaty is the key provision offered in Article 26. Like all carefully drawn agreements, the Peace Treaty recognized that Japan's situation or behavior might change in future years, and so Article 26 of the 1951 Treaty of Peace with Japan provided for this by stating in part: "Should Japan make a peace settlement or war claims settlement with any State granting that State greater advantages than those provided by the present Treaty, those same advantages shall be extended to the parties to the present Treaty."[5]

Japan did, in fact, sign several treaties with other nations in subsequent years, which granted more favorable conditions than those agreed to by nations that had signed the 1951 treaty. Documents recently unearthed in the archives of the British Public Records Office and by this writer at the National Archives show clearly that American and British diplomats were very well aware of this fact. In 1998, Keith Martin, chairman of the Association of British Civilian Internees–Far East Region, discovered a series of internal memoranda exchanged in May and September 1955 between ministers at Britain's Foreign Office and Treasury, commenting on treaties signed by Japan with Burma in December 1954, and with Switzerland in March 1955.

The Foreign Office memorandum observes: "In agreeing to the San Francisco Treaty Her Majesty's Government waived a very large proportion of their just claims against Japan in order to avoid ruining the Japanese economy," but recommends "That we should not invoke Article 26. . . . We should not of course give any publicity to this decision." In a handwritten comment, Lord Reading, minister of state at the Foreign and Commonwealth Office, wrote: "I agree. We are at present unpopular enough with the Japanese without trying to exert further pressure which would be likely to cause the maximum of resentment for the minimum of advantage." And a Treasury official also agreed "On the general ground of foreign relations, despite the possibility of domestic political embarrassment in connection with Allied prisoners of war."[6]

Meanwhile, in June 1955 an internal memorandum circulated at the American Embassy in Tokyo, commenting on the treaty then being negotiated between the foreign ministers of Japan and the Netherlands. It is known as the Yoshida-Stikker Agreement, concerning compensation to Dutch citizens, thousands of whom were interned by the Japanese. The memorandum reads in part:

> It may be a little awkward for us to explain to American civilians who were interned by the Japanese in the Far East why they should receive no compensation if the Dutch Government succeeds in getting some compensation from Japan for Dutch civilian internees. You will recall we had a lot of explaining to do to American prisoners of war about their being cut out of the Article 16 fund.[7]

The explaining referred to involved detailed claims ex-POWs filled out, with the assistance of military personnel right after the war, listing all the personal property confiscated by the Japanese, and estimating the dollar worth of their pain and suffering. They were told that they would be entitled to hefty compensation, but the treaty agreement barred this from happening.

Otto Schwarz remembered: "We filled out long forms and listed everything we would think of. I never heard another word about it." Apparently all the original POW claims were filed in a drawer somewhere.

In 1957 Japan signed a treaty with Sweden, once again offering more favorable terms, prompting this comment from Mr. Fraleigh of the American Embassy staff in Tokyo to the State Department in Washington: "The settlement raises a question concerning the applicability of a Peace Treaty provision obliging Japan to extend to Peace Treaty signatories the same advantages as are accorded to any other governments in war claim settlements." Fraleigh then quotes from Article 26, but rationalizes that the U.S. government "Still retains the proceeds from the liquidation of Japanese assets within its borders."[8]

Clearly, renewed interest in the subject of compensation for ex-POWs should prompt a fresh look by scholars, legal experts, members of Congress, and government officials at the 1951 Treaty of Peace, as recently discovered memoranda have shed new light on deliberations within the U.S. government about the full provisions of that treaty.

Claims against individual organizations are much more clear-cut than claims against nations, a fact that ex-POWs have known for a long time. Their efforts got a real boost in January 1999, when a California Superior (state) Court ruled that a foreign-based company doing business in the state of California could be sued there, even if the basis for the claim dated back to World War II.[9] That decision, involving an Italian insurance company, prompted state lawmakers to provide a legislative framework enabling World War II slave-labor and forced-labor victims, civilian and military, to deal directly with the companies that exploited them, since so many of those companies do a significant amount of their business in California.

When state senator Tom Hayden successfully steered a landmark legislative bill through the California Senate early in 1999, ex-POW Lester Tenney was ready. Tenney, like Bob Aldrich, was a survivor of Bataan and Mitsui's coal mine at Omuta. A retired professor of finance at Arizona State University, Tenney knew about Aldrich's effort, because he had helped Aldrich calculate how much back pay, with interest, Mitsui owed him.

The Hayden bill, which became effective in July 1999, enables any World War II slave-labor or forced-labor victim to bring an action in California state court "To recover compensation for labor performed from any person who received the benefit of that labor," and extends the statute of limitations for filing such claims to the year 2010. The bill defines "compensation" as "The present value of wages and benefits that individuals should have been paid and compensation for injuries sustained in connection with the labor performed. Present value shall be calculated including interest compounded annually to date of full payment without diminution for wartime or postwar currency devaluation."[10]

This bill is what Bob Aldrich was waiting for—but his time ran out. The bill also states:

> Any Second World War slave labor victim, or heir of a Second World War slave labor victim, Second World War forced labor victim, or heir of a Second World War forced labor victim, may bring an action to recover compensation for labor performed as a Second World War slave labor victim or Second World War forced labor victim from any person or entity who received the benefit of that labor. That action may be brought in a superior court of this state, which the court shall have jurisdiction over that action until its completion or resolution."[11]

Tenney filed his claim August 12, 1999, against Mitsui Co. of Japan and New York, and the Mitsui Mining Co. About a month later, on September 13, 1999, a claim was filed in Albuquerque, New Mexico, on behalf of Frank Bigelow, Robert Dow, Harold Feiner, Edward Jackfert, John Oliver, Leo Padilla, Melvin Routt, Gap Silva, Alvin Silver, Herbert Zincke, and about 250 other ex-POWs against Kawasaki Heavy Industries, Mitsubishi, Mitsui, NKK, and Showa Denko.[12] The next morning eight ex-POW claimants appeared at a press conference in New York City, to announce the filing of the claim, tell their stories, and take questions from some fifty broadcast, print, and wire service journalists. Columbia Law School dean David Leebron reviewed the claim at the request of the *International Herald Tribune,* and told the *Tribune* he thought the suit was crafted in a way that would allow it to be heard.

"It gets around some of the most basic problems such as whether the treaty ending the war prohibited these claims," he said, adding, "Even if the claims are relatively weak from a legal point of view, they may be enough of concern both on the law and the public-relations aspect of them to suggest some settlement by the companies."[13]

Dean Leebron may have been right on target. Since the Tenney suit was filed, dozens of ex-POWs living in California, joined by fellow survivors from all over the United States, have filed similar claims in California state courts. All of the companies named do big business not only in California, but throughout the United States. The "public-relations aspect" mentioned by Dean Leebron is considerable.

For example, in addition to the container ships Bob Aldrich counted weekly in St. Augustine harbor, Mitsui operates a rolling fleet of truck container transports that travel throughout the country, to and from just about every large coast port in the United States. The company also makes a

News conference, New York City, September 13, 1999, announcing POW lawsuit against five Japanese companies. Left to right: Ex-POWs Agapito Silva (standing), Melvin Routt, and Paul Reuter (seated). THE ASSOCIATED PRESS

vitamin B$_4$ additive used in animal feed. The megacorporation is involved in real estate, chemicals, foodstuffs, machinery, lumber, steel, and electronics—a long list for a corporation that has been ranked for several years as the third largest in the world.

As mentioned earlier, in December 1998, Kawasaki Heavy Industries was awarded a $190 million contract by the Metropolitan Transit Authority of New York to supply 100 new subway cars for New York City, along with a further multimillion dollar commitment for trains and engines on the Long Island Railroad, as well as railcars for transit systems in Massachusetts and Maryland. For many years the company has built freight and tank cars for our nation's railroads. Kawasaki makes turbines for Rolls Royce engines in Boeing 777 aircraft, among others, and motors for water JetSkis and hydrofoil ferry boats. Kawasaki is probably best known for its motorcycles.

Mitsubishi's cars and trucks are everywhere, heavily advertised in print and on television. In the state where so many of its former slave laborers live, New Mexico, Mitsubishi has for several years been part owner of a copper mine in Silver City; the company also has mine holdings in several other locations. It is a large international trading company, and is Japan's largest oil company as a result of a recent merger. Mitsubishi operates lumber, electronics, construction, insurance, shipping, and textile businesses—another very long list.

Nippon Steel (Nippon Ko-Kan) is the world's largest steel company. In 1999, NKK was cited by the International Trade Commission for "dumping" steel on the U.S. market; the company promised to modify its trade practices.[14] NKK makes semiconductors and silicon wafers, among other products, and is involved in real estate and transportation worldwide.

Showa Denko, as mentioned earlier, supplies components such as magnetic alloys for many household appliances sold in the United States. The company also makes computer components, semiconductors, aluminum, and a wide range of chemical products, including ammonia, fluorocarbons, and chlorine. Its environmental and safety track records have long been a source of concern.

All in all, the companies of Japan doing business in the United States have a lot at stake, in the court of public—and consumer—opinion. In the long run, these may be more important than courts of law.

Balancing the Books

THERE IS NO DOUBT THAT JAPAN'S POSTWAR "ECONOMIC MIRACLE" WAS fueled by many factors: enterprising industrialists, $2 billion in economic aid from the United States, an extremely favorable trade climate for Japanese products, and the banning of American products from sale in Japan for several years; to name just a few.

But for Americans who were forced to work in the war production for at least forty-four Japanese companies, the haunting perception is that their slave labor also fueled the postwar prosperity of those organizations. Too often, the miraculous recovery of Japan's industries began on the backs of our prisoners of war.

The stark reality is that on the last day of World War II, nearly all of these companies were in full production at most of their locations, because they were using a full workforce of American and other Allied prisoners of war. As mentioned earlier, in some company locations, prisoners were the *only* workforce. Without them, the factory or shipyard or mine would very likely have had to shut down.

A second stark reality is that American men who survived slave labor in Japanese companies came home to a lifetime of lingering medical problems and permanent injuries caused by that labor. In what should have been the prime of their life, these survivors lost their good health forever in Japan, or somewhere else in Asia under Japanese control. They ask: Aren't they owed something by the companies that caused it to happen?

"I don't give a damn about the money; I just want them to apologize for what they did to us," Frank Bigelow declared in February 1996. For Frank, "them" means the Mitsui Mining Company, for whose Omuta managers' war production quota he lost a leg and almost lost his life.

Other ex-POWs state that just some acknowledgment, some common gesture of compensation from the companies of Japan, might help their nightmares to stop, and give them some peace of mind in their old age.

Jack Edwards put it more directly: "The Allies rebuilt Japan and Germany and Italy—nobody rebuilt our lives."[1] Maybe it was just easier for the

U.S. government to look the other way—the typical reaction of an embarrassed person.

For six decades, what happened to Americans in the Pacific and Asia during the opening months of World War II has been an embarrassment to the government, or so it would seem. It was embarrassed when the entire Army of the Pacific was killed or captured within months. It was embarrassed when the Asiatic Fleet was decimated in a matter of weeks. It was horrified and embarrassed at its powerlessness to stop the atrocities of the Bataan Death March; embarrassed at the rounding up of American civilians and its inability to retrieve most of them.

The U.S. government was frustrated—and embarrassed—that its protests, through the Swiss, about the treatment of American citizens fell on deaf Japanese ears; especially since it had served as Japan's diplomatic protector nation during three previous wars. In every way, the Japanese humiliated the United States and its people—except, thankfully, in combat.

The government was so embarrassed at the condition of liberated prisoners that it made some of them wait until nightfall to disembark from a ship in San Francisco—after the welcoming crowds and bands and politicians had left, and there was only a bus with darkened windows to whisk them to Letterman Hospital.

What is more, U.S. intelligence officers told many returning ex-POWs not to talk about their treatment by the Japanese, or to discuss their POW experiences in newspaper and radio interviews, unless they received clearance from the military. Some were even ordered to sign papers to that effect.

Melvin Routt said the verbal instructions he received were so intimidating that for many years he refrained from describing to doctors his treatment as a POW, which had caused many of his postwar ailments.

Roy Gentry was reminded, as he prepared to be interviewed by his hometown Indianapolis radio station, not to discuss specifics of his captivity. He remembered repeatedly saying to the interviewer, "I can't discuss that."

James Brennan and a fellow ex-POW from Pawtucket, Rhode Island, had been contacted by the *Providence Journal,* which sent a reporter to meet their ship in San Francisco. But a military intelligence officer entered the room and terminated the interview.

Several ex-POWs reported that when they returned home and tried to discuss their captivity with friends and relatives, they were met with stares of disbelief. Very little information about POWs had appeared in the local press during the war. Soon, ex-POWs stopped mentioning it altogether.

The wartime suppression of information and the postwar "gag" orders many ex-POWs received served to underscore their impression that their experience was something the government wanted to forget—and wanted the American people to forget.

CINCPAC-CINCPOA

5 September 1945

SUBJECT: Publicity in Connection with Liberated Prisoners of War.

1. In conformity with directive of the War Department Chief of Staff contained in dispatch WARX-59052 (031929(of 3 September 1945, which amends AG Letter 383.6 of 24 March 45, OB-S-B-M subject: Publicity Concerning Evaders, Escapers, and Prisoners of War, the following is published:

2. Released prisoners of war may release stories of their experiences after clearance with theater Bureau of Public Relations headquarters or War Department Bureau of Public Relations with the following exceptions:

(a) There will not be published in any form whatsoever, or either directly or indirectly communicated to press, radio or any persons except to representatives of the appropriate theater intelligence section, as designated by theater commanders or to American military attaches or to the AC of S-G2, WDGS any details or references concerning the following:

(1) Unannounced organizations which have assisted evaders and escapers or methods used by these organizations.

(2) Any means of identifying helpers, such as names, pictures, descriptions, etc.

(3) Evasion and Escape equipment and special intelligence activities within the prison camps.

3. Commanding officers will be responsible for instructing all subject personnel in the provisions of this directive, and insuring that the attached certificate be executed.

SECURITY CERTIFICATE

I certify that I have read and fully understand all the provisions of the Directive of the Secretary of War as is printed on this sheet, and will at ALL TIMES hereafter comply fully therewith.

I understand that disclosure of secret military information to unauthorized persons will make me liable to disciplinary action for failure to safeguard such information.

I realize that it is my duty during my military service, and later as a civilian, to take all possible precautions to prevent disclosure, by word of mouth or otherwise, of military information of this nature.

Name (print) EDGAR N. LANGLEY   Signed Edgar N. Langley

Rank PFC   A.S.N.   Date Sept. 13, 1945 Place Hosp. #103 GUAM

Unit Wake Island Det.-1st Def. Bn.   Witness C.E. Pruitt 2LT USMCR

POW "gag order." This copy is signed by Edgar M. Langley. Identical orders were supplied by Frank Bigelow and Terence Kirk. This is the clearest of the copies obtained by the author. COLLECTION OF UNITED STATES MARINE CORPS HISTORICAL CENTER

The government told the Japanese it would make them pay after the war, and a few did, with their lives—or with "life" sentences, none of which lasted longer than a decade. In 1950 investigations of war criminals in both Germany and Japan were ordered to be stopped by Washington because we were helping to rebuild those nations' economies, and it simply wasn't in our best interests to continue reminding them of their war crimes. By 1958, Sugamo Prison was closed because it was empty. All of the convicted Japanese war criminals had been released.

In its effort to avoid embarrassing the Japanese in postwar years and in cautioning Americans against "Japan bashing," it seems as if the U.S. government, perhaps inadvertently, has instead indulged in "survivor bashing." Beginning with the homecoming orders to ex-POWs not to discuss their captivity and continuing in repeated rebuffs by the State Department to ex-POWs and members of Congress seeking a means of compensation from the Japanese on their behalf, the government has made ex-prisoners of the Japanese feel that their experience was not as worthy of redress as that of German slave-labor victims, or people of Japanese anscestry interned in the Unted States during the war years. In many ways, for over half a century, Pacific ex-prisoners of war have been made to feel like the forgotten victims of World War II.

But no amount of suppression has broken the spirit, or the patriotism, of these survivors. As one general remarked about them: "When death was preferable, these men dared to live."[3] And now, at long last, it appears as if their determination may be paying off.

As this book went to press, momentum was gaining in courts, in state legislatures, and in Congress to recognize that indeed, these men who somehow survived the darkest chapters of the Pacific War deserve recognition—and compensation.

In the ledger of every Japanese company that used prisoners of war during World War II, there is a debit column written in invisible ink, headed: "Slave Labor, 1942–45." Now we have begun to sprinkle lemon juice on that column and the numbers have started to reappear. This debt needs to be paid. The honorable business of each company requires no less.

Do Japan's companies really expect the world to hold them to a different, lower standard of accountability than the companies of Europe? And can the State Department expect American ex-prisoners of war to accept continued rebuffs, after their own government has been so active in helping victims of German slave labor get justice?

It is this writer's hope that when the subject of unpaid debts to ex-prisoners of war is again brought up in their boardrooms, this time the companies of Japan will be proud of their response, instead of continuing to be ashamed of their past.

Appendix A

Japanese companies known to have used American prisoners between 1942 and 1945.

Source: Official Japanese Government list of companies using POW forced labor in World War II.

Asano Dockyard
Electric-Chemical Company
Fujinagata Shipbuilding, Kobe
Furukawa Mining, Omine Machi
Hitachi Shipbuilding
Hokkai Electric Chemical
Hokkaido Coal (Sorachi Mining Co.)
Imperial Special Copper Works,
    Noetsu
Ishihara Industries, Narumi
Kajima Coal, Ohnoura
Kawaminami Shipbuilding, Yahata
Kawasaki Heavy Industries, Kobe
Kinkaseki Copper Mine, Formosa
Kobe Stevedore, Kobe
Kumagai Enggr. Co.
Manshu Leather, Mukden,
    Manchuria
Manshu Machinery, Mukden
Manshu Tent
Meiji Mining
Mitsubishi Heavy Industries
Mitsubishi Mining Co.
Mitsubishi Chemical
Mitsui Industries

Mitsui Mining
Moji Transportation Association
Namura Shipyards
Niigata Iron & Steel
Niigata Transport, Kawasaki
Nippon Express
Nippon Ko-Kan (Japan Iron Co.)
Nippon Metallurgy
Nippon Mining
Nippon Soda
Nippon Steel Pipe
Nippon Vehicles
Nisshin Mill
Nisshin Oil
Nittetsu Mining
Ohsaka Shipbuilding
Radio Tokyo (government-
    operated)
Shinetsu Chemicals
Showa Electrical Engineering
Showa Electrode (Showa Denko)
Sorachi Mining Co.
Sumitomo Mining
Taihoku Locomotive Works, Taiwan
Tobashima Construction Co.

Tokyo-Shibaura Electric
Tsuruga Stevedore, Osaka
Tsurumi Shipbuilding

Yawata Iron Works, Ohasi
Yodogawa Steel

List in formation as of April 2000.

Note: Many companies used prisoner labor at more than one site.

Appendix B

List of Japanese-owned merchant ships transporting prisoners of war 1942–45.

Name of ship	Built by	Registered owner
Amagi Maru	Yokohama Dock Co.	Nippon Yusen K.K.

Amagi Maru Soerabaja, Java, to Ceram Island, April 1943–2,000 POWs.

Argentina Maru   Mitsubishi Shipbuilding   Osaka Shosen K.K. (Mitsui OKS Lines, Ltd.)
Guam to Japan, January 10, 1942–400 POWs.

Arisan (Armisan) Maru   Mitsui   Mitsui Bussan Kaisha Ltd.
Manila to Japan–1,800 U.S. POWs–torpedoed, 8 survived: 5 escaped on a life raft to China; 3 taken by Japanese to Formosa.

Asaka Maru   Mitsubishi   Nippon Yusen K.K.
Singapore to Japan, July 4, 1942–700 POWs—shipwrecked, most survived; transferred via Formosa to Japan.

Brasil Maru   Kawasaki Heavy Industries   OnoShoji Gomei (Mgr.)
Philippines to Japan, December 27, 1944–1,105 POW survivors of *Oryoko Maru*—ship attacked in Formosa Harbor, fewer than 300 survivors; ship eventually arrived in Japan.

Clide Maru (not listed in Lloyd's Registry)
Manila to Moji, Japan, August 1943–500 U.S. POWs.

Dai Nichi (Dainiti) Maru   Mitsubishi   Itaya Shosen K.K.
Singapore to Japan, October 30, 1942–500 POWs–arrived November 24.

England Maru   Kawasaki   Yamashita Kisen K.K.
Singapore to Taiwan, 1942–1,100 POWs aboard.

Enoura (Enzyu) Maru   Canadian-built   Okada Gumi K.K.
Attacked in Takeo harbor, Formosa, January 8, 1945—1,311 POWs, 619 survived; transferred to *Brasil Maru* to Japan, 300 survivors.

Name of ship	Built by	Registered owner
Fukaye Maru	British-built	Mitsubishi Kogyo

Singapore to Formosa, August 16, 1942–mostly civilians.

Fukuichi Maru	Kawasaki	Tokai Yenyo Gyogo K.K.

Moji, Japan, to Manchuria, November 9, 1944—354 high-ranking military and civilian POWs.

Hakusan Maru	Mitsubishi	Nippon Yusen K.K.

Keelung, Formosa, to Japan—700 POWs off the *Asaka Maru.*

Haru (Haruna) Maru	Mitsubishi	Nippon Yusen K.K.

Manila to Formosa, October 3, 1944–1,100 U.S. POWs, put in two holds, filled with coal and horse manure; 60 died en route.

Hohuku (Fuku) Maru	Kawasaki	Kokusai Kisen

Manila, September 20, 1944–1,289 POWs, British/Dutch–sunk in Subic Bay, 63 POWs survived; transfered to *Oryoko Maru;* also sunk.

Junyo (Junyei) Maru	Aoki Shipbuilding	Wada Kenzo

Batavia, Java, September 15, 1944–2,200 POWs: 14 U.S., 1,700 Dutch/British/Australian, 4,320 Javanese conscript laborers, 506 Indonesian POWs—torpedoed in Java Sea, 5,640 men died, 15 survived: greatest maritime disaster in history.

Kachidoki Maru	NY Shipbuilding, Camden N.J.	

Captured December 1941, renamed; sunk September 13, 1944— 900 POWs, 360 survived.

Kamakura Maru	Yokohama Dock Co.	Nippon Yusen K.K.

Singapore to Japan, November 29, 1942–2,200 POWs, 500 U.S.

Kibibi Maru	U.S.-built	

Whaling ship, September 16, 1944—received 656 survivors of *Rakuyu Maru, Kachidoki Maru;* arrived Moji September 28, 8 died en route.

Kinai Maru	Mitsubishi	Osaka Shosen

Batavia, Java, to Singapore, October 10, 1942—1,200 POWs including Australian Pioneers and USS *Houston*/HMAS *Perth* survivors.

Name of ship	Built by	Registered owner

Kuramasan Maru   Mitsui   Mitsui Bussan Kaisha
Soerabaja, Java, to Ambon, April 22, 1943–1,500 POWs.

Kyokko Maru   Taihoku Steamship Co.   Yamashita Kisen
Singapore to Moji, April 26, 1943–1,500 POWs.

Lisbon Maru   Yokohama Dock Co.   Nippon Yusen K.K.
Hong Kong to Japan, September 25, 1942–1,816 British POWs—
torpedoed, 970 survivors continued to Japan on the *Shinsei Maru;*
6 survivors escaped to China and eventually the United States.

Matu Maru (Canadian Inventor)   Shimizu, Nagasaki   Matsumoto Sojiro
Manila to Japan, July 24, 1943-August 9–500 POWs;
Manila to Japan, July 1944–1,000 U.S. POWs, sixty-three days at sea.

Mayebassi Maru ?
No Lloyd's listing, but Australian army captain Harry Bishop was on
board and wrote account of voyage; also carried USS *Houston* and HMAS
Perth survivors, from Singapore to Moulmein, Burma.

Montevideo Maru   Mitsubishi   Osaka Shosen K.K.
Rabaul to Japan, torpedoed January 7, 1942 off Luzon–1,050 POWs
and civilians, 3 crew survived; Japan failed to report loss to ICRC or
Allies; postwar discovery, charges at Tokyo Trials.

Nagato Maru   Kawasaki   Nippon Yusen
Manila to Japan, November 7, 1942–1,700 U.S. POWs, 7 died at
sea; 150 dying were left on docks at Moji on Thanksgiving Day and
never seen again.

Nissyo Maru   Mitsubishi   Syowa Tanken K.K.
Manila to Japan, July 17, 1944–1,500 U.S. POWs.

Nitta Maru   Mitsubishi   Nippon Yusen K.K.
Wake Island to China via Yokohama, January 12, 1942–489 POWs,
746 civilians; 5 beheaded for "misbehaving."

Nittai Maru   British built   Nissan Kasai
Singapore to Moulmein, Burma, January 10, 1943–1,000 POWs—
sunk by British planes, most POWs were rescued.

Name of ship	Built by	Registered owner
Noto Maru	Mitsubishi	Nippon Yusen

Manila to Japan, September 1944–1,035 POWs.

Oryoko Maru	Mitsubishi	Osaka Shosen

Manila to Japan, December 14, 1944—1,619 U.S. POWs.—sunk by U.S. planes; 1,122 died, some when second ship was bombed.

Rio de Janiero Maru	Mitsubishi	Osaka Shosen

Makassar to Batavia, Java, October 2, 1943–200 POWs.

Rokyo (Rokko) Maru	Mitsubishi	Toakaien K.K.

Ryukyu Maru	Mitsubishi	Dairen Kise

Singapore to Japan, September 1944–torpedoed September 12–1,318 POWs, Australian, British, U.S.; 1,159 drowned, 157 rescued by submarine.

Shinsei Maru	Ohara, Osaka	Chosen Kisen K.K.

Shanghai to Japan October 5, 1942–840 British POWs from *Lisbon Maru*

Shinyo Maru	Tsurumi Shipbuilding.	Suisan Koshu Japanese Govt. Dept. Agri/Forest

Philippines to Japan, September 3, 1944–750 U.S. POWs— torpedoed, 667 died.

Singapore Maru	Kawasaki	Kobe Sanbashi KK

Singapore to Japan, late 1942; in 20 days, of 1,100 POWs aboard, 60 died at sea and 180 died within weeks of arrival.

Suez Maru	Uraga Dock Co.	Kuribayashi Syosen KK

Ambon—1,150 POWs—torpedoed in Java Sea November 29, 1943–548 POWs, all drowned.

Taga Maru	Tsurumi Shipbuilding	Hinode Kisen

Manila to Japan, September 1943–850 U.S. POWs, 70 died on board.

Tango Maru	Mitsubishi	Nippon Yusen KK

Java to Japan, February 1944—torpedoed, 3,500 POWs, 3,000 died.

Name of ship	Built by	Registered owner
Thames Maru	Kawasaki	Kawasaki Kisen KK

Singapore, May 5, 1943–2,150 Indian/Indonesian POWs, 200 died.

Tohoku Maru	Senkyo Kaisha	Aomori Shosen KK

Formosa to Japan, June 1944—torpedoed near Nagasaki, 772 POWs, 43 U.S., 559 died, 29 U.S.

Tottori Maru	Glasgow, Russell Co.	Nippon Yusen KK

Captured from English at Singapore; Manila to Japan via Pusan, Korea, October 8, 1942–1,930 POWs, 10 died at sea.

Toyama Maru	Mitsubishi	Ono Shoji Gomei Kaisha

Hong Kong to Moji, 1944–500 Canadian POWs.

Umeda (Ume)Maru	Kawasaki	Tochiki Shoji KK

Manila to Japan, November 7, 1942–1,500 U.S. POWs, 15 died at sea.

Yoshida Maru renamed *Yosida*	Uraga Dock Co.	Yamashita Kisen

Batavia, Java, to Singapore, October 1942–3,000 POWs transferred to *Dainiti Maru*.

Primary owners of POW transport ships:

Nippon Yusen (Japan Mail & Steamship Co. Ltd., a subsidiary of Mitsubishi), Tokyo.
President in 1941: N. Ohtani

Osaka Shosen (Osaka Mercantile Steamship Co.), Mitsui OSK Lines, Ltd.
Director in 1941: T. Mitaya

Kawasaki Dockyard Co.
President in 1941: Vice Admiral Y. Yoshioka

Yamashita Kisen, Kobe
President in 1941: K. Yamashita

Note: Official Japanese government records list forty-eight Asia-Pacific Japanese merchant vessels that successfully transported Allied POWs between 1942 and 1945, and an additional twenty-one that were sunk, for a total of sixty-nine. Of these, forty-three were registered in *Lloyd's Ship Registry,* and they are listed here, identifying shipbuilding companies and owner/operators. Two ships not listed with Lloyds, but known to have transported POWs, the *Clide Maru* and the *Mayebassi Maru,* are also included. Some ships not registered with Lloyd's may have been misidentified by surviving ex-POWs or by researchers. Dutch ex-POW Van Waterford (*Prisoners of the Japanese in World War II* [Jefferson, N.C.: McFarland, 1994]) was one of fifteen survivors of the *Junyo Maru,* and spent considerable time compiling the list of fifty-six POW transport ships, using as a primary source E. Bartlett Kerr, *Surrender and Survival* (New York: William Morrow, 1985). Also Clay and Joan Blair, in *Return From the River Kwai* (New York: Simon and Schuster, 1979) located and interviewed a considerable number of surviving POWs from torpedoed ships. I have gathered personal accounts from at least fifty ex-POWs. Shawnee Brittan, whose father perished on the *Arisan Maru,* interviewed all eight survivors (1,792 U.S. POWs drowned) and created a videotape of that voyage. I also interviewed a survivor of that ship, Glenn Oliver, in May 1996.

Appendix C

Official Japanese government list of successful POW transports, 1942–1945.

Transport	Departure	Arrival	POWs Alive
1942			
Shinsei Maru	Shanghai	Moji	930
Tottori Maru	Manila	Osaka	1,992
Shoun Maru	Manila	Kobe	50
Tenshin Maru	Manila	Moji	50
Tofuku Maru	Singapore	Moji	1,200
England Maru	Singapore	Takao	1,100
Dainichi Maru	Takao	Moji	1,200
Shonan Maru	Singapore	Moji	1,100
Miike Maru	Shanghai	Moji	70
Nagato Maru	Manila	Moji	1,482
Asama Maru	Molucas	Nagasaki	1,000
1943			
Kamakura Maru	Singapore	Nagasaki	1,700
Yuzan Maru	Manila	Takao	6
Aki Maru	Singapore	Takao	74
Tatsuta Maru	Hong Kong	Nagasaki	1,200
Hawaii Maru	Singapore	Moji	1,000
Kyokko Maru	Singapore	Moji	1,500
Wales Maru	Singapore	Moji	900
Clide Maru	Manila	Moji	500
Banryo Maru	Hong Kong	Osaka	501
Muroto	Shanghai	Osaka	520
Kohho Maru	Manila	Moji	883
Uslii Maru	Singapore	Moji	506
Matsue Maru	Singapore	Moji	1,155
Hawaii Maru	Singapore	Moji	1,229

Transport	Departure	Arrival	POWs Alive
1944			
Toyama Maru	Hong Kong	Moji	500
Kenwa Maru	Manila	Moji	200
Taihoki Maru	Manila	Osaka	300
No. 5028	Hong Kong	Osaka	220
Kosuei Maru	Singapore	Moji	505
Hioki Maru	Singapore	Moji	400
Teiwa Maru	Singapore	Moji	1,123
Tamahoku Maru	Singapore	Nagasaki	212
Sekiho Maru	Manila	Moji	1,021
Hokusen Maru	Manila	Moji	150
Rashin Maru	Singapore	Moji	1,065
Hakushika Maru	Singapore	Moji	609
Hakusan Maru	Singapore	Moji	690
Nissho Maru	Manila	Moji	1,539
Noto Maru	Manila	Moji	1,036
Oryoku Maru	Chilung	Moji	259
Kibitsu Maru	Singapore	Moji	656
Hokusen Maru	Manila	Takao	1,170
1945			
Brazil Maru	Takao	Moji	581
Melbourne Maru	Takao	Moji	500
Enoshima Maru	Chilung	Moji	564
Awa Maru	Singapore	Moji	525
Taiko Maru	Chilung	Moji	702
		Total	36,378

Official Japanese government list of shipwrecked POW transports, 1942–1945.

Ship	Date Sunk	POWs Overboard	Survivors
Montevideo Maru	July 1, 1942	1,045	0
Lisbon Maru	October 1, 1942	1,816	977
Moji Maru	January 15, 1943	1,001	992
Nichimei Maru	January 15, 1943	1,000	947
Suez Maru	November 29, 1943	548	0
Chuyo (Navy)	December 4, 1943	20	0
Ogajima Maru	January 20, 1944	7	0
Katori (Navy)	February 17, 1944	8	0
Kokai Maru	February 21, 1944	27	0
Eiho Maru	April 30, 1944	1	0
Tamahoko Maru	June 24, 1944	772	212
Chiran Maru	June 26, 1944	720	543
Shinyo Maru	September 7, 1944	750	0
Kachidoki Maru	September 12, 1944	950	520
Rakuyu Maru	September 12, 1944	1,317	136 (159)
Junyo Maru	September 18, 1944	2,200	723
Toyofuku Maru	September 21, 1944	1,287	383
Arisan Maru	October 24, 1944	1,782	4 (5)
Navy submarine	November 29, 1944	2	0
Oryoko Maru	December 14, 1944	1,619	1,311
Asaka Maru	1944	709	690
Enoura Maru	January 9, 1945	1,311	619
Tenryo Maru	May 29, 1945	3	0
	Totals	18,901	8,048

Appendix E

Some additional documents of interest mentioned in the text.

Document No. 2690

TO: Chief of POW Information Office, Tokyo

FROM: Taiwan Army Chief of Staff
        Radio #854
        2 April 1942

        Reference Radio #165.

        Reply to POW Information Office Radio #165

        We will use the POW's principally as laboring power for Taiwan
agricultural production and on another hand as material for education
and guidance of local islanders. For this we would like for the time
being about two or three thousand British and American POW's. (Here-
ever, informal consultation has been completed on this matter with the
Hong Kong Governor-Generalship.

Chopped by:

C. of S. HIGUCHI and Chief-of-Section-in-Charge, TANAKA and for the
staff section by HIRAI. Checked by or for the C. G.

(Translator's note: On the margin is written, "The Taiwan Governor-
                    Generalship also concurs").

        I hereby certify that this is a true translation of a radio
on page 2 of Taiwan Army H.Q. Staff Files concerning POW's Vol. 1,
2 April 1942 to 24 August 1942.

                            Signed: Stephen H. Green
                                     STEPHEN H. GREEN

        This is Exhibit marked "C" referred to in the Affidavit of
JAMES THOMAS NEHEMIAH CROSS.

        Sworn before me this 19th day of September 1946.

                            /s/ P. A. L. Vine

                                 Major, R.M.

Radio message of April 2, 1942, from Tokyo to Japanese Army chief of staff on Taiwan regarding treatment and deployment of prisoners of war.

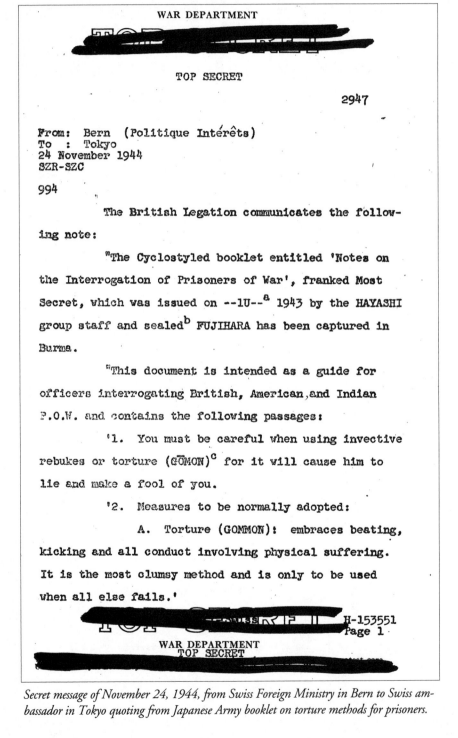

TOP SECRET

2947

From: Bern (Politique Intérêts)
To : Tokyo
24 November 1944
SZR-SZC

994

          The British Legation communicates the follow-
ing note:

          "The Cyclostyled booklet entitled 'Notes on
the Interrogation of Prisoners of War', franked Most
Secret, which was issued on --1U--[a] 1943 by the HAYASHI
group staff and sealed[b] FUJIHARA has been captured in
Burma.

          "This document is intended as a guide for
officers interrogating British, American, and Indian
P.O.W. and contains the following passages:

          '1. You must be careful when using invective
rebukes or torture (GŌMON)[c] for it will cause him to
lie and make a fool of you.

          '2. Measures to be normally adopted:

          A. Torture (GOMMON): embraces beating,
kicking and all conduct involving physical suffering.
It is the most clumsy method and is only to be used
when all else fails.'

H-153551
Page 1

WAR DEPARTMENT
TOP SECRET

*Secret message of November 24, 1944, from Swiss Foreign Ministry in Bern to Swiss am-
bassador in Tokyo quoting from Japanese Army booklet on torture methods for prisoners.*

WAR DEPARTMENT

███████████████████████

TOP SECRET

(Note: This passage is specially marked
in text.)

'When violent torture is used change interrogation officer and it is beneficial if new officer
questions in sympathetic fashion.

B. Threats

1. As a hint of physical discomforts
come, e.g., murder, torture, starving, deprivation of
sleep, (?solitary?) confinement, etc.

2. (?As mental?) discomforts come,
e.g., (?the threat that he?) will not receive same
treatment as other prisoner of war; in event of exchange
of prisoners, he will be kept till last; he will be
forbidden to send letters, will be forbidden to inform
his home that he is a P.O.W., etc.'

"The British Ministry want Mr. GORGE to bring
these extracts to the notice of the Japanese authorities;
Mr. GORGE should point out that the Japanese government
recently indignantly denied that they used torture. (See
your wire #790[d].)

███████████████████████ H-153551
Page 2

WAR DEPARTMENT ██████████

WAR DEPARTMENT

TOP SECRET

"It is presumed, therefore, that these instructions which envisage the use of torture when interrogating
P.O.W. were issued without the knowledge of the Japanese
government. The British government, therefore, expect
that Japan will not only cancel these instructions, but
will punish the person or persons who issued them without
authority.[e]"

Please make the démarches which have been requested and wire --2U--

a - A date.

b - As in text.

c - GŌMON or GOMMON - Japanese for "third degree".

d - Not available.

e - Quoted portion is in English.

Inter 24 Nov 44 (1)   Swiss   H-153551
Rec'd 25 Nov 44   Page 3
Trans 1418 28 Nov 44 (3816-s)

WAR DEPARTMENT

TOP SECRET

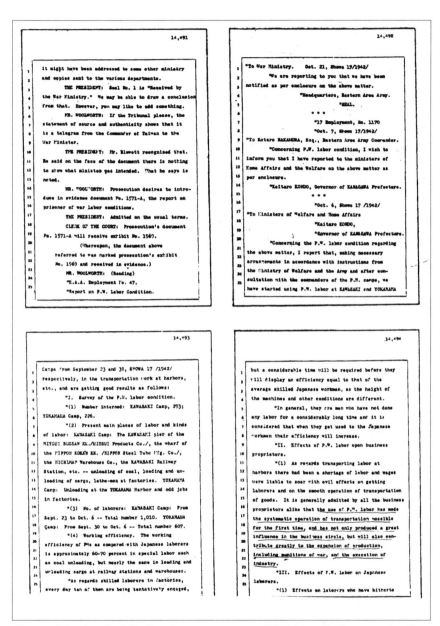

Report of October 6, 1942, from Japanese governor of Kanagawa Prefecture on benefits to companies of POW labor. (Pages from transcript of Tokyo War Crimes Trials.)

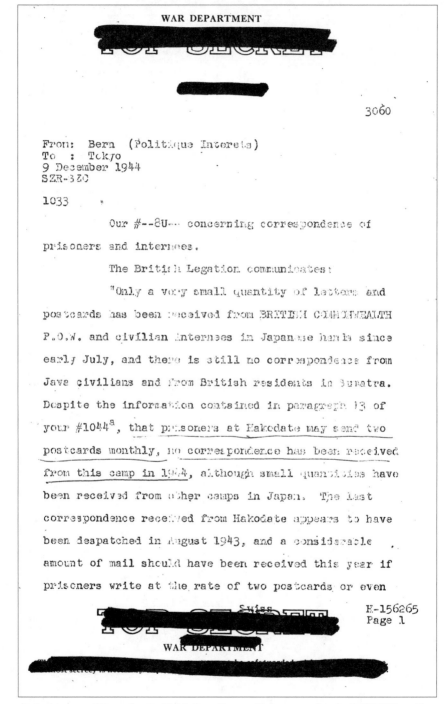

WAR DEPARTMENT

3060

From: Bern (Politique Intérets)
To : Tokyo
9 December 1944
SZR-320

1033

Our #--8U--- concerning correspondence of
prisoners and internees.

The British Legation communicates:

"Only a very small quantity of letters and
postcards has been received from BRITISH COMMONWEALTH
P.O.W. and civilian internees in Japanese hands since
early July, and there is still no correspondence from
Java civilians and from British residents in Sumatra.
Despite the information contained in paragraph 13 of
your #1044[a], that prisoners at Hakodate may send two
postcards monthly, no correspondence has been received
from this camp in 1944, although small quantities have
been received from other camps in Japan. The last
correspondence received from Hakodate appears to have
been despatched in August 1943, and a considerable
amount of mail should have been received this year if
prisoners write at the rate of two postcards or even

Swiss   E-156265
                                                                       Page 1

WAR DEPARTMENT

Swiss message of December 9, 1944, from Bern to Tokyo regarding lack of POW mail.

WAR DEPARTMENT

~~████████████████████~~

TOP SECRET

one a month, and correspondence is duly forwarded.

"The British Ministry would therefore be glad
if Mr. CORGE would renew representations as regards:

A) Definite quota of outgoing mail to be
allowed everywhere to BRITISH COMMONWEALTH P.O.W. and
civilian internees, and to be despatched regularly;

B) Complete lack of mail from Java civilians,
and from British residents in Sumatra; and

C) Position outlined above as regards
Hakodate."

Intervene, (?make demarches?) requested, and
cable result.

a — H-147574.

~~████████~~

WAR DEPARTMENT

~~████████████████████~~

SRA

WAR DEPARTMENT

14601

From: Tokyo (NERNS (VICE-CHIEF, GEN. STAFF))
To: Budapest (RIKUGUN)
12 December 1944

547

PART 1 *

Propaganda notice #103.

1st. On the 7th in the Mukden raid by B-29's
the prisoner of war shelter was hit, causing about
4 deaths. In the future please propagandize the fact
that such indiscriminant bombing will result in self-
destruction of the enemy.

* - Only part available.

Inter 13 Dec 44 (1)   Japanese   D 8546
Rec'd 13 Dec 44
Trans 15 Dec 44

Secret message of December 12, 1944, from vice-chief general staff of Japanese Army to attaché in Budapest about making propaganda use of the POW camp at Mukden, Manchuria, being hit during a B-29 air raid.

AUG-20-1997 17:00 FROM CTRL BK SERVICES TO 1749 P.02

OFFICE CORRESPONDENCE

DATE April 24, 1944

To Mr. Cameron

FROM D. J. Liddy

SUBJECT:

As a result of discussions between the Treasury Department and Swiss authorities dealing with the transfer of funds from this country to Switzerland for humanitarian purposes, we have opened a new dollar account on our books designated "Banque Nationale Suisse Account T" and we, as fiscal agent of the United States, requested the Banque Nationale Suisse in our cable No. 223 dated April 20, 1944 to open a Swiss franc account on its books designated "Federal Reserve Bank of New York Account No. 4". These accounts were opened on April 22, 1944.

COPY

sg

FEDERAL RESERVE BANK
OF NEW YORK

OFFICE CORRESPONDENCE

DATE July 31, 1944

TO Mr. Kelley

FROM B. E. Webber

SUBJECT:

On April 22, 1944 you opened an account on your books designated Banque Nationale Suisse Special Account "T". Mr. Liddy has instructed that the quotation marks be deleted in the name of the account. Will you, accordingly, see to it that the present statement and all subsequent statements show the designation of the account

Banque Nationale Suisse
Special Account T

Interoffice memoranda of April 24, 1944, and July 31, 1944, from files of Federal Reserve Bank of New York discussing creation of secret relief fund bank accounts.

WAR DEPARTMENT

483

From: Bangkok (SIEGENTHALER)
To: Bern
6 October 1944
SZB

378.

    My #359[a].

    Funds are exhausted. Please speed up
remittance. (Your #233).[b]

    On October 6 in #45[c] I cabled GORGE:

    "On 19 September the Department authorized
a transfer of 500,000 for me via TOKYO for the
relief program for war prisoners. Because of
exhausted cash funds I have to discontinue the
program (."?).

    I therefore request intercession with Japanese
authorities so that transfer will be speeded up.

a - Not available.
b - SMM 7976.
c - Available if requested. Highly imperfect text.

Inter 8 Oct 44   (92)   Swiss   #146610
Rec'd 17 Oct 44
Trans 2025 20 Oct 44   (10849-r)

TOP SECRET

TOP SECRET

WAR DEPARTMENT

**This sheet of paper and all of its contents must be safeguarded with the greatest care.
Utmost secrecy is necessary to prevent drying up this sort of vital intelligence at its source.**

Message of October 6, 1944, from Swiss chargé d'affaires in Bangkok to Foreign Ministry in Bern stating he has no funds left for relief supplies.

SCHWEIZERISCHE NATIONALBANK
BANQUE NATIONALE SUISSE
BANCA NAZIONALE SVIZZERA ⊹

Bundesplatz 1	Telefon 031 312 02 11
	Telefax 031 312 19 53
3003 Bern	Telex 911 310 snb ch

Mrs Linda G. Holmes

United States

Your reference:

Our reference: CR

Zurich, July 01, 1997

Yokohama Specie Bank Accounts at the Swiss National Bank

Dear Mrs Holmes,

Referring to the fax you sent to our Governor on June 16th, 1997, we can give you the following information related to the accounts that the Yokohama Specie Bank (YSB) had at the Swiss National Bank (SNB).

The Swiss banking law requires to keep the book entries of an account for a period of 10 years. Hence, those related to the YSB accounts were destroyed a long time ago. Nevertheless, a brief investigation into the records of our Governing Board has permitted us to partially trace out the evolution of the YSB accounts at the SNB.

- The YSB opened two accounts at SNB after a clearing settlement was reached (August 17th 1944) between Switzerland and Japan in order to funnel U.S. and British governments' help to their POW held by Japan. In rough outline, the funds were transferred according to the following steps :

  1. The US government paid dollars into the SBN account at the Fed in New York.

  2. The SNB paid the equivalent in Swiss francs (SFR) into one of the two YSB accounts at the SNB in Berne.

  3. The YSB paid the equivalent in yen into the account of the Swiss Legation at the YSB in Tokyo.

  4. The yens should have been used to pay for POW relief packages under the supervision of the International Committee of the Red Cross (ICRC).

  The first three steps were executed simultaneously and were not a matter of concern. Regarding the forth one, it happened that Japan refused to allow the ICRC access to POW camps in Asia and diverted part of the aid.

- The YSB accounts at the SNB were opened in August 1944. In January 1945, they amounted to SFR 30 million. In August 1945, the Japanese assets in Switzerland were

Letter of July 1, 1997, to the author from Swiss National Bank representatives giving an accounting of the wartime secret relief funds.

SNB
BNS✛

---

blocked. At that time, the YSB accounts had reached SFR 60 million. Moreover, the Japanese Legation held also an account at the SNB which amounted to SFR 9 million.

According to Swiss diplomatic documents, the Allies were regularly informed about the evolution of the transfer payments. When Switzerland handed over its role as a defender of the Allied interests in Japan at the end of WWII, an accounting supervision was carried out and the corresponding archive material transferred to the Allies.

- The liquidation of the Japanese possessions at the SNB (the YSB accounts and the account of the Japanese Legation in Berne) were carried out in several steps, all of them with the consent of the allied governments and the YSB liquidators in Japan.

    – In February 1948, the account of the Japanese Legation was liquidated. SFR 6,5 million were transferred to the Allies and SFR 2,5 million were kept by the Swiss government in provision for Swiss claims against Japan until a settlement between Switzerland and Japan would have been reached.

    – In June 1949, SFR 10 million of YSB accounts were transferred to the ICRC.

    – In July 1952, SFR 4,3 million of YSB accounts were transferred to the British Legation in compensation for POW help diverted by Japan during WWII.

    – In March 1955, a settlement was reached between Japan and Switzerland. The Swiss government kept SFR 13,5 million to compensate for Swiss claims against Japan. The remainder (SFR 33 million) was set free. It should have been transferred to the ICRC, according to the Treaty of San Francisco.

We hope that this information will be useful for your research. Some documents related to the role of Switzerland in the funnelling of POW help have been published in „*Les documents diplomatiques suisses*". Another useful source of information would be the Swiss Confederation Archives in Berne. We are also aware that a closer look in our archives could bring more information on the subject. As you know, our archives have been opened to researchers since the beginning of the eighties and we are willing to make them available to you.

Yours sincerely,
BANQUE NATIONALE SUISSE

Vincent Crettol   Enzo Rossi

WAR DEPARTMENT
~~TOP SECRET ULTRA~~

2575

From: Bern (Politique)
To : Washington (Swiss Legation)
3 November 1945

1060

On 17 August 1944 we concluded with the Japanese
Government a clearing agreement of an absolutely confidential
nature, in accordance with which 40 per cent of the franc
payments by the British and American governments for prisoners
of war and internees in Japan are utilized for the transfer of
Swiss claims in Japen, and 60 per cent are at the free disposal
of the Japanese Government.

The account for the transfer of Swiss claims shows a
balance of 14 million francs. After Japan's capitulation
Minister GORGE had come to an agreement with the Japanese
Government to transfer via this account the savings, and the
expenses for the homeward voyage, of the members of the Swiss
colony, in return for the release of corresponding sums for
the repatriation of Japanese.

After the Allied assumption of control in Japan,
Headquarters, to be sure, did declare the retention of clearing
to be incompatible with Japan's present position, but

Swiss
~~TOP SECRET ULTRA~~
WAR DEPARTMENT

H-215101

Page 1

Secret message from the Swiss Foreign Ministry in Bern to the Swiss Legation in Washington discussing intention to use some of the relief funds for repatriation expenses of Swiss nationals.

nevertheless [it] had GORGE put in a request for permission
to transfer $1,400 for the voyage and $800 for the purchase
of necessities in behalf of each individual returning home,
which [request] the military authority forwarded to the
American Treasury with a recommendation. We request you to
bring the matter up for discussion with the State Department
immediately and as far as possible to give it your urgent
support.

We are willing to adjust the clearing rate of exchange
of 1 franc equals 1 yen to the new establishment of the dollar-
yen exchange rate. We reserve the intention to make use of
the clearing balance for the transfer of additional Swiss
claims, but request that you make no mention of this question
for the time being.

Inter 3 Nov 45   (76 Y)   Swiss   H-215101
Rec'd 7 Nov 45
Trans 1739 26 Nov 45 (10849-S)   Page 2

OFFICE OF THE UNITED STATES POLITICAL ADVISER

Tokyo, February 15, 1946

CONFIDENTIAL

No. 258

SUBJECT: Views of Some Leading Japanese Businessmen

The Honorable

The Secretary of State,

Washington.

Sir:

I have the honor to forward as an enclosure a memorandum of remarks made to a member of the staff of this Office by a group of Japanese businessmen, representative executive members of various Mitsui corporations.

The problems which appear to worry Japanese businessmen most, as brought out in the memorandum, are obscurity of the future no matter how severe it may be, the uncertainties of reparations payments, failure to receive guidance from their Government concerning rehabilitation of Japanese economy, question of hastening required dissolution of the "Zaibatsu" in order to provide for creative economic and industrial ability to "get on with the job", mounting unemployment resulting from inaction, and finally, the danger, which, to them at least, is real, that help may be sought from non-American nationals to the detriment of future American trade relations with Japan. The additional danger of economic chaos resulting from too rapid a disintegration of the large combines is stressed, with a clear implication that such chaos will hasten the communization of Japan.

These opinions are frankly those of leading businessmen who, rightly or wrongly, have come under a cloud. The word "Zaibatsu" has been so blithely and almost indiscriminately bandied about in both the United States and Japan that the views of anyone formerly or presently connected with large Japanese industries are apt to be discredited before expression. It is believed, however, that it should not be forgotten that many Japanese industrialists were formerly international traders and well-connected with American business. These same "Zaibatsu" represent the best proven economic ability in Japan.

Their

ASSIFIED

Confidential memorandum of February 15, 1946, from Max Bishop, Foreign Service officer in Tokyo, to the secretary of state in Washington regarding William Sebald's luncheon meeting that day with Mitsui executives.

-2-

Their universal attachment to the controlled-economy theories
of the Japanese militarists is open to question, at least in
some instances. In the belief that the blanket incrimination
of all economic leaders in Japan has not yet been proved, it
is submitted the remarks of these persons will be of real value
to the Department as presenting another view of the Japanese
situation.

Respectfully yours,

Max W. Bishop
Foreign Service Officer

Enclosure:

Copy of Memorandum of
Conversation dated
February 12, 1946.

Original and hectograph to Department
Copy to General Headquarters, SCAP .

Enclosure to despatch No. 258 dated February 15, 1946, from the Office
of the United States Political Adviser, Tokyo, Japan, on the subject
"Views of Some Leading Japanese Businessmen".

MEMORANDUM OF CONVERSATION

CONFIDENTIAL   February 12, 1946

Participants: Mr. MITSUI Taknatsu, Partner of Mitsui Holding Company;
                Mr. MIYAZAKI Kiyoshi, President, Mitsui Trading Company;
                Mr. MATSUMOTO Kisashi, Managing Director, Mitsui Head Office;
                Mr. SASAKI Shiro, President, Mitsui Real Estate Company;
                Mr. OKADA Shinji, President, Sanki Kogyo K. K.;
                Mr. MASUDA Katsunobu, President, Taiwan Sugar Company; and
                Mr. Sebald.

Subject: Views of Leading Japanese Businessmen.

───

        Mr. MITSUI Taknatsu invited Mr. Sebald to an informal luncheon on
February 12, 1946. The luncheon was held in an executive dining room
of the Mitsui Main Bank Building and the other guests present were representative executive members of various Mitsui corporations. The
Japanese guests expressed themselves with unquestionable sincerity and
frankness seldom found among Japanese except those who have become
accustomed to Western thoughts and ways of business. In view of the
important positions held by these men and their past broad experience,
it is believed that their ideas, probably typical of most successful
Japanese industrialists and businessmen, are worthy of some consideration. It is also believed that these remarks serve in a measure to
throw light on the thinking, political and economic, of a section of
Japanese society which for the most part has not heretofore actively
presented its views on the situation in Japan. Their remarks are
summarized in following paragraphs:

        The greatest worry of Japanese business leaders today
    is the uncertainty which circumscribes their every effort,
    plan, or suggestion. It is obvious to anyone with even a
    smattering knowledge of economics, that the fundamental
    problem of Japan today is the failure quickly to rehabili-
    tate industry in some form. Without production, inflation
    is a certainty, and such attempts at alleviation as the
    capital levy are only temporary step-gaps which will, in
    the final analysis, only increase the problem.
        The Mitsui organization has the capital, organization,
    brains, know-how, and connections throughout Japan to under-
    take practically anything which is desired, but is baffled
    at every turn in its efforts to assist in improving Japan's
    present condition. For example, immediately after the sur-
    render, the Mitsui organization prepared a practical plan
    whereby the big companies were to be mobilized in an en-
    deavor to attack the problem of housing in Japan. The plan
    envisaged the formation of a new non-profit company which
    would draw on the entire business world in Japan for this
    purpose. The plan had two objectives: to alleviate the
    housing situation and to furnish work for the numerous
    unemployed in Japan. At first, the General Headquarters
    were sympathetic, but eventually, the plan was disapproved,
    but no alternative was offered.
        If the Mitsui organization is to be dissolved, and
    every one was in agreement that it will be, what can be

                                                        done

Confidential report of February 12, 1946, by William Sebald, political advisor to General MacArthur, about his luncheon meeting that day with Mitsui executives.

-2-

done to hurry along the process? What can the organization do to democratize itself? Those questions are funda-
mental. The Mitsui interests are vast, employ many thousands
of people, their capital is frozen, and no credit is forthcoming from the banks. The result of this stagnation is
that the organization is cannibalizing itself: employees
have to be paid or laid off; in the latter event, the unemployment problem is increased and the Government is doing
nothing to insure the livelihood of the jobless. The result is the disintegration of an organization which could
be put to work to assist in Japan's economic rehabilitation, and also an increase, by leaps and bounds, of social
unsettlement and unrest.

The problem of reparations must be settled. The so-
called Zaibatsu is not concerned that a certain proportion
of its heavy industry is to be taken for reparations. What
does concern the business leaders is the fact that no decision is made. It would be better to decide that all
heavy industry is to be taken for reparation payments
than allow this uncertainty to continue. The capitalists
see no point in attempting to convert to peace-time industry, even if this were possible, only to have the installations taken away at some future date for reparations payments. Even if they were told to convert, banks will not
advance money, and the capitalists' own capital is frozen.
Even attempts to take the initiative are generally denied.
Thus, an application was recently made to start a soap factory, one of the critical needs of Japan. The application
was denied. The general rule that the Mitsui and other
large interests can start no new enterprises obviously
prevents a peace-time economy from beginning. Small entre-
preneurs are given permission to construct various factories
and plants, but lack of the required organization, capital,
"know-how", and ability severely limits their effectiveness.
That the result is a wasteful process in an already desperate
economy is proven by the general economic stagnation in
Japan today.

The Mitsui organization has attempted not to add to
the unemployment problem, but cannot carry on alone. In
the case of certain Mitsui enterprises which are continuing operations, labor now insists that part of their
wages be paid in rice. When application is made to the
Government for rice, the reply invariably is that there
is none available. Mitsui recently applied to the Government for permission to increase cultivation of staple products on a large scale. The Government disapproved of the
plan submitted on the pretext that the Government is working on its own plan. Thus time is wasted, and time is of
the essence, and the situation continues to deteriorate.

Either the Government must "grab the ball" and start
the wheels of industry, or industry itself must do it.
However, industry cannot, because it is frozen by lack of
capital, refusal to allow new undertakings, and general
uncertainty and bewilderment. In consequence, the general
atmosphere is one of frustration at every turn. The very
people who can most help the General Headquarters in carrying out its policies, and they are only too willing so to
help, are barred by Governmental red tape, refusal to
clarify policies except in vague, general terms, and the
propensity for giving negative decisions with no alterna-
tives offered.

The large

-3-

The large business interests in Japan have always been pro-American in their sentiments, but the present seemingly destructive trend of American policy, without encouragement or assistance in reconstruction, is rapidly alienating previous ties of good will. As a result, business leaders in Japan are beginning to think about the possibilities of help from non-American quarters. This would be most unfortunate, but desperation makes for strange bed-fellows.

The so-called Zaibatsu cannot understand why there is so much commotion to "break up" the big combines. As a matter of fact, with the present tax structure in Japan, it is practically impossible for any large organization to continue in existence and also make a profit. After all, even Americans must admit that profit is one of the impelling motives of business; without profit, any organization will eventually fall apart. This is well illustrated by the fact that many of the "Mitsui" companies competed among themselves. Furthermore, Mitsui enterprises were not solely financed by the Mitsui Bank. On the contrary, Mitsui companies placed their business with those banks which advanced loans at the lowest rate of interest.

Mere "bigness" should not necessarily be taken as "badness". American Telephone and Telegraph Company, General Motors, United States Steel, Du Pont, Ford, and other large American corporations were cited as precedents for "bigness" which yet had the blessing of the American people. As Japanese companies, under the lash of the military, it is hardly reasonable to expect the large Japanese combines to do otherwise than carry out the instructions of the Government during the war.

Too rapid a disintegration of the large combines can only result in economic chaos in Japan. Once such chaos does result, Japan will be ripe for Communism, already growing as a result of the clever infiltration of Communists among the workers in all branches of industry. Is it believed that a Communistic Japan is in the best interests of the United States?

Mr. Sebald found the Japanese so eager to present their views that it was generally unnecessary for him to offer direct comment or actively to enter the discussion which was in both Japanese and English. He confined himself to occasional general questions designed to elicit their views on certain aspects of the situation.

William J. Sebald

Confidential interoffice memorandum of June 9, 1955, from Mr. Fraleigh at the American Embassy in Tokyo acknowledging that ex-prisoners of war were cut out of the 1951 Peace Treaty compensation provisions.

FOUCH

UNCLASSIFIED

(Security Classification)

FOREIGN SERVICE DESPATCH

DO NOT TYPE IN THIS SPACE

294.5841/10-457

XR 294.1141

FROM : AMEMBASSY, Tokyo

TO : THE DEPARTMENT OF STATE, WASHINGTON.

REF :

Action Assigned to AE/

Action Taken

2945841

SUBJECT: Japanese-Swedish War Claims Settlement

Summary: Japan has agreed to pay Sweden about $1.5 million in settlement of Swedish claims for physical suffering and property damage arising during World War II. The principal Swedish claimants are match companies, which suffered damage to property in the Philippines and Burma, and Swedish ship companies. Coincident with the settlement, but not mentioned in public announcements, is an agreement by Sweden to release Japanese assets in Sweden valued at about $1 million. The Swedish settlement is the third war claims settlement by Japan with a neutral country; the others were with Switzerland and Spain and were each in the amount of $5.5 million. The settlements raise a question concerning the applicability of a Peace Treaty provision obliging Japan to extend to peace treaty signatories the same advantages as are accorded to any other governments in war claims settlements.

On September 21, 1957 the Japanese Ministry of Foreign Affairs announced the conclusion of an agreement between Japan and Sweden for the settlement of claims of Swedish individuals and corporations against the Japanese Government for physical suffering and for property damage during the Second World War. It was agreed that Japan would pay a lump sum of 7,250,000 Swedish crowns (about ¥505,000,000 or $1,402,777) in settlement and that the Swedish Government would distribute the sum among the claimants. The agreement was signed in Stockholm on September 20, 1957. It is expected to take effect between January and March of 1958, provided that it is approved by the Swedish Riksdag.

The Embassy has obtained additional information concerning the settlement from Mr. Kenjiro CHIKARAISHI, Chief of the First Section of the European Affairs Bureau of the Japanese Ministry of Foreign Affairs and from Mr. Carl George CRAFOORD, First Secretary of the Swedish Legation. The Swedish Government issued a public notice in 1949 calling upon Swedish nationals with claims against Japan arising out of World War II to file their claims. The claims were referred to a Swedish court which submitted a report in 1952 on the appropriate amount of compensation. On the basis of this report the Swedish Government in 1952 entered into negotiations with the Japanese for a lump sum settlement.

AFraleigh/es

UNCLASSIFIED

ACTION COPY — DEPARTMENT OF STATE

The action office must return this permanent record copy to DC/R files with an endorsement of action taken.

Memorandum of October 4, 1957, from Ben Thibodeaux, minister of Economic Affairs at the American Embassy in Tokyo to the Department of State in Washington, quoting provisions of Article 26 of the 1951 Peace Treaty.

Although the public announcement concerning the war claims settlement makes no mention of the release of Japanese assets in Sweden, agreement on the release of such assets was reached simultaneously with the settlement of the Swedish war claims. Mr. Chikaraishi acknowledged that the release of the assets had played a significant part in the settlement, but he noted that the value of Japanese assets in Sweden, which he estimated at slightly more than $1 million, was less than the amount of the war claims settlement by almost half a million dollars.

The principal beneficiaries of the war claims settlement are Swedish match companies whose branches in the Philippines and in Burma suffered substantial war damage, and also Swedish shipping companies two of whose ships were seized and sunk during the war. Mr. Crafoord said that there was no damage to any Swedish property in Japan. Swedish nationals did file claims for damages suffered in China due to Japanese action prior to 1939, but the settlement speaks only of claims arising during the Second World War. It remains to be seen, therefore, whether the Swedish Government will subsequently press pre-war claims, or whether it will include the pre-war claimants in distributing the lump sum settlement among Swedish nationals.

According to Mr. Crafoord, the Swedish Government has made war claims settlements with a number of countries including Yugoslavia and Hungary. The Japanese Government has previously made settlements with Spain ($5.5 million) and Switzerland (also $5.5 million) as reported by the Embassy in item 7 of despatch 711 of January 18, 1957. It is still negotiating with Denmark and, according to Mr. Chikaraishi, this negotiation will take some time.

The settlements by the Japanese Government with the neutral countries raise a question concerning the possible application of Article 26 of the Japanese Peace Treaty which reads in part as follows:

" . . . . Should Japan make a . . . war claims settlement with any State granting that State greater advantages than those provided by the present Treaty, those same advantages shall be extended to the parties to the present Treaty."

Japan, by making payments to the neutral countries for damages suffered by their nationals in China and in the countries of Southeast Asia as a result of World War II, may be said to have accorded greater advantages to the nationals of neutral countries than those accorded to American nationals who are not entitled under the Peace Treaty to receive compensation for war losses occurring outside of Japan. However, the United States Government, unlike Sweden, still retains the proceeds from the liquidation of Japanese assets within its borders.

For the Ambassador:

Ben H. Thibodeaux
Minister for Economic Affairs

Endnotes

INTRODUCTION

1. Report from U.S. military records, entered into the Congressional Record, December 1942.
2. Figures published by American Ex-Prisoners of War national headquarters, Arlington, Tex. compiled from official U.S. military records.

CHAPTER 1

1. P. Scott Corbett, *Quiet Passages* (Kent, Ohio: Kent State University Press, 1987), 6.
2. Ibid.
3. Testimony before the House Interstate and Foreign Commerce Committee, March 20, 1947.
4. Reprinted in *Air Force News,* August 1995, 15.
5. Corbett, *Quiet Passages,* 20.
6. Cited in the *New York Times,* December 9, 1999, in a story written by Howard W. French.
7. Interview with the author, February 25, 2000.
8. Louis Morton, *The Fall of the Philippines,* (Washington, D.C.: Office of the Chief of Military History, Department of the Army, 1953), 71.
9. Interview with Robert J. Hanyok, senior historian, Center for Cryptologic History, Fort Meade, Md. February 19, 2000.
10. Associated Press wire story, May 29, 1942; from the library of the Associated Press, New York.
11. Corbett, *Quiet Passages,* 32.
12. Congressional Record, December 15, 1941.
13. Figures compiled from official military records by American Ex-Prisoners of War, Arlington, Tex.
14. Remarks at the National Museum of the Pacific War (Admiral Nimitz Museum) symposium March 18, 1995, Fredericksburg, Tex. supplemented in an interview with the author, March 2, 2000.

CHAPTER 2

1. State Department files, RG 59, "Summary of Communications between the Department of State and the Japanese Government, 18 December 1941–24 August 1945," National Archives, College Park, Md. (cited hereafter as NA).

2. Van Waterford, *Prisoners of the Japanese in World War II* (Jefferson, N.C.: McFarland, 1994), 38.

3. Gavan Daws, *Prisoners of the Japanese* (New York: William Morrow, 1995), 133.

4. International Committee of the Red Cross, *Report of the International Committee of the Red Cross on its activities during the Second World War* (May 1948), 2:263 (cited hereafter as ICRC Report).

5. Message from Gen. Douglas MacArthur to Stimson, February 1, 1942, RG 59, NA.

6. Associated Press wire story, May 29, 1942.

7. Letter to the author, March 2, 2000.

8. National Security Agency files (cited hereafter as NSA files), RG 457, NA.

9. Cited by John Toland, *The Rising Sun: The Decline and Fall of the Japanese Empire* (New York: Random House, 1970), 342–44.

10. Letter to the author, 1999.

11. Radio message, April 2, 1942, recovered after the war as part of a complete file on the treatment and deployment of POWs kept by the Japanese camp commandant at Taihoku, Taiwan (International Prosecution Section [cited hereafter as IPS]), RG 331, NA; see appendix C.

12. Ibid. Instructions undated but entered in the July 1942 commander's log.

13. Secret message from the Swiss Ministry in Bern to its ambassador in Tokyo, November 24, 1944, NSA files, RG 457, NA; see appendix C.

14. Secret message from the Japanese Embassy in Bern to Tokyo asking for confirmation of the radio broadcast, July 10, 1944. NSA files, RG 457, NA.

15. Conversation with the author, April 28, 1998.

16. ICRC Report, 262.

17. Secret message from Swiss Ministry in Bern to its embassy in Tokyo, December 9, 1944, NSA files, RG 457, NA; see appendix C.

18. International Labor Organization Convention concerning forced or compulsory labor, adopted June 28, 1930. United Nations Treaty Series, no. 612.

CHAPTER 3

1. International Prosecution Section (cited hereafter as IPS), RG 331, NA.

2. Cited by Prof. Sumio Adachi in his study, *Unprepared Regrettable Events* (Yokosuka: National Defense Academy, 1982), 23.

3. IPS, RG 331, NA.

4. Ibid.

5. Ibid.

6. Ibid.

7. Ibid.

8. Deposition of General Tanaka, March 18, 1946. IPS, RG 331, NA.

9. Map and list as presented to General MacArthur, September 1945, the MacArthur Memorial, Norfolk, Va.; supplemented by official Japanese report, 1955, and further augmented by the author's research.

10. News conference, New York City, September 14, 1999; supplemented by interview with the author, March 3, 2000.

11. Foreign Affairs Monthly Report, September 1942, published by the Foreign Section of the Police Bureau of the Home Ministry, excerpt, 58; Exhibit no. 1971–1971A, the Tokyo War Crimes Trials, 14,508.

12. Excerpts from October 6, 1942, report from Kaitaro Kondo, governor of Kanagawa Prefecture, to the ministers of Welfare and Home Affairs; Tokyo War Crimes Trial transcript, 14,494–14,496 (New York, Columbia University Law School Library, Special Collections); see appendix E.

13. Interview with the author, September 15, 1999.

14. Taped interview with the author, Louisville, Ky. May 20, 1998.

15. *Furyo Joho Kyoku,* Summary Record of Treatment of Prisoners of War, December 1955, and Collected Documents of National Legislation concerning Prisoners of War, December 1946, cited repeatedly by Prof. Sumio Adachi as primary sources for his 1984 study on the wartime treatment of Allied prisoners, titled *Unprepared Regrettable Events.*

16. Taped interview with the author, Louisville, Ky. May 20, 1998.

17. Adachi, *Unprepared Regrettable Events,* 43.

18. Interview with the author, October 5, 1999.

19. Interviews with the author, May 20, 1998, and March 3, 2000.

20. Adachi, *Unprepared Regrettable Events,* 5, 44.

21. Geoffrey Pharoah Adams, *Destination Japan* (Dorset, England: self-published, 1980.)

22. Secret message from Swiss minister Camille Gorgé in Tokyo to the home office in Bern, intercepted by Allied intelligence November 20, 1944. It is a point-by-point response to an eighteen-point protest delivered by the United States to Japan through the Swiss on February 5, 1944. The response consists of answers given to a Swiss representative who was finally allowed to visit a POW camp at Osaka, but allowed no direct access to POWs.

23. Excerpt from an August 1999 letter to the author.

24. Excerpt from a July 18, 1999 letter to the author.

CHAPTER 4

1. A list of POW transports, except for three, which carried fewer than seventy POWs, is shown in appendix B. This list was compiled by the author using official Japanese records, adding the name of the company that built each ship, and the registered owner as listed in *Lloyd's Ship Registry,* 1942–45.
2. Adachi, *Unprepared Regrettable Events,* 16.
3. Affidavit signed December 14, 1985, and sent to the author in August 1999; Mr. Menozzi is deceased.
4. Excerpt from an undated letter to the author, 1998.
5. Excerpt, reprinted in the *Ex-POW Bulletin,* May 1992, from Robert Dow's memoir, *Guest of His Imperial Highness* (self-published, December 1993).
6. Cited by fellow passenger Sidney Stewart, who used the phrase as the title for his book, *Give Us This Day* (New York: Norton, 1957), 228.
7. Recollections of ex-POW Melvin Routt, USN, in an interview with the author February 22, 2000, Los Angeles, Calif.; see also William Evans, *Soochow and the 4th Marines* (Rogue River, Oreg.: self-published, 1987), 129.
8. Messages between Secretary of State Cordell Hull and Ambassador Leland Harrison at the U.S. Consulate in Bern, January 11, 1944, and May 9, 1945; RG 59, NA.
9. Report by Australian major H. S. Williams, entered as evidence at Tokyo War Crimes Trials, October 6, 1945.
10. Interview with the author, Melbourne, Australia, October 1991.
11. Based on the first Geneva Convention of 1864; modified at The Hague in 1907 and Geneva in 1929; cited by Corbett, *Quiet Passages,* 3.
12. Robert Dow, *Guest of His Imperial Highness.*
13. Tom Woody, *Railroad to Nagasaki* (Pensacola, Fla.: self-published, 1992), 58.
14. NSA files, RG 457, NA.

CHAPTER 5

1. Conversation with the author, San Antonio, Tex. May 22, 1999.
2. Letter to the author, June 22, 1998.
3. Series of interviews with the author, Louisville, Ky., May 1998.
4. Marcel Junod, *Warrior without Weapons: The Story of Dr. Marcel Junod of the International Committee of the Red Cross* (Geneva: International Committee of the Red Cross, 1982).
5. Swiss inspector's report August 15, 1944, on file at New Mexico National Guard headquarters, Santa Fe, N.Mex.
6. Frank Stecklein, unpublished memoir, sent to the author July 1998.
7. Series of conversations with the author, March 1996–March 2000.

8. Statement written to the author, June 18, 1998.
9. Extract from service record, sent to the author, July 1998.
10. Extract from report by Col. Thomas Hewlett, M.D., to a reunion of the American Defenders of Bataan and Corregidor, August 1978. In 1997 the author discovered the reason for undistributed Red Cross boxes. It is the subject of a later chapter.
11. Ibid.
12. Conversations with the author, September 14 and December 8, 1999.

CHAPTER 6
1. Herbert L. Zincke, *A Guest of the Emperor,* unpublished diary, 54.
2. Excerpt from a 1979 account prepared by David English for the Veterans Administration, and sent to the author in 1998.
3. From an interview taped in Louisville, Ky., May 20, 1998.
4. Letter to the author, June 1998.
5. Taped interview, Louisville, Ky., May 20, 1998.
6. Conversation with the author, November 15, 1999.
7. Secret message from Swiss Foreign Ministry in Bern to its Ministry in Tokyo, July 14, 1944, intercepted by Allied Intelligence; NSA files, RG 457, NA.
8. Letter from John Britton circulated to his fellow ex-POWs, July 31, 1947.
9. Statement by ex-POW Wilburn Snyder to the author, January 25, 1999.
10. Conversation with the author, January 25, 1999.

CHAPTER 7
1. Zincke, *A Guest of the Emperor,* 93.
2. The Mitsushuma POW site was not listed on the map and key given to General MacArthur prior to his acceptance of the Japanese surrender, or on the official list compiled by the Japanese government after the war. It was one of the thirty-three additional POW locations in Japan discovered by War Crimes Trials investigators in 1945–46. As one investigator commented: "The unlisted camps were the *real* horror stories."
3. Leslie G. Chater, diary, unpublished; excerpts sent to the author, October 1999.
4. Interview with the author, March 19, 2000.
5. Legal Section Informational Summary, no. 25, issued July 31, 1947, by General Headquaters, Supreme Commander for the Allied Powers; sent to Captain Chater by Major Hewitt.
6. From the personal files of Captain Chater, sent to the author, October 1999.
7. *St. John's University Law Review* 66, no. 3 (fall 1992): 748.

8. Interview with the author, August 4, 2000.

9. Showa Denko and Kanose gained international notoriety two decades after the Tokyo trials concluded when "Minimata Disease" became a symbol of environmental disaster and corporate liability after it was established that Showa Denko's plants at Kanose and Chisso had discharged deadly mercury waste into the Agano and Minimata rivers. The discharge affected the central nervous systems of over 10,000 people, as well as birds and dogs, in the tiny fishing town of Minimata, on the Yatsuhiro Sea, Kyushu.

   In the United States Showa Denko's entry into the diet supplement market, L-tryptophane, was withdrawn from sale after several people taking it became ill.

CHAPTER 8

1. Interview with the author, September 3, 1999.
2. Diary of Robert Renfro, unpublished; sent to the author June 1998.
3. Letter sent to the author, July 29, 1999.
4. Letter to the author, July 1999.
5. Stephen N. Kramerich, excerpt from unpublished memoir; sent to the author September 1999.
6. Excerpt of a report on Hirohata POW Camp No. 12, released by the Liaison and Research Branch, American Prisoner of War Information Bureau, July 31, 1946.
7. Affidavit by Joseph Sterner, made on behalf of a fellow POW seeking disability benefits; sent to the author July 1999.
8. John Aldrich, summary of POW experience sent to the author February 25, 1998.
9. Taped interviews with John Aldrich and Paul Reuter, San Antonio, Tex., May 1999.
10. John Burton, *Traveling Life's Twisting Trails* (New York: Vantage Press, 1992), 84, 87, 99, 101, 104.
11. Excerpt of report compiled by Liaison and Research Branch, American POW Information Bureau, completed July 31, 1946; supplied to the author by Kokura ex-POW Walter B. Helhowski.
12. Terence Kirk, *The Secret Camera* (Cotati, Calif.: La Boheme Publishing, 1982), 189.
13. Ibid., 191.
14. From a series of interviews with the author, beginning August 30, 1998.

CHAPTER 9

1. Letter to the author, September 3, 1999.
2. Letter to the author, July 28, 1999.

3. Letter to the author, August 15, 1999.

4. Excerpt from a daily informational summary at the war crimes trial of Lieutenant Asaka and others, issued by the Legal Section, General Head-quarters, Supreme Commander for the Allied Powers.

5. Excerpt from a recollection sent to the author, September 9, 1999.

6. Excerpt of recollection sent to the author, June 1999.

7. Conversation with the author, May 21, 1999, San Antonio, Tex.

8. Interview with the author, July 23, 1999.

9. Interview with the author, February 17, 1999.

10. Interview with the author, March 10, 2000.

11. Excerpts from diary of British major Robert Peaty, camp commander for British POWs, Mukden, entries December 7–10, 1944 (Major Peaty is deceased); from the collection of Melvin L. Routt.

12. Secret message from Tokyo to Budapest, NSA files, RG 457, NA; see appendix C.

13. Excerpt from a letter from Mrs. Bridges to the author, June 1999 (Wilson Bridges died in 1987).

14. Interview with the author, July 23, 1999.

15. Interview with the *San Leandro Times,* May 27, 1999.

16. Interview with the author, July 20, 1998.

17. Interviews with the author March 5, 1999, and May 20, 1999.

18. Excerpt of an interview with reporter Bob St. John for the November/December 1995 issue of *Philippine Notebook;* reprinted in the *Ex-POW Bulletin,* March 1998.

19. Letter to the author, August 27, 1999.

20. Letter to the author, July 31, 1999; interview with the author, November 28, 1999.

21. Interview with the author, March 22, 1999.

22. Junod, *Warrior without Weapons,* 262–264.

23. Ibid., 268, 269, 312.

24. Interview with the author, February 2, 2000.

25. Letter to the author, January 18, 2000.

CHAPTER 10

1. *Journal News,* Westchester-Rockland edition, Gannett Newspapers, September 9, 1999, 1A.

2. *Lloyd's Ship Registry,* London, England, 1941 and 1942 editions.

3. Interview with the author, November 8, 1999.

4. Frank R. Mace, ed., *The Story of Wake Island Before, During, and After: Life as a Prisoner of War of the Japanese,* sketches by Joe Astarita (Spokane, Wash.: self-published, 1998), 48.

5. Interview with the author, March 31, 2000.

6. Mace, *The Story of Wake Island,* 47.

CHAPTER 11

1. Figures from the Allied War Graves Commission and the Lost Battalion/USS *Houston* Survivors Association.

2. Interviews with several former Office of Strategic Services (OSS) Pacific agents, March through September 1997.

3. Documents from the U.S. Treasury and Swiss National Bank files at the Federal Reserve Bank in New York; released to the author with permission of the Swiss National Bank, by letter dated August 15, 1997; see appendix E.

4. State Department document filed in the Federal Reserve Bank, New York.

5. Secret Japanese diplomatic message intercepted by Allied Intelligence, decoded May 26, 1944, and translated July 18, 1944. NSA files, RG 457, NA. Unless otherwise indicated, messages subsequently cited in this chapter are from the same source and record group.

6. ICRC Report, 267.

7. Letter to the author, March 17, 1997.

8. State Department files, Federal Reserve Bank, New York.

9. Interoffice files, Federal Reserve Bank, New York.

10. Report of Swiss historian Michele Coduri: "Bonnes offices et bonnes affaires?" (Good intentions and Good Conduct?: Financial implications of the protection of Allied interests by Switzerland in the Far East during the Second World War). Mr. Coduri's report was prepared at the request of the Swiss government after the author's findings appeared in the worldwide press February–March 1997. Copy of his report sent by Mr. Coduri to the author, July 1997.

11. Junod, *Warrior without Weapons,* 264.

12. Personal experience related to the author by Jos Hagers, a correspondent for the newspaper *De Telegraaf,* March 1997. Ms. Hagers was born in the Sumatra internment camp where this incident took place, and spent nearly the first four years of her life there.

13. Junod, *Warrior without Weapons,* 276.

14. News magazine of Dutch ex-POW organization, *Stichting Japanese Ereschulden,* December 1995, 10; statistics from official Dutch government sources.

15. The Dutch refused to sign the 1951 Peace Treaty with Japan until a provision was made allowing the Dutch to negotiate a separate compensation agreement with Japan, which would recognize the extraordinary suffering

of 120,000 Dutch citizens in Japanese internment camps, and the deaths of 26,000 Dutch men, women, and children in Japanese hands. In March 1957, the Yoshida-Stikker agreement was signed, named for the two foreign ministers who negotiated it. Under the agreement, Japan paid the Netherlands about $10 million from the Japanese treasury.

16. Letter from Vincent Crettol and Enzo Rossi of the Swiss National Bank to the author, July 1, 1997, listing disbursement of funds in the special account; confirmed by letter dated September 1, 1997 from Asataro Miyoke, Bank of Tokyo–Mitsubishi; see appendix E.

CHAPTER 12

1. Jack Edwards, *Banzai, You Bastards!* (Hong Kong: Pioneer Printers, 2000), 258.
2. Telephone interview with the author, July 7, 1995.
3. Ibid.
4. Letter to the author, February 16, 1995.
5. Interview with the author, October 6, 1996.
6. Interview with the author, October 1, 1996. The Japanese governor-general's copy of the execution order, written on rice paper, is part of the IPS files, RG 331, NA.
7. Interview with a former Pacific agent in the OSS, November 16. 1995.
8. Telephone interview with the author, July 7, 1995.
9. Arnold Brackman, *The Other Nuremberg* (New York: William Morrow, 1987), 264.
10. Tokyo War Crimes Trials transcript, 14,728.
11. John Dower, *Embracing Defeat* (New York: W. W. Norton, 1999), 460.
12. Interviews with John E. Taylor, senior archivist, Military History and Intelligence section, NA, June–July 1995.

CHAPTER 13

1. Atcheson had also formed a friendship at the University of Pennsylvania with the emperor's uncle, Prince Fumimaro Konoe, when both were undergraduates there. The prince committed suicide December 16, 1945, the day he was to enter Sugamo Prison after being placed under arrest as a suspected war criminal. Prince Konoe reportedly told his close friend and former Penn roommate, Jimmy Kawasaki, that he couldn't stand being put on trial by his American friends. According to Robert Donihi, a prosecutor at the trials, our Foreign Service had mistakenly added Prince Konoe's name to the list. Interview with the author, June 3, 1998.
2. Excerpts from memorandum written by William Sebald February 12, 1946, SCAP files, RG 331, NA, declassified for the author March 28,

2000; copy obtained with the assistance of researcher Kristin Bonneau. see appendix E.

3. SCAP files, RG 331, NA; excerpt quoted in the summary of a symposium at the MacArthur Memorial, Norfolk, Va., April 13–15, 1978.

4. Excerpt of message radioed to General MacArthur from Washington, Radio NR WX 68524, September 24, 1945; the MacArthur Archives, Norfolk, Va., RG 9, Box 160.

5. Dower, *Embracing Defeat,* 223.

6. Brackman, *The Other Nuremberg,* 54.

7. Ibid., 86.

8. Excerpt from wire story: "U.S. Spares Top Nippon War Criminals," Soviet Far East Service, April 24, 1948, intercepted by Allied intelligence, SCAP Files, RG 331, NA, declassified for the author under the Freedom of Information Act, March 28, 2000.

9. Interview with the author, November 29, 1999.

10. Brackman, *The Other Nuremberg,* 191–93.

11. Interviews with the author, March 16 and April 10, 2000.

12. William R. Gill, *War Crimes Investigations in Japan 1945–48: A Personal Remembrance* (Auburn, Ala.: self-published, 1995), 34.

13. Brackman, *The Other Nuremberg,* 42.

14. Ibid., 41.

CHAPTER 14

1. U.S. Department of State, *American Foreign Policy, 1950–55, Basic Documents,* vol. 1, Department of State publication 6446.

2. Excerpt from form letter May 22, 1952, sent by War Claims Commission, Washington, D.C., to claimants; collection of Harold Feiner.

3. U.S. Department of State, *American Foreign Policy.*

4. *Report on the Activity of the International Committee of the Red Cross for the Indemnification of Former Allied Prisoners of War in Japanese Hands: Article 16 of the Peace Treaty of 8 September 1951 between the Allied Powers and Japan* (Geneva: ICRC, 1971), 4.

5. U.S. Department of State, *American Foreign Policy.*

6. Excerpt of letter dated September 19, 1955 from E. R. Copleston of the Treasury to W. D. Allen, Foreign Office; RG 59, NA.

7. Excerpt from June 9, 1955, internal memorandum from Mr. Fraleigh to Mr. Hemmendinger, American Embassy, Tokyo, RG 59, NA; see appendix E.

8. Excerpt of October 4, 1957, Foreign Service Despatch signed by Ben H. Thibodeaux on behalf of Mr. Fraleigh to the State Department in Washington, RG 59, NA; see appendix E.

9. *New York Times,* January 31, 1999.
10. Sec. 354.6, California Code of Civil Procedure.
11. Ibid.
12. The suit was subsequently withdrawn without prejudice; this enables the plaintiffs to refile their lawsuits separately.
13. *International Herald Tribune,* September 15, 1999, 1.
14. *New York Times,* January 20, 1999, and November 19, 1999.

CHAPTER 15

1. Edwards, *Banzai, You Bastards!,* 264.
2. Interviews with and documentation from Frank Bigelow, James Brennan, Roy Gentry, Terence Kirk, and Melvin Routt; additional documentation from directives from the adjutant general's office, RG 407, NA.
3. Brig. Gen. A. S. Blackburn, AIF, in a foreword to the memoirs of ex-POW Walter Summons, *Twice Their Prisoner* (Melbourne: Oxford University Press, 1946.)

Bibliography

PRIMARY SOURCES

Interviews with over 400 American, Australian, British, Canadian, and Dutch World War II ex-prisoners of war captured by both Japanese and German forces.

Interviews with present and former U.S. government officials at the National Archives, the National Security Agency, the Central Intelligence Agency, the Office of Strategic Services, and the State Department.

Archival material at the following museums: the National Museum of the Pacific War (Admiral Nimitz Museum), Fredericksburg, Tex.; the Australian War Memorial, Canberra; the MacArthur Memorial, Norfolk, Va.; the Marine Corps History Museum, Washington, D.C.; the Office of Naval History, Washington, D.C.; the U.S. Army Military History Institute, Carlisle Barracks, Pa.; the Congressional Record; International Military Tribunal of the Far East, transcripts of the Tokyo War Crimes Trials, 1946–48.

Officials and staff at the Consulate General of Australia, New York; the Consulate General of Japan, New York; the Japanese Embassy, Washington, D.C.; the Consulate General of the Netherlands, New York; the Consulate General of the United Kingdom, New York.

Officials and staff at the International Committee of the Red Cross, Geneva and New York.

Officials at the following banking institutions: the Bank of Tokyo–Mitsubishi, Tokyo, Japan; the Federal Reserve Bank of New York; the Swiss National Bank, Bern, Switzerland.

PUBLISHED WORKS AND UNPUBLISHED MEMOIRS

Adachi, Sumio. *Unprepared Regrettable Events.* Yokosuka, Japan: National Defense Academy, 1982.

Adams, Geoffrey Pharoah. *Destination Japan.* Dorset, England: self-published, 1980.

Brackman, Arnold. *The Other Nuremberg.* New York: William Morrow, 1987.

Burton, John. *Traveling Life's Twisted Trails.* New York: Vantage Press, 1992.

Chater, Leslie G. *Diary.* Collection of Leslie G. Chater.

Coduri, Michele. "Bonnes offices et bonnes affaires?" Geneva: International Committee of the Red Cross, 1997.

Corbett, P. Scott. *Quiet Passages.* Kent, Ohio: Kent State University Press, 1987.

Daws, Gavan. *Prisoners of the Japanese.* New York: William Morrow, 1995.

Dow, Robert. *Guest of His Imperial Highness.* Albuquerque, N.Mex.: self-published, 1993.

Dower, John. *Embracing Defeat.* New York: W. W. Norton, 1999.

Edwards, Jack. *Banzai, You Bastards!* Hong Kong: Pioneer Printers, 2000.

Gill, William. *War Crimes Investigations in Japan, 1945–48: A Personal Remembrance.* Auburn, Ala.: self-published, 1995.

International Committee of the Red Cross. *Report of the International Committee of the Red Cross on its activities during the Second World War.* Vol. 2, *The Central Agency for Prisoners.* Geneva: May 1948.

Junod, Marcel. *Warrior without Weapons: The Story of Dr. Marcel Junod of the International Committee of the Red Cross.* Geneva: International Committee of the Red Cross, 1982.

Kirk, Terence. *The Secret Camera.* Cotati, Calif.: self-published, 1982.

Lloyd's Ship Registry. London: 1941 and 1942 editions.

Mace, Frank, ed. *The Story of Wake Island Before, During, and After: Life as a Prisoner of War of the Japanese.* (Spokane, Wash.: self-published, 1998.

Morton, Louis. *The Fall of the Philippines.* Washington, D.C.: Office of the Chief of Military History, Department of the Army, 1953.

Renfro, Robert. *Diary.* Collection of Robert Renfro.

Stecklein, Frank. Memoir. Collection of Frank Stecklein.

Stewart, Sidney. *Give Us This Day.* New York: W. W. Norton, 1957.

Summons, Walter. *Twice Their Prisoner.* Melbourne: Oxford University Press, 1946.

Toland, John. *The Rising Sun: The Decline and Fall of the Japanese Empire.* New York: Random House, 1970.

U.S. Department of State. *American Foreign Policy, 1950–55, Basic Documents.* Vol. 1. Department of State Publication 6446.

Waterford, Van. *Prisoners of the Japanese in World War II.* Jefferson, N.C.: McFarland, 1994.

Woody, Tom. *Railroad to Nagasaki.* Pensacola, Fla.: self-published, 1992.

Zincke, Herbert. *A Guest of the Emperor.* Diary. Collection of Herbert Zincke.

PERIODICALS AND WIRE SERVICES
Air Force News
Associated Press
Journal News, Gannett Newspapers
New York Times
International Herald Tribune
Niewsmagazine, published by Stichting Japanese Ereschulden,
    The Hague, Netherlands

Index